'Special'
No More

Anglo-American Relations:
Rhetoric and Reality

———

JOHN DICKIE

WEIDENFELD & NICOLSON
London

First published in Great Britain in 1994
by Weidenfeld & Nicolson
The Orion Publishing Group Ltd
Orion House
5 Upper St Martin's Lane
London WC2H 9EA

A catalogue reference is available
from the British Library

ISBN 0 297 81486 9

Photoset in Monophoto Ehrhardt by
Selwood Systems, Midsomer Norton
Printed and bound in Great Britain by
Butler & Tanner Ltd, Frome and London

For Lorna and Nigel,
remembering all the good times
of our special relationship

Contents

Preface

President Clinton's inauguration as the 42nd President of the United States of America on 20 January 1993 symbolized the transition to a new era of international politics. After decades of confrontation between East and West, the Cold War was over. The collapse of the Communist empire in Eastern Europe after the Berlin Wall came down on 9 November 1989 and the disintegration of the Soviet Union into independent republics totally transformed the basic power structures which governed policies in Western capitals. Despite expectations of a lucrative 'peace dividend', however, the legacy of the crumbling Communist systems remained a threat to the stability of large areas of the world. The United States, as the one surviving superpower, was left facing awesome challenges and responsibilities as the twentieth century wound to a close amid warnings of even more perplexing problems emerging in the twenty-first century.

It was not just a moment of historic change for America, a time for re-examining the problems of leadership and assessing where and how American influence is best exerted to serve the interests of the United States. It was also a transatlantic turning point, signalling fundamental change for America's partners – and none more so than for the British. In the course of five decades they had nurtured a partnership of unparalleled trust with the Americans. It was no accident that it was described by successive generations of political leaders as the Special Relationship, for it was a unique bond. Unlike any other, it was based on kinship, not on contract. Nothing was written down: no agreement, no treaty of friendship and co-operation was ever signed.

Its existence was difficult to define. Like theatregoers who ask '*Why must the show go on?*' and fail to get a satisfactory answer, commentators have searched in vain for the essence of the mystique enshrouding the Special Relationship. For some, the essential element which created the 'specialness' was disclosed in Bismarck's observation:

'The most important fact of the modern world is that Britain and America speak the same language.' It is certainly true that university-trained Americans are often more familiar with Shakespeare and Shaw than with Goethe and Heine or Molière and Racine. But it was Shaw who described Britain and the United States as 'two nations separated by a common language'. Historical bonds – from the sailing of the *Mayflower* in 1620 to the comradeship of two world wars in the twentieth century – are usually acknowledged to be important factors, as are the long-standing links between the legal, academic, artistic and professional communities on both sides of the Atlantic. Senior officers in the armed services, especially in the two navies, and members of the Diplomatic Services have a tradition of operating together with an affinity unmatched in other foreign countries.

Even the origin of the term 'Special Relationship' has been a matter of controversy. It came into prominence following the 'Iron Curtain' speech delivered by Churchill at Fulton, Missouri, on 5 March 1946, when he said that the only certain way to prevent war was through a fraternal association of the English-speaking peoples: 'This means a Special Relationship between the British Commonwealth and Empire and the United States.' In fact, Churchill used the term in a note to Richard Law on 16 February 1944 when he wrote: 'It is my deepest conviction that unless Britain and the United States are joined in a Special Relationship including Combined Staff Organization and a wide measure of reciprocity in the use of bases – all within the ambit of a world organization – another destructive war will come to pass.'

The use of the term from the outset has been almost entirely in English accents. The partnership has been appreciated on both sides of the Atlantic, but not the phrase. On his arrival in London on 3 May 1991 to take up his appointment as United States Ambassador, Raymond Seitz made a vow, despite being an unashamed Anglophile, that he would never use the term nor quote Churchill – and he stuck to his pledge. The term is rarely heard in Washington – even in the British Embassy. The only occasions when it has been used on the White House lawn are in front of the television cameras, as a gesture from the host to make his visitor feel that he is held in particular affection in the hearts of Americans. Politicians are so well practised in massaging each other's egos that the rhetoric about the relationship is poured out automatically regardless of the reality.

Cynics have tended to portray this perception of 'specialness' as largely sustained on the British side of the partnership. Yet the strength of feeling in the United States on the eve of Prime Minister Harold Wilson's application in 1967 to join the Common Market was conveyed to London in an extraordinary statement from New York which headed the Letters columns of *The Times*. Signed by the Governors of Vermont, Illinois, Utah, Oregon and Delaware, 10 leading Senators, 28 Congressmen and 36 University Presidents, it saluted the relationship, saying 'Whether Britain enters Europe or not, we believe this friendship should remain a cornerstone of American foreign policy. We hope it will likewise remain a fundamental part of British foreign policy.'

However, despite a long history of shared concepts and traditions, these common values have not always resulted in the pursuit of common interests or common policies. All states act according to what their leaders perceive to be in the best national interest at the time, a guiding principle shrewdly described by the Italian Prime Minister Antonio Salandra at the outbreak of World War I as 'sacred egoism'. On many occasions when advance consultation was expected in London or Washington it was denied on the grounds that national interest overruled any claims for 'special' treatment. Even in the halcyon days of the relationship there was never a period of total harmony or complete frankness right across the board. Some areas of policy were reserved as the exclusive concern of the White House – and sometimes 10 Downing Street preserved a similar secretiveness.

Even so, throughout the ups and downs of the relationship one constant theme – with only occasional variations or aberrations – was predominant in Downing Street: a heavy political emphasis on equating whenever possible the best interests of Britain with being in the closest possible harmony with the United States. Yet from the outset the rhetoric of the hands-across-the-sea partnership far outstripped the reality. The closeness of the kinship was hyped – shamelessly on occasion – by Churchill not only in his public utterances but in his private correspondence with President Roosevelt. The Prime Ministers who followed him – with the exception of Edward Heath when his priorities were determined by the need to convince his Common Market partners that he was a 'good European' – often went out of their way to extol the links with America. For many years at summit meetings it was regarded as politically rewarding for most statesmen – Conservative or Labour, Democrat or Republican – to salute the common bonds fulsomely in public even when there were sharp differences never far beneath the surface cordiality.

Habits die hard even when circumstances are radically changed. Despite the complete transformation of the international balance of power, Prime Minister John Major sent congratulations to Bill Clinton on his election as President in terms that might have been drafted decades earlier: 'I have no doubt ... that the United States and Great Britain will continue to work together very closely and that the Special Relationship we have had for so many years will be maintained.' Only a few months beforehand, setting out his vision of the future to the Conservative Party Conference after his election victory, Major had pledged to 'preserve and strengthen our Special Relationship with the United States'.

Major's determination to pursue the aspirations of the Special Relationship's founding father defied the realities of the post-Cold War world. Yet the rhetoric was easier to justify than the gloomy predictions peddled for years. To some analysts the Special Relationship never really survived in any meaningful way after World War II. The abrupt termination of Lend-Lease seven days after the war against Japan ended was seen by many observers as a stark reminder that there was nothing 'special' left in the relationship. Nonetheless, three years later Foreign Secretary Ernest Bevin's vigorous rallying of the West in the NATO alliance to face the Communist challenge revived the trans-atlantic partnership.

It was not long, however, before historians and political pundits decided that its days were over. They wrote it off as a nostalgic symbol of a bygone age so frequently that it became like an *in memoriam* column every time Prime Minister and President met. Even the most ardent upholders of the Special Relationship found it difficult to argue against the academics who buried it in the sand after bitter clashes between John Foster Dulles and Sir Anthony Eden over the Suez War in 1956. Yet within two years Harold Macmillan had brought it back glowing again in a remarkable fence-mending operation with Dwight D. Eisenhower. Two years later the cordiality between Macmillan and President John Kennedy restored it to a warmth unknown since the Roosevelt–Churchill era. In that period Macmillan secured the 'special status' of Britain in two agreements, one with Eisenhower on nuclear co-operation in the production of warheads, and the other with Kennedy making Polaris missiles available to Britain.

By the mid-1960s much of the gloss had faded. Regardless of the familiar rhetoric dispensed by President Johnson in a public relations exercise for the benefit of Prime Minister Harold Wilson, the wide gap between the two statesmen over Vietnam left the relationship virtually in limbo. Britain's role on the international stage was grievously reduced in American eyes by the decision of the Wilson Government to withdraw all British forces from East of Suez. In a cogently argued monograph entitled 'The Special Relationship: An Anglo-American Myth', Lord Beloff stated: 'It could thus be maintained that the "Special Relationship" was something in which many British public figures felt the need to believe, so as to be able to argue that the displacement of power from Britain to the United States need not directly damage British interests.' In January 1967 the message to Young Conservatives from an aspirant to Cabinet office was emphatic: 'That long-dead myth of the "Special Relationship" between John Bull and Uncle Sam must be finally buried.' That young undertaker was John Selwyn Gummer, who 20 years later became Agriculture Minister with a determination to save as much as possible of the transatlantic harmony amid clashes with Europe.

The prophets of doom appeared to have been right all along in the 1970s, when few contested that relations between the United States and Britain had reached their lowest point since the Special Relationship was established. The aloofness of Prime Minister Edward Heath towards Washington was epitomized in his refusal to let the words cross his lips. Less than six months after a Labour Government succeeded him, *The Times* published an article on 12 August 1974 under a headline across seven columns stating: 'Mr Wilson Must Realize the Special Relationship Is Dead'. Despite attempts by James Callaghan on taking over the premiership from Harold Wilson in 1976 to be more Atlanticist, even amid renegotiating the terms of Britain's membership of the European Community, it was not until the Reagan–Thatcher era that the transatlantic relationship was fully resuscitated and became 'Special' again.

For almost the entire decade of the 1980s the United States and Britain collaborated across a wide area of international issues – although by no means the whole spectrum – with an identity of views only previously achieved during their wartime alliance. Not since Churchill had a Prime Minister's views received such an attentive hearing in the White House as Margaret Thatcher's did at Ronald Reagan's side. Although Thatcher could not claim that they were always in step – since she would have been sharply reminded of the rows over the

Siberian gas pipeline contracts, the American invasion of Grenada and other controversies – the academic assertions that the Special Relationship no longer existed were made to look ridiculous by America's vital clandestine role in ensuring the victory of the British task force in the Falklands War and, less spectacularly, by the close cooperation in getting Soviet President Gorbachev to make the first major arms-reduction agreements.

That the Special Relationship lasted as long as it did surprised sceptics on both sides, and when it foundered there was undisguised astonishment in Washington that Mrs Thatcher seemed unaware of how far she had drifted apart from President George Bush. For the best part of a year the Thatcher Government was so much out of step with the United States over the process of German unification that the Prime Minister was marginalized by Washington and the Special Relationship was virtually irrelevant. It was only the fortunate coincidence of Bush and Thatcher being in Aspen, Colorado, at the time of the Iraq invasion of Kuwait on 2 August 1990 that set the transatlantic relationship back on course again. When John Major took over as Prime Minister and cemented the new bonds of the partnership in Operation Desert Storm to liberate Kuwait, it proved to be the last chapter of the Special Relationship.

When there was no longer a Communist threat requiring Britain to be the alliance standard-bearer in Europe for the Americans, the principal *raison d'être* of that relationship had gone. Its sudden disappearance from the political landscape tempted some historians to question whether it had ever really existed and to revive familiar theories that it was a myth; neither Britain nor the United States, they felt, had enjoyed any special benefits from their association. These arguments were undermined, however, by one singularly important thread stitching the relationship together infinitely more tightly than any other partnership – the Intelligence connection. While British Intelligence chiefs acknowledge that ten times more information crossed from Washington to London than the other way round, the Central Intelligence Agency highly valued what came back for its quality, especially when the one-tenth was from Oleg Gordievsky, the Russian KGB agent 'turned' by the British. Information from the Gordievsky file was for the Americans in a category of its own, of crucial value, at one particular juncture, in defusing a dangerously escalating crisis between Russia and the United States. It was the Intelligence connection, as will be revealed in Chapter VII, which enabled

Prime Minister Macmillan to become aware of the Cuban missile crisis in 1962 six days before President Kennedy officially informed his allies.

The way the Special Relationship survived throughout its five decades until the international agenda was so changed as to make it special no more is a fascinating phenomenon of what Charles de Gaulle, in his irritation with the kinship between London and Washington, called Anglo-Saxon attitudes. In analysing how the Special Relationship endured and what ultimately made it cease to endure, I have had the advantage of living through the period and writing about the partnership as it evolved instead of being confined to the study of documents, diplomatic telegrams and the memoirs of statesmen. In the course of over 30 years as a diplomatic correspondent, travelling with every Foreign Secretary from Lord Home to Douglas Hurd and attending international conferences with American Presidents and British Prime Ministers, I have had the opportunity to observe the Special Relationship in its triumphs and tribulations at first hand. I have also been greatly assisted by many people involved in the making and execution of policy in the context of Anglo-American relations. In research for this study I have conducted over 100 interviews with ministers and ambassadors of both governments, members of the Intelligence services, Cabinet Office officials, senior officers of the armed services and officials of allied governments. To ensure frank discussion these interviews were off-the-record with the assurance that the names of the participants would not be revealed. For that trust and the friendship which went with it I am extremely grateful. Assistance over printed material came generously from several quarters. At the top of the list is the Library of the Royal Institute of International Affairs at Chatham House in London where everyone is a model of efficiency and enthusiasm for any researcher. My thanks are due to Librarian Susan Boyde and her colleagues Mary Bone, Maggie Julian, Stephanie Alman, Linda Bedford, Dante Burford, Philip Chrimes, Susan Franks, Sarah Hibberd, Olga Olver, Lilian Pearce, John Peel and Mary Wood. I am also grateful for helpfulness at the George C. Marshall Library at Lexington, Virginia, at the Reference Library of the US Embassy in London, the Daily Mail Library and the Newspaper Library at Colindale in tracing items from newspapers, and at the Naval Historical Branch at the Ministry of Defence. Much appreciated assistance over Cabinet papers and Foreign Office telegrams came from the Public Record Office.

My greatest debt of gratitude is to my wife, Inez, for sustaining my morale with her *cordon bleu* dinners and for accepting with infinite patience and grace the long periods of neglect during the preparation of this book.

John Dickie,
Brooklands,
Oxshott,
November 1993

I

'Special' in Action

*'I felt that naked aggression, as practised by the Argentinian
military dictatorship, should not be encouraged nor indirectly
supported by our indifference or neutrality, which in this case I
took to mean the same things.'*

US Defence Secretary Caspar Weinberger: 1982

As the hands of the clock ticked away the seconds towards noon at the
residence of the British Defence Attaché in Washington on Easter
Sunday 1982, Major-General Tony Boam knew there was no need to
check his wrist-watch. The telephone would ring precisely on the hour.
The General knew it would not be an enquiry about chocolate Easter
eggs. It was a call from the Ministry of Defence in London with the
first of the urgent requirements for the British task force sailing towards
the Falkland Islands.

Officially, the United States was neutral in the confrontation triggered
off by the Argentine invasion of the tiny British colony in the South
Atlantic 8,000 miles from the United Kingdom. President Reagan had
commissioned Secretary of State Alexander Haig on 5 April as mediator
between Britain, his NATO ally, and Argentina, his partner in the
Organization of American States. That status of neutrality was to
remain the official US Government position until the Haig mediation
foundered on 30 April and America came off the fence on Britain's
side. But right from the start some Americans were much less disposed
than others to be strictly neutral.

General Boam knew such a person – and he knew his home telephone
number. As soon as he called Lieutenant-General Bill Richardson,
Director of Military Operations at the Pentagon, on Easter Sunday it
was apparent from his tone that the matter was not appropriate for
discussion on an open telephone line, so Boam was invited to drive

over to see General Richardson at his house with the priority request. It was from Sir Terence Lewin, Chief of the Defence Staff, for Stinger missiles. They were required for men of the Special Air Service (SAS) spearheading the assault on South Georgia. The SAS believed that the Blowpipe missile they normally used would be too heavy for this operation and thought the latest version of the Stinger would be ideal. 'My God! You don't want much, do you?' the Pentagon General snapped. The heat-seeking, shoulder-held Stinger missiles had not been allowed out of American hands. But after five minutes on the telephone he beamed back to General Boam: 'They will be on their way in six hours.' As a bonus, an extra Stinger went secretly to London by an overnight plane in the knapsack of a US officer who flew over to demonstrate the potential of the weapon. The consignment of Stingers costing $4 million was completed without an invoice or a signature from General Boam. It was just sealed with a handshake.

Another key member of the British Embassy, Air Vice-Marshal Ron Dick, had his own special relationship with the Joint Chiefs of Staff at the Pentagon that enabled him to resolve the most pressing problem at the very beginning of the war – a desperate shortage of aviation fuel at Ascension Island, the staging post for the task force, 4,000 miles from the Falklands. Although the island was a British colony, Wideawake Air Force Base was run by the Americans and its oil storage facilities were minuscule. All it normally required was enough aviation fuel for the C-141 that made a weekly flight there to service the American tracking station. When Air Vice-Marshal Dick spelled out his requirements, the American admiral at J4 Logistics in the Pentagon was flabbergasted: a complete tanker load in seven days and the same again next week. 'You cannot use that much fuel, surely?' exclaimed the American. 'Just give us the chance,' he was told.

As there was no British tanker available, the admiral scoured the charts on his wall plotting the course of every American tanker with a full load of aviation fuel. When he located the ideal candidate his next problem was how to offload the fuel. That was solved by making arrangements to run pipes from the shore to the tanker, which would lie off Georgetown on the west coast of Ascension as a floating fuel station. But these plans went awry when the designated tanker, the USNS *Neches*, was forced to abandon its voyage to Ascension because of a broken shaft. Finding a replacement tanker capable of arriving within the seven-day deadline was impossible. Air Vice-Marshal Dick was dreading having to report failure back to London when he hit on the idea of asking for the US 'war stocks' of emergency aviation fuel kept under lock and key at Wideawake Air Force Base. These emergency supplies would just fill the gap until the delayed tanker arrived. Under US defence regulations top-level authorization was required to enable 'war stocks' to be used. But the admiral was not to be baulked: 'Hell! There is a war on, isn't there?' The fuel was released – without a piece of paper being signed. By the end of the Falklands campaign the total amount of aviation fuel supplied by the Americans was six million US gallons – and all on credit.

By far the most important item of American assistance was the latest version of the deadly American air-to-air Sidewinder missile, the AIM9L. Fitted to Harriers operating from the carriers *Invincible* and *Hermes*, the Sidewinders had a demoralizing impact on the Argentine air force. The AIM9L, and especially its earlier version the AIM9G, were responsible for destroying more of the Argentine Skyhawks and Daggers than any other weapon. Provision of the first 105 Sidewinders meant that the supplies had to be taken from America's NATO stocks. A further 95 were delivered even though this meant delaying supplies to American squadrons. A team of US Air Force officers was flown to Ascension to instruct British air crews on the most effective ways of using Sidewinders.

A sophisticated new piece of equipment recently tested by the Americans in the Middle East was the next priority item on Air Vice-Marshal Dick's 'shopping list' at the Pentagon. Because of the danger of casualties occurring through pilots becoming fatigued by long flying duties and uncomfortable accommodation in tents, he made a bid for a 'Concertina City'. This provided a mobile package of air-conditioned accommodation sound-proofed against the noise of nearby generators running 24 hours a day. Again, the Special Relationship cleared all obstacles – and bureaucratic paperwork. After two telephone calls Major-General Mike Ryan confirmed that a 'Concertina City' was being loaded aboard a C-141 at Holloman Air Force Base in New Mexico for immediate delivery to the British at Wideawake. When this was reported to London, a crusty admiral was concerned that the package, which was intended to accommodate 160 people, included an elaborate kitchen capable of serving 500 people. Luckily for the British air crews it was too late to change the C-141 load, so they enjoyed cafeteria meals well beyond their expectations on active service.

From the beginning of the Falklands crisis 'ghost flights' took supplies every night from Andrews Air Force Base in Washington to

Ascension Island. The British Defence staff in Washington numbered 128 from all three Services and Intelligence, many of them on 24-hour duty rotas. Army, Navy and Air Force had their separate lists of requirements, but there was never a clash of priorities. At the centre General Boam had a small command team run by his chief of staff, Marine Colonel Michael Reece. In view of the scale of the operation it was extraordinary that it remained a secret. US Air Force staff at Andrews Air Base had been used to seeing weekly trooping flights of RAF VC10s and from time to time C-130s, but no one at the base could have avoided noticing the intense activity night and day at the British corner of the airfield. Yet even during his diplomatic shuttle Secretary of State Alexander Haig appeared unaware of the military shuttle. He gave an assurance to the Argentines on 14 April with what appeared to be genuine sincerity: 'The United States has not acceded to requests [from Britain] that would go beyond the customary patterns of co-operation based on existing bilateral agreements.'

Not even the most eloquent lawyer could have convinced a jury that the vast quantities of weapons and equipment supplied by the Americans were either customary or in accordance with bilateral agreements. The total cost excluding the aviation fuel and the Sidewinder missiles was estimated at over $60 million. The list read like pages from an inventory of new stock at a military emporium: Shrike anti-radar missiles; the newly developed Vulcan Phalanx close-in anti-aircraft system; torpedo exhaust valves, an engine for a C-47 helicopter, Harpoon anti-naval missiles, crates of mortar ammunition, flare cartridges, 40mm high-explosive shells and air-drop containers. Apart from the hardware, the troops were pleased to get American ration packs and night-vision goggles for patrols.

When they came to the end of the military shopping list the Pentagon had thought that they were no longer capable of being surprised by anything the British might want. But Lieutenant-General Philip Gast and Rear-Admiral Robert Hilton were bowled over by the last item: a complete airfield. Air Vice-Marshal Dick explained that once Port Stanley was recaptured there would be an urgent need for an effective large-scale airbase to replace the old airfield, which had been badly damaged in British bombing raids during the Argentine occupation. The three officers sat down at the planning table and worked out the details: length of the runway, space for taxiways, size of the parking apron and the amount of arrester gear. The total calculation for prefabricated steel-mesh AM2 matting was 4,700 tons. This clearly meant making more than a five-minute telephone call. One of the difficulties was that the most conveniently available matting was in war stocks earmarked for the US Marines, but Admiral Hilton had his own special relationship with the Marines and 24 hours later had circumvented the regulations. The consignment was 'borrowed' from east coast war stocks and delivered to Baltimore for shipping to the Falklands. RAF Group Captain Dougal McGregor went to Baltimore to supervise the dispatch so that there would be no delay in reporting 'mission accomplished' to London.

Some of the most crucial assistance came clandestinely on the Old Pals network between senior members of the Intelligence Services. Initially there was even greater readiness than usual among American Intelligence chiefs to help because they felt that on the eve of the invasion they had let their 'British pals' down. Despite their vastly superior resources and equipment, the Americans were unable to give the British any advance warning of the Argentine moves towards the Falkland Islands. Even when the British Ambassador, Sir Nicholas Henderson, went to tell Alexander Haig 48 hours before the invasion that it was imminent, the Secretary of State refused to believe him at first. It was only after Haig instructed his own Intelligence staff to investigate the situation and they returned later in the afternoon with confirmation that an invasion was 'probable' that he took Henderson's warnings seriously.

Another important factor encouraging American Intelligence to even more generous collaboration with the British was the widespread conviction on both sides of the Atlantic that the task force faced enormous odds against achieving a decisive victory. Senior American admirals made no secret of their assessment that a seaborne assault would be very dangerous and could easily fail. US Air Force chiefs believed that the RAF, despite its skills and courage, could not give adequate protection to the Navy. Even in Whitehall there were warning voices at the Ministry of Defence which rated the operation too hazardous. Faced with these gloomy forecasts, American Intelligence officers were determined to make sure that they would not be blamed for depriving the British of assistance which could make the difference between success or failure.

One of the most urgent Intelligence tasks required secret Anglo-American collaboration to recover from the damage caused 24 hours after the invasion by a disclosure from a Labour MP, Ted Rowlands, who had been the minister responsible for Falklands affairs in the

Callaghan Government. In a flush of enthusiasm to blame the Thatcher Government for not reading the danger signals, Rowlands inadvertently blurted out: 'The Secretary of Defence asked "How can we read the mind of the enemy?" I shall make a disclosure. As well as trying to read the mind of the enemy, we have been reading its telegrams for many years.' Naturally, the Argentines changed their diplomatic code immediately. But with the assistance of the Americans, the backroom boys at British Intelligence cracked the new code within a week.

Since British Intelligence operations in South America were on a very meagre scale, one of the first priorities after the invasion was to seek assistance from the CIA. There was no hesitation from CIA Director William Casey when Ambassador Henderson sent his co-ordinator, Roger Carrick, to see him. Anything that the American Intelligence network had of value to the British was immediately made available. Casey telephoned the Cabinet Office to assure the Joint Intelligence Committee that orders had been given for any Intelligence material which would be useful to the British to be conveyed instantly to London. There was no question of seeking authorization from the White House: the long-standing tradition of co-operation on Intelligence matters made emergency assistance automatic. As proof of their eagerness to help, the Americans moved one of their satellites to operate a 'spy-in-the-sky' monitoring service over Argentina.

Difficult weather conditions over the South Atlantic, however, severely reduced the precision of American satellite pictures, so American SR-71 reconnaissance planes were assigned to special missions for the British. They produced pictures which enabled the British to pinpoint airfields being used to transport Argentine troops and equipment to the Falklands. American listening posts in Chile provided valuable information on Argentina's military movements. Messages from these sources beamed by the Americans to the Government Communications Headquarters (GCHQ) at Cheltenham were instantly decoded by computer. At the end of the war American Intelligence claimed that they were responsible for the vast bulk of movement information acquired by Britain.

Some Americans in influential positions, however, were inclined to be much more neutral than others. There was a formidable group inside the American Administration led by UN Ambassador Jeane Kirkpatrick and Thomas Enders, Under-Secretary for Latin American Affairs at the State Department. Nicknamed the 'Latin lovers', that group saw the issue largely in terms of a colonial dispute between Britain and Argentina. Whatever the value of the Special Relationship, there was no justification in their eyes for automatically backing Britain, particularly if such a policy damaged American interests in Latin America. While they deplored the use of force by Argentina, they saw no reason why Britain should retaliate with force in an attempt to resolve the dispute – and certainly no reason why the US should help the British to do so. Even seven years after the Falklands War Jeane Kirkpatrick remained highly critical of America's involvement, stating in an article in the *National Interest*: 'I found it a miserable example of unnecessary carnage and an unnecessary squandering of Western resources, efforts and lives.' Her vigorous arguments at the time for a policy of neutrality posed a serious challenge to Ambassador Henderson and his UN colleague Sir Anthony Parsons.

From the very start Sir Nicholas Henderson made a dramatic impact in television interviews which focused the attention of ordinary Americans on the rights of Britain's case and won support from influential members of Congress. When he was asked what he thought of Jeane Kirkpatrick attending a dinner in honour of Argentina's Ambassador Esteban Takacs on the very day of the invasion, he retorted: 'What would you think if I had dined with the Iranian ambassador on the night the US hostages were seized?' Behind the scenes Robin Renwick, later to become ambassador in Washington but then counsellor, worked on Anglophiles such as Under-Secretary Lawrence Eagleburger to get State Department backing for Britain at the United Nations despite Kirkpatrick's strong resistance.

At the United Nations, Britain's Ambassador Sir Anthony Parsons was quick off the mark in the Security Council where his task was eased by Jeane Kirkpatrick having to hand over the rotating presidency to Zaire's Ambassador Wa Kamanda Kamanda 24 hours before the crisis began. After getting an emergency session convened on 1 April he had his draft for Resolution 502 all ready – affirming that there was a 'breach of the peace' by Argentina and calling for 'immediate withdrawal of Argentine forces' – within hours of the actual invasion on 2 April. Outsmarting Kirkpatrick, who wanted the vote delayed, Parsons – with the help of Prime Minister Thatcher who telephoned King Hussein of Jordan to win his support – secured the passage of Resolution 502 by ten votes to one (Panama) with Russia and China eschewing the veto and abstaining together with Poland and Spain. A crestfallen Kirkpatrick avoided having to register America's vote in support of Britain by getting her deputy, Charles Lichenstein, as head of the US delegation in the chamber, to do so instead.

One leading American politician was prepared to defy the fence-sitting posture of the Administration from the first day and proclaim himself 100 per cent on Britain's side: Defence Secretary Caspar Weinberger. Ambassador Henderson promised him cash on the nail for all equipment, but it had to be delivered very quickly. Weinberger cleared 15 in-trays to speed the process, since the normal procedures meant that each application was assessed by several different divisions of the Pentagon on a strict American calculation about the need for supplies being given. He insisted on being told personally if a British request was not met within 24 hours and the reason why. Assistant Under-Secretary Dov Zakheim was told to ensure that everything was moved instantly: 'Anything the Brits want, find it and give it to them. We'll work out the cost later.'

Pentagon chiefs dealing with General Boam and Air Vice-Marshal Dick were instructed to handle all requirements on the spot without waiting for authorization. There was not a single occasion when a request for help – weapons, equipment stores or Intelligence – was refused. On two or three occasions, including the request for additional Sidewinder missiles which were to leave gaps in America's front-line air defence, there were some bureaucratic hesitations. But these were immediately overruled by Secretary of State Weinberger. All assistance short of actual American participation in the war was given unstintingly.

During the first four weeks after the Argentine invasion, Weinberger did not worry about the criticism in Britain of America sitting on the fence. He did not want publicity which would have caused a backlash in Congress for breaching America's official neutral status. At one stage in the war he became so concerned about the risks of Britain's two aircraft carriers, *Hermes* and *Invincible*, being knocked out by the Argentines without any replacements readily available that he made a secret offer to hand over the USS *Guam* to the Royal Navy. Since it was capable of launching Harriers and helicopters from its deck, Weinberger foresaw no problem in switching it to a British crew with British command. This boundless enthusiasm to the point of total commitment was never put to the ultimate test – fortunately, since it would have caused such a row in Congress that it might have seriously jeopardized support for Britain.

Weinberger's secret supply was able to come out into the open after the passage of Senate Resolution 382 by 79 votes to one (that of right-wing Jesse Helms) on 29 April which stated: 'Resolved that the United States cannot stand neutral with regard to the implementation of Security Council Resolution 502 and recognizes the right of the United Kingdom and all other nations to the right of self-determination under the United Nations Charter, should therefore prepare, through consultations with Congress, to further all efforts pursuant to Security Council Resolution 502, to achieve full withdrawal of Argentine forces from the Falkland Islands.'

After the defeat of Argentina, Secretary of State Weinberger was modest about his contribution to the British victory which earned him an honorary knighthood from the Queen in February 1988. He described his role as that of 'assistant Supply Sergeant or an assistant Quartermaster'. It was, however, much more than opening the stores to a friend. America's help demonstrated the Special Relationship in action as a partnership without parallel. No other nation at war – with the possible exception of Israel – has received such generous assistance from the United States. Without the abundance and alacrity of US supplies the Falklands War might not have been won or else would have gone down as a costly victory after a long and bloody conflict. Admiral Sandy Woodward, assessing the campaign in *One Hundred Days*, highlighted two crucial factors: the decisiveness of the Sidewinder missile in combat and American co-operation on Ascension Island. 'Never mind the other ways that help was provided, lack of these two alone would probably have reversed the outcome.'

Politically, the Falklands War was a test case of historic importance for the future of relations between the United States and Britain. Regardless of whether the outcome had been victory or stalemate, if the Americans had failed to support the United Kingdom in fighting against an act of aggression in what President Reagan called 'that little ice-cold bunch of land', they would have done irreparable damage to the partnership. In the final analysis this glowing chapter in the Special Relationship showed how carefully it had been nurtured from the days of Roosevelt and Churchill, 40 years earlier, and makes it appropriate to go back to the beginning and examine how well the foundations were laid.

II

How It All Began

'*A conference between us would proclaim the ever closer association of Britain and the United States, would cause our enemies concern, make Japan ponder, and cheer our friends.*'

Winston Churchill: July 1941

'*A productive and creative relationship, perhaps one of the most durable in the history of nations.*'

Henry Kissinger: 1982

Bold headlines across the front page of the *New York Times* on 11 September 1939 proclaimed the surge of the Nazi war machine against Germany's neighbours: 'Poles Repel Attacks on Warsaw: Nazis Report Trapping Two Armies'. Yet it was a much less prominent dispatch from England at the bottom of the page that gripped the attention of the Americans and, it is believed, their President. The war clouds over England seemed closer than the plight of the distant Poles. Under the headline 'London Grimly Pushes War Preparations; Gas Mask Boxes Give Picnic Appearance', the movingly written report from Raymond Daniell conveyed the stark transformation of the peaceful way of life in England which was so familiar to his readers.

The fact of war falls with brutal impact upon a traveller arriving in England. The most depressing sight of all were ships painted in funereal colours, waiting for the grim tasks ahead of them in this movement to smash Hitlerism. Everyone who boards the liner at Customs – Immigration men and Intelligence officials – carries a gas mask in a brown pasteboard box, slung from the shoulder by a yard of string. These boxes seen everywhere make it look as though the whole population were heading for a gigantic picnic.

The boat train to London is lightless and it puffs across an invisible countryside whose beauties are hidden under blackness and gloom. At the railway station in London porters help passengers select their baggage in inky shadows with the aid of shaded flashlights. One identifies the station only because the guard tells us we have arrived. Outside the station it is the blackest black. There is no other word to describe that darkness. Shaded taxicab sidelights seem mere glow-worms in the murk and as the taxi bumps away between solid but unseen buildings even the curbstones are invisible. Piccadilly, the Strand and Trafalgar Square all look alike in the blackness. Even their monuments are hidden. It is as though London's landmarks had been magically erased from the scene. In fact, the British capital after dark now is like the inside of a cinema theatre when the travelogue film is broken and the audience is waiting for the lights to come on.

While the advertisements in the *New York Times* ran tempting offers of a grilled fillet of Boston sole at the Longchamps restaurant for 65 cents, readers realized that any prospect of such a menu for the British was fast disappearing. With a picture showing people running across Parliament Square in London during a test of an air-raid warning, there was the sombre statistic that two more merchant ships had been sunk by German submarines, bringing the losses of British ships carrying food supplies to a total of 11 in the first eight days of the war. It may have been that grim portrait of London in the blackout, and the memories evoked by the hymns at the service on the previous day at the tiny episcopal church where President Franklin Roosevelt had worshipped with King George VI only three months previously, that prompted the first tentative steps towards the creation of the Special Relationship.

The initiative came from the American side of the Atlantic, not the British, as is commonly supposed. It was taken by President Roosevelt on that very day, 11 September 1939, in a letter to Winston Churchill eight days after the Tory rebel became a member of Neville Chamberlain's War Cabinet as First Lord of the Admiralty, a post he had held in World War I. There was no offer of help. Roosevelt was in no position to do that. A presidential election was only a year away and the isolationists in the 'America First' lobby were unlikely to be enthusiastic about any 'foreign adventures'. On the day Roosevelt wrote his letter, the *New York Times* reported that his neighbour had gone to war. Alongside the proclamation by Canadian Prime Minister Mackenzie King, there was a report that President Roosevelt had announced an arms embargo against Canada in accordance with the Neutrality Act.

That stance caused unease at the *New York Times*, which stated in its editorial: 'As matters stand we are committed to a line of action which violates our traditional neutrality and throws the weight of our influence, unnecessarily and unwisely, against the very nations which are engaged in defending decent standards of international conduct and our own democratic way of life.' A sharply contrasting view was expressed in the leading letter to the Editor of the *Washington Post*. It stated: 'When Hitler said to the British Ambassador "You dirty English (British); you are the cause of all the trouble in Europe", he certainly hit the nail on the head. The United States cannot go to the defence of British stupidity and perfidy again. If this country does get in, it should be on the side of Germany.' It was signed by Carl A. Neibling, President of the German League of the United States, from Kansas City. Totally different advice was given in the leading letter in the *New York Times* from Edwin Trent who called for the repeal of the Neutrality Act with one fundamental assertion: 'It should be realized that it is our own democratic government which is at stake. The issue is by no means confined to Europe. The war going on now will inevitably be our battle if France and Britain are defeated. In the circumstances this country should be ready, anxious and willing to furnish all the material equipment and supplies which Great Britain and France require of us. To do this now without delay may obviate the necessity of spilling our own blood in defence of our democratic form of government.' Middle-of-the-road opinion was expressed in the first sermon preached by the Revd Jesse Stitt at Greenwich Presbyterian Church and reported under the headline 'God on Both Sides in War'.

What President Roosevelt offered in his brief, 123-word letter was a sense of concern in these direct practical terms:

My Dear Churchill,
It is because you and I occupied similar positions in the World War that I want you to know how glad I am that you are back again at the Admiralty. Your problems are, I realize, complicated by new factors but the essential is not very different. What I want you and the Prime Minister to know is that I shall at all times welcome it if you keep me in touch personally with anything you want me to know about. You can always send sealed letters through your pouch or my pouch. I am glad you did the Marlboro volumes before this thing started – and I much enjoyed reading them.

With my sincere regards,
Faithfully yours,
Franklin Delano Roosevelt

Such was the start of a secret correspondence from the former Assistant Secretary of the Navy in Woodrow Wilson's administration, to which Churchill responded, as he admitted later, 'with alacrity' (correcting the spelling of Marlborough in his own memoirs!), initially under the code name 'Naval Person' and subsequently on becoming Prime Minister as 'Former Naval Person'. It was not the resumption of an old friendship. There had been only one glancing meeting during World War I when they exchanged salutations at a dinner at Gray's Inn in London. Nor was it a calculated move towards an association which Roosevelt foresaw would develop into a historic partnership. At best it was a shrewd assessment by Roosevelt that it would be in the interest of the United States for him to have a personal rapport with an English politician whose global perspective could make him Britain's wartime leader when events swept Chamberlain aside. The greeting on 11 September 1939 was a fresh start with someone who could keep him well informed.

Churchill enjoyed writing letters and had what generations before him called a 'fine epistolary style'. Sometimes in short telegraphic messages, at other times in long strategic and philosophic surveys, the letters were often written well after midnight at the end of exhausting days in the War Cabinet Room at Downing Street. With the five-hour time lag, a message dispatched from London before 3 a.m. could be answered by Roosevelt before going to sleep and be in London for Churchill to read at breakfast. The correspondence, amounting to some 950 messages sent by Churchill and some 800 from Roosevelt until his death over five years later, makes totally fascinating reading in a three-volume collection edited and annotated with immense dedication by Warren F. Kimball for publication by Princeton University Press. In its day it provided the intimacy and confidentiality which nowadays is achieved by the hot-line conversations between heads of government.

During the 'phoney war' in the first nine months of the conflict, and in the testing time leading to the fall of France, it was extremely important for Churchill to have direct access in order to influence the thinking of the President and to have the opportunity to enlist his support. He was aware that Ambassador Joseph Kennedy at the United States Embassy in London had no faith in the capacity of Britain to survive the onslaught of German bombers and fight back to turn the tide against the Nazis. The Ambassador's telegrams to Washington arguing that making war material available to Britain would be a wasted effort were intercepted and deciphered by the British Code and Cipher School, thus enabling Churchill to counter that despair and present the case for helping Britain in his own compelling terms. It was not, however, until after Churchill had become Prime Minister on 10 May 1940, as the Nazi blitzkrieg began punching holes in the French defences at Sedan, that he pitched a direct plea for help to the White House. In his first message as a 'Former Naval Person' on 15 May 1940, marked 'Most Secret and Personal', he urged Roosevelt to move from neutrality to non-belligerency 'which would mean that you would help us with everything short of actually engaging armed force'. For the first time he introduced a note of anxiety: 'I trust you realize, Mr President, that the voice and force of the United States may count for nothing if they are withheld too long. You may have a completely subjugated, Nazified Europe established with astonishing swiftness, and the weight may be more than we can bear.' It was the first time, too, that he called for the loan of '40 or 50 of your older destroyers'.

Five days later, with no response to his plea, Churchill put a nightmare scenario to Roosevelt. He conjured up the prospect of the Churchill Government, being denied American help but refusing to surrender, having to yield to a group of appeasers.

> If members of the present administration were finished and others came into parley amid the ruins, you must not be blind to the fact that the sole remaining bargaining counter with Germany would be the fleet, and if this country were left by the United States to its fate no one would have the right to blame those then responsible if they made the best terms they could for the surviving inhabitants. Excuse me, Mr President, putting this nightmare bluntly. Evidently I could not answer for my successors who in utter despair might well have to accommodate themselves to the German will.

The perilous state of Britain's defences after the fall of France was exposed at St Margaret's at Cliffe, three miles east of Dover, where all that was available to repel invaders along a coastline of four miles were three anti-tank guns, each with only six shells. An immediate appeal went to President Roosevelt to help replace the vast losses of equipment sustained in the evacuation of 338,226 troops from Dunkirk. General George Marshall, US Army Chief of Staff, gave his ordnance staff 48 hours to produce a list of reserve stocks of equipment and ammunition available for immediate shipping to Britain. He got the list on time and authorized the allocation of 500,000 rifles with ammunition, 900 field guns with one million rounds, 80,000 machine guns and other arms for sale at $37 million.

However, it was not until September 1940, standing alone facing a Nazi-occupied Western Europe and defying the *Luftwaffe* in the Battle of Britain, that Churchill was able to negotiate a deal for 50 destroyers which were to ensure that the lifeline of the British Isles was not severed. He did so by bypassing Ambassador Kennedy – who, he suspected, might try to sabotage the deal – and going instead through Britain's Ambassador in Washington, Lord Lothian. The Lend-Lease arrangement providing destroyers for Britain in return for the Americans getting bases on a 99-year lease in eight places – Antigua, Bahamas, Bermuda, British Guiana, Jamaica, Newfoundland, St Lucia and Trinidad – was described by Churchill as 'the most unsordid act in the history of any nation'. Once more he hyped it up to Parliament, telling MPs:

> Undoubtedly this process means that these two great organizations of the English-speaking democracies, the British Empire and the United States, will have to be somewhat mixed up together in some of their affairs for mutual and general advantage. For my part, looking out upon the future, I do not view the process with any misgivings. I could not stop it if I wished; no one can stop it. Like the Mississippi, it just keeps rolling along.

Subsequently, sceptical historians have sought to discredit Churchill for being duped into accepting destroyers which some critics believed were fit only for the scrapyard in return for giving the Americans a strategic foothold in significant British territories. However, they ignore the peril facing Britain at a time when any warship, no matter how old, could make the difference between vessels in convoy getting sunk or reaching port. One statistic from the autumn of 1940 – before the American destroyers came into service for Britain – undermines the arguments of these historians: between 17 and 19 October in the north-western approaches, German U-boats sank 33 ships – 22 of them British. Churchill had the answer for his critics in a letter written three years later on 14 October 1943, when he insisted that the destroyers 'although very old were most helpful at the critical time', but he acknowledged that they could not be compared to the strategic benefits of the bases. His justification was simple: 'I never defended the transaction as a business deal. I proclaimed to Parliament, and still proclaim, that the safety of the United States is involved in these bases, and that the military security of the United States must be considered a prime British interest.'

Where the cynics have a much stronger case is in highlighting American pressure in the conduct of the Cash-and-Carry system. Under diplomatic coercion not far short of blackmail from the United States, Britain had to sell the American division of Courtaulds at a depressed price only to discover later that it had fetched a substantially higher figure when put up for sale again on the market. While London was burning from the nightly air raids, the Americans were so eager to lay their hands on Britain's gold reserves held in South Africa that they sent a warship to Cape Town to speed its acquisition by Fort Knox. In a long review on 7 December 1940 of problems such as shipping losses, which had mounted to 420,300 tons in five weeks, Churchill warned Roosevelt of the financial strains that Britain faced:

> The moment approaches when we shall no longer be able to pay cash for shipping and other supplies. While we will do our utmost and shrink from no proper sacrifice to make payments across the exchange, I believe that you will agree that it would be wrong in principle and mutually disadvantageous in effect if, at the height of this struggle, Great Britain were to be divested of all saleable assets so that after victory was won with our blood, civilization saved and time gained for the United States to be fully armed against all eventualities, we should stand stripped to the bone.

Although how far the United States should go in helping Britain was not an issue in the election of November 1940 when Roosevelt's opponent, Wendell Wilkie, was equally firmly pledged to 'giving aid to the heroic British people', the renewal of the President's mandate enabled him to be much more open in his commitment. His message to the American people in a fireside chat on 30 December 1940 was more direct than before: 'We cannot escape danger by crawling into bed and pulling the covers over our heads. If Britain should go down, all of us in all the Americas would be living at the point of a gun. We must produce arms and ships – we must be the great arsenal of democracy.' That led to arrangements for American yards to repair British merchant ships and destroyers crippled by U-boat attacks. In the three months to May 1941, these attacks sank 142 ships – 99 of them British.

An even more important consequence was Roosevelt's decision to send his closest confidant, Harry Hopkins, to London on 10 January

1941 with a message of total commitment: 'The President is determined that we shall win the war together ... there is nothing that he will not do so far as he has human power.' As someone who knew Roosevelt's mind more intimately than anyone else, Hopkins was to become the ideal interlocutor and trusted channel of communication. Until he became seriously ill in 1944 he was on both sides of the Atlantic the fixer, the trouble-shooter and the subtle remover of ripples on the pool. In his war memoirs Churchill saluted Hopkins as an 'extraordinary man who played a sometimes decisive part in the whole movement of the war'. Hopkins was so trusted that Churchill insisted on his attending Cabinet meetings from time to time – an extension of the Special Relationship which did not always meet with general approval. Sir Alexander Cadogan's diary for 21 July 1941 revealed the irritation: 'Cabinet at 5. Lasted till nearly 8. Hopkins there again. This is rather absurd, and we had to get rid of him before the end on the excuse that we were going to discuss home affairs, and then discussed – America and the Far East!'

It was largely due to Hopkins, however, that after almost two years of correspondence arrangements were made for the two leaders to meet and cement their Special Relationship at a conference which Churchill believed 'would proclaim the ever closer association of Britain and the United States'. Their summit – the first of nine – at Placentia Bay, Newfoundland, from 9 to 12 August 1941, established its place in the history books for the declaration which became known as the Atlantic Charter. That in itself was ironic since the United States was not in the war, and Roosevelt did not want to antagonize his anti-interventionist lobby by seeming to become more involved. Yet he was eager to set out guidelines for the post-war world 'after the final destruction of Nazi tyranny'. Much of the declaration was pious platitudes holding forth the vision of men leading their lives 'in freedom from fear and want' and being able to 'traverse the high seas and oceans without hindrance'. But underneath the cordiality, which for many was the main benefit of bringing the statesmen together, there were the first indications of differences which subsequently caused controversy. Roosevelt's advisers pushed for wording on economic liberalization which clearly had Britain's attachment to Imperial Preference as the target. It was a signal of gathering irritation in the United States that America might be induced not only to help Britain win the war but also prolong the British Empire in the post-war world. Nimble diplomatic footwork enabled Churchill to avert an immediate clash by having Article Four of the Atlantic Charter refer to all states having 'access, on equal terms, to the trade and to the raw materials of the world'.

Five months later, on 7 December 1941, came the Japanese attack on Pearl Harbor and Roosevelt's terse comment to Churchill, 'We are all in the same boat now.' Churchill admitted: 'This certainly simplifies things.' For the first time in 18 months he no longer had to stand alone, and he went off to bed for what he described as 'the sleep of the saved and thankful'. On being asked at a meeting of the Chiefs of Staff the next day about continuing the gentle approach to the United States as before, Churchill was impishly dismissive, according to Sir Arthur Bryant in *The Turn of the Tide*. Apparently his response, with what Field Marshal Alanbrooke described as a 'wicked leer', was: 'Oh, that is the way we talked to her while we were wooing her: now that she is in the harem, we talk to her quite differently.'

At once the new partnership went into top gear. In less than a week, Churchill set sail for the United States to work out with Roosevelt a comprehensive programme of joint action: 'The whole plan of Anglo-American defence and attack has to be concerted in the light of reality.' In the course of three weeks at the Arcadia Conference in the White House, the two leaders agreed on a unity plan which concentrated land, sea and air forces under a Supreme Commander in each theatre of operations. There was genuine integration across the globe except for the Pacific where, as one Washington observer put it, Admiral Ernest J. King and General Douglas MacArthur 'preferred to keep foreigners, so to speak, in the waiting room'. Overall command was centralized in the Combined Chiefs of Staff Committee in Washington to control the general military strategy, supplies and reinforcements to the various theatres. Much of the success of this war machine was due to the harmony achieved by the two men at the top. Alanbrooke had persuaded Churchill to appoint Field Marshal Sir John Dill as Head of the British Military Mission in Washington – 'one of my most important accomplishments during the war,' Alanbrooke said later. Dill struck up a rare partnership with General George Marshall, the US Chief of Staff.

Meshed together under that superstructure, a network of co-ordinating units was established: the Munitions Assignment Board, the Combined Raw Materials Board, the Anglo-American Shipping Adjustment Board and the Combined Production and Resources Board. This resulted in the creation of an administrative force of 9,000 senior British experts – one and a half times the numbers in the Foreign

Office today – shipped from Britain to the United States. One British embassy official in Washington at the time who rose to become Head of the Diplomatic Service, Lord Gore-Booth, described it as 'a constellation of stars ... a concentration of British industrial and financial talent as can never before have lived for so long in a foreign capital'.

It was not until the Arcadia Conference that Churchill disclosed in detail to Roosevelt what Marshal of the Royal Air Force Sir John Slessor called Britain's 'priceless secret' – the Intelligence resources provided by Ultra which deciphered secret messages transmitted by the Nazis through their 200,000 Enigma machines in all branches of their armed forces. With the clandestine gift of an Enigma machine from the Poles – it arrived in a diplomatic bag at Victoria Station in London on 16 August 1939 – the British Code and Cipher School pulled off one of the most amazing coups of the war. The codebreakers, established in a country house at Bletchley, Buckinghamshire, under the disguise of Station X, Room 47, the Foreign Office, were a brains trust of outstanding Cambridge University mathematicians such as Alan Turing and Gordon Welchman together with some brilliant chess champions – Hugh Alexander, Harry Golombek and Stuart Milner-Barry.

After the first breakthrough in decoding in April 1940, Ultra was of crucial importance in revealing how hopeless the position of the British Expeditionary Force was in May, providing sufficient warning for the evacuation from Dunkirk. It was equally important for Air Chief Marshal Sir Hugh Dowding in assessing the build-up of the *Luftwaffe* and supplying advance notice of raids during the Battle of Britain. As an addict who could never get enough Intelligence material, Churchill would sometimes telephone Bletchley to enquire about the latest Ultra messages from the chief cryptanalysts whom he called 'the geese who laid the golden eggs but never cackled'. When he made his 'eggs' available to the Americans, they got what Ronald Lewin, the assiduous chronicler of the Bletchley operations, described as 'an enormous inheritance which they did not squander'.

By means of a machine called the Colossus Mark II set up at Bletchley to match the German *Geheimschreiber*, the secret writing apparatus made by Siemens which was 'guaranteed unintelligible' to any potential decoder, Station X intercepted the Nazi High Command's instructions to generals in the field. Operating at what in those days was an amazing speed – 250,000 characters a second – the Colossus was the forerunner of the modern electronic computer. Once sufficient American officers had been trained at Bletchley, the US commanders had special liaison units with them throughout the campaigns in Africa, Europe and the Far East. During the final preparations in March 1944 for the Normandy landings on 6 June, General Marshall reminded General Eisenhower: 'You are undoubtedly aware of the supreme importance the War Department attaches to Intelligence known as Ultra.' General George S. Patton became a devotee of Ultra, making sure that its service was always available at his command post, unlike Field Marshal Montgomery who had no time to read the warnings from Ultra in September 1944 that the Germans had secretly moved up two Panzer regiments to trap his forces at Arnhem in the disastrous airborne assault in south Holland.

Churchill's eagerness to make sure that Anglo-American co-operation went smoothly meant that he took great care over the smallest details. When General Bedell Smith, Chief of Staff to the Supreme Commander, raised a complaint from American officers who thought they were being charged extortionate amounts for accommodation in London, Churchill sent a stiff memorandum on 14 March 1944 to the Lord Chancellor, the Chancellor of the Exchequer, the Minister of Works and the Minister of Health. He demanded an immediate investigation of reports that Americans were having to pay £28 a week for a flat and £35 a week for a small house. 'There is no reason why the Americans should not pay a fair and equitable price for accommodation, which they are quite willing to do, but I do not think extortion or profiteering should be allowed.' Churchill's ability to turn from high strategy to the minutiae of Treasury accounting was exemplified in the midst of tortuous wrangling with the Russians over Poland on 18 March 1945, when he sent a memorandum to the Chancellor of the Exchequer stating: 'I see that the Foreign Office salaries are up by £666,893 – what are the principal causes of this very large increase?'

Scientific co-operation on atomic research, leading to the Manhattan Project which produced the bombs dropped on Japan, was not so smooth. There were times when it became exceedingly bumpy for the British. The Americans are apt to argue that the fault lay with the British who were originally overzealous in seeking to protect their independence. The British were well ahead of the United States in nuclear fission research and were only prepared to co-operate fully when the American side had overtaken them; the Americans, in their turn, were suspicious of the British seeking post-war benefits. However, there is no doubt that the impetus came from scientists in Britain, albeit German refugees at Birmingham University: Professor Rudolf Peierls and Dr Otto Frisch. Their three-page paper 'On the Construction of a "Super-Bomb" based on a Nuclear Chain Reaction in Uranium' in March 1940 resulted in the establishment of the Maud Committee which became the catalyst for nuclear research. Professor Margaret Gowing, the eminent authority on the history of atomic energy developments, is emphatic: 'Without the work of the Maud Committee ... the Second World War might well have ended before an atomic bomb was dropped.'

When the Maud Report was handed to the Americans, they were so taken aback by the progress in Britain that Roosevelt instructed Dr Vannevar Bush, the Director of the Office of Scientific Research and Development, to make overtures to the British for close collaboration to develop an atomic bomb. Roosevelt wrote to Churchill before their Arcadia Conference suggesting discussions 'in order that any extended efforts may be co-ordinated or even jointly conducted'. But Sir John Anderson, the Cabinet minister in charge of the project – code-named Tube Alloys – with the ultimate object of building a production plant in Britain for an atomic bomb, rejected the American overtures in what Professor Gowing called 'a most superior tone'. His reservations were endorsed by Lord Cherwell whose advice on scientific matters carried great weight with Churchill. A memorandum from Lord Cherwell to Churchill warned: 'However much I may trust my neighbour, and depend on him, I am very much averse to putting myself completely at his mercy and would, therefore, not press the Americans to undertake this work.'

Subsequently, after calculating the cost of going it alone, Sir John changed his tune. In a memorandum to Churchill dated 31 July 1942, he admitted that since entering the war after the Japanese attack on Pearl Harbor the Americans had outstripped the British in nuclear research: 'The Americans have been applying themselves with enthusiasm and lavish expenditure, which we cannot rival, over the whole field of Tube Alloys.' Although the British method was still considered the best, 'it has little chance so long as work on it is handicapped by the limited resources available in this country'.

It was now Britain's turn to advocate a joint effort, but the mood of the Americans had changed. Much of this was due to the project being put under the control of an officer from the US Army Corps of

Engineers in September 1942. One day 46-year-old Leslie Groves was a Colonel in charge of building ordnance depots and army camps; the next he was promoted Brigadier-General in charge of the Manhattan Project with the job of building the world's first atomic bomb. Groves had strict ideas about how to handle security. He put the 'long hairs', as he called America's scientists, into uniform and kept the Limey scientists from Britain outside the secret research centres. For over a year the British were cut off from the American scientists without even any exchange of information. It was not until August 1943 that Churchill persuaded Roosevelt – with backstairs manoeuvring by Harry Hopkins – to lift the barriers.

Under the Quebec Agreement of 19 August 1943, arrangements were made 'to ensure full and effective collaboration between the two countries'. For the British there was an added dividend: a veto on the use of the bomb – 'we will not use it against third parties without each other's consent'. In return, however, Britain accepted restraint on what could be gained after the war because of 'a far greater expense' having fallen on the Americans. 'The Prime Minister expressly disclaims any interest in these industrial and commercial aspects beyond what may be considered by the President of the United States to be fair and just and in harmony with the economic welfare of the world.' The immediate benefits were in bringing the British scientists into direct involvement with the advances being made in gaseous diffusion and the engineering aspects of the bomb. The doors of the American installation at Los Alamos were opened to some 50 British physicists and engineers, but under the tight security imposed by General Groves everything was carefully compartmentalized so that scientists were not able to move freely from one laboratory to another. That meant that no British scientists were allowed into the plutonium section of the installation.

Although there was relief on the British side that they were back in partnership with the Americans in a special nuclear relationship, it was clearly established from then onwards that Britain was to be at best a junior partner and on occasion just a minor one. Churchill, however, was always reluctant to concede that the relationship was anything less than a partnership of equals. Realizing that this concept would be increasingly difficult to sustain in the post-war era when the predominance of the Americans would be too obvious to deny, Churchill deployed all his persuasive powers to secure Roosevelt's agreement for a formal guarantee of co-operation continuing indefinitely after the war. Article Two of a secret 'Aide-Memoire of Conversation between the President and the Prime Minister at Hyde Park on September 19, 1944' stated: 'Full collaboration between the United States and the British Government in developing Tube Alloys for military and commercial purposes should continue after the defeat of Japan unless and until terminated by joint agreement.' Armed with that pledge Churchill thought he had stilled the anxieties of British scientists, but, as subsequent events were to demonstrate, controversy over co-operation kept erupting for more than a decade.

The idea of extending what Churchill called 'a righteous comradeship' in his first address to the United States Congress on 26 December 1941 was always close to his heart, but the lengths to which he was prepared to go in the hope of preserving the partnership after the war took his righteous American comrades aback. During his third visit to Washington for the conference on strategy codenamed Trident, he aired his ideas of 'a fraternal association' at a luncheon on 22 May 1943 in the British Embassy attended by Vice-President Henry Wallace, Secretary of War Henry Stimson and Secretary of the Interior Harold Ickes. He floated the proposition of Americans and Britons having equal rights in each other's country. The memorandum of the meeting sent to Roosevelt elaborated it: 'There might be a common passport or a special form of passport or visa. There might even be some common form of citizenship, under which citizens of the United States and of the British Commonwealth might enjoy voting privileges after residential qualification and be eligible for public office in the territories of the other, subject, of course, to the laws and institutions there prevailing.' Vice-President Wallace politely categorized the conversation as the most encouraging he had had for years but left Churchill's grand design at the bottom of the files.

Churchill's proposals were a reflection of his anxiety about the slippage in the Special Relationship which he had worked so hard to perpetuate. As he began to see Britain's influence waning, Churchill became more sensitive to the gap between Britain and the United States over a wide range of issues. His faithful physician Lord Moran observed in his memoirs that Churchill had been very careful in his handling of Roosevelt up to a certain stage in the war:

> At first all went well. ... He would listen for hours – and listening did not come easily to him – to stories he had heard before. ... When things began to go wrong I cannot tell. As America came to make all the decisions that mattered and to take over the control of operations,

the PM became sorely worried about the future. He was sure he knew how the war could be won, and now that England's survival was no longer at stake he felt free to speak about his misgivings. As time passed, it was noticed that he got more and more outspoken.

For Churchill, the warning signals of change came as Roosevelt became convinced that he was best placed to deal with Russia in planning not just the conduct of the war but in the disposition of power afterwards. As early as 18 March 1942, Roosevelt served notice of Churchill's diminishing status: 'I know you will not mind my being brutally frank when I tell you that I think I can personally handle Stalin better than either your Foreign Office or my State Department. Stalin hates the guts of all your top people. He thinks he likes me better and I hope he will continue to do so.' When Roosevelt started pushing for a faster convoy service of supplies to help Russia, Churchill replied stonily: 'With great respect what you suggest is beyond our power to fulfil.'

A year later, while Roosevelt was in correspondence with Churchill over meeting Stalin and claiming 'You and I are completely frank in matters of this kind', he was shown to have been manoeuvring behind Churchill's back. Despite denying that he had suggested a Big-Two meeting without Churchill and blaming 'Uncle Joe' for suggesting it, Roosevelt was found guilt of a straight lie. Thereafter Churchill was apt to fret, as he did at the Teheran summit in November 1943, when Roosevelt had any private exchanges with Stalin. Suspicions were mutual. When Churchill insisted on flying to Moscow in October 1944 to see Stalin on his own about questions concerning Poland and the working of the United Nations, there was unease in Washington. Regardless of Roosevelt's reservations and his decision to end Averell Harriman as an observer, Churchill made it clear that Harriman's presence would not 'preclude private tête-à-tête between me and U.J. [Uncle Joe]'.

Throughout the wartime partnership there was an undercurrent of anxiety on the American side that Churchill was using it to perpetuate the control of the British over their empire. In American eyes the first joint declaration by the two leaders on 12 August 1941 established 'the freely expressed wishes of the people concerned' as one of the main themes of the Atlantic Charter. For them, Article Three – which stated that the two sides 'respect the right of all peoples to choose the form of government under which they live' – was a commitment to end colonialism. Not so for Churchill. For him the second part of that article about sovereign rights and self-determination being 'restored to those who have been forcibly deprived of them' was the key commitment since it was for the victims of aggression by the Germans, Italians and Japanese.

Roosevelt's concern for India riled Churchill when it was raised on his first visit to Washington in December 1941. After the Japanese stormed into Burma and seized Rangoon in March 1942, bringing the threat of war close to the Indian subcontinent, Roosevelt sent a long message to Churchill urging him to consider moves towards liberalization by setting up a temporary Dominion Government with representatives from 'different castes, occupations, religions and geographies'. He renewed his plea a month later when the mission of Sir Stafford Cripps to Delhi failed to break the deadlock over constitutional reform. Roosevelt was blunt about where the blame lay: 'The feeling is almost universally held that the deadlock has been caused by the unwillingness of the British Government to concede the right of self-government, notwithstanding the willingness of the Indians to entrust technical, military and naval defence control to the competent British authorities.' Churchill, however, was in no mood to take advice from someone who, in his view, saw the issue nostalgically in terms of the 13 American colonies trying to throw off the yoke of George III. To set up a national government in India at that stage would have been, in Churchill's opinion, 'an act of madness'.

American criticism of his policy in Africa provoked Churchill into sharp exchanges. What stung him most was a report by five senators – one of whom was Henry Cabot Lodge, the Republican from Massachusetts – which he would have denounced before a Senate Committee if he had been in the United States at the time. Instead, he wrote a long letter on 14 October 1943 to Harry Hopkins, which he knew would be shown to the President, explaining how 'cruel and churlish' were the senators' suggestions that 'in Africa the Americans were conquering territories and the British ruling them afterwards'. He put the record straight by pointing out that AMGOT – Allied Military Government of Occupied Territories – was an Anglo-American operation. 'We have nowhere "taken over" territory alone except in Italian East Africa which we liberated alone.' He also set out some 'simple facts' for his American critics to ponder: 'In the fighting in Tunis, Sicily and Italy up to the present the British have lost more than twice as many men killed, wounded and missing as the United States.'

Inevitably, as the war reached its climax and attention in the United

States and Britain began to focus more on the problems of the post-war world, the divergences in the relationship became more obvious. National interests asserted themselves in economic and political issues despite the rhetoric in public about common objectives. The two governments started off in harmony at the United Nations Monetary and Financial Conference in July 1944 at Bretton Woods in New Hampshire. Each assembled a vast array of talent: on the British side Lord Keynes led a team of experts which included Sir Kingsley Wood, Sir Percival Liesching and Sir John Anderson; on the American side the formidable Harry Dexter White was surrounded by powerful delegates such as Dean Acheson, Winthrop Brown and Henry Morganthau. The struggle between them over international monetary reform resulted in what was diplomatically described as a judicious compromise, but the terms for the conference's two main achievements – the International Monetary Fund and the International Bank for Reconstruction and Development – were largely dictated by the Americans.

Politically, the divergences had a much sharper edge because of the passions aroused in public by the struggles for power in the liberated territories. One of the biggest controversies centred on the clash with the Communists in Greece after the British forces drove out the Germans. House-to-house fighting between British troops and snipers of the Communist controlled ELAS – People's National Army of Liberation – earned vehement condemnation in the United States and a stern comment from the State Department. There was outrage over the mistaken belief that Churchill was trying to reimpose King George II on the Greeks. Taking the temperature on the sidelines, Churchill's doctor, Lord Moran, observed: 'There were angry exchanges between the President and the Prime Minister, and our relations with the White House became very strained.' The six-week crisis was only resolved when Churchill gave up his Christmas holiday, flew to Athens and calmed the situation with a settlement establishing a regency under Archbishop Damaskinos.

The Greek crisis was a prelude to tougher struggles over the structure and balance of power in post-war Europe at the Yalta Conference in February 1945. Realizing that there would be harsh clashes with Stalin over Poland, Churchill was eager to have two or three nights with Roosevelt in advance at Malta to co-ordinate tactics. Roosevelt, however, said that he could not spare the time, so Churchill had to be content with a working dinner on the President's warship,

USS *Quincy*, before flying on to the Black Sea. That proved to be a serious miscalculation which reduced the cohesion of the joint negotiating position at Yalta. The partnership was further weakened by the failing health of the President. Churchill, himself understandably showing signs of strain after five gruelling years of wartime leadership, was unaware at the time of the steady deterioration in Roosevelt's grip on affairs. Writing in his war memoirs, Churchill acknowledged what he should have observed on the way to their final meeting: 'In my long telegrams I thought I was talking to my trusted friend and colleague as I had done all these years. I was no longer being fully heard by him.' Roosevelt's condition was disguised by those around him. Sometimes the telegrams from the White House were drafted by General Marshall. Normally Harry Hopkins would have taken an increased share of the burden, but by then his own state of health was fragile.

Even a vigorous Roosevelt–Churchill partnership might not have been able to block Stalin's determination to have the Communist-controlled Lublin Government as his puppet in Poland. But Stalin's objectives were made much easier to achieve when Churchill lacked the fulsome support of Roosevelt in opposing the excesses of the Communist take-over. Although the question of Poland's borders and the way the government was to be formed occupied over 80 per cent of the conference time at Yalta, it was not the issue which was of supreme importance to Roosevelt. That was raised at the end during a private meeting between him and Stalin: the terms for Russia entering the war against Japan after the surrender of Germany. Churchill was not even consulted on the negotiations. The first time he saw the agreement was on 11 February 1945 when he was asked to sign the document. It underlined again how the Americans marginalized Britain in matters concerning the Pacific area. For once, however, Churchill was not disconcerted at being left on the sidelines. In view of the subsequent criticism of the concessions made to Stalin's territorial demands, such as the restoration of southern Sakhalin, Churchill was relieved not to have had any part in the negotiations.

When the Russians continued to ignore commitments made at Yalta to allow a wide range of consultations on the formation of a Polish government, Churchill became impatient with Roosevelt's slowness in accepting the need for tough talking to Stalin and persistent pressure. In one further plea for Roosevelt to take firm joint action, Churchill warned on 13 March: 'I do not wish to reveal a divergence between the British and the United States Governments, but it would certainly be necessary for me to make it clear that we are in presence of a great failure and an utter breakdown of what was settled at Yalta, but that we British have not the necessary strength to carry the matter further.' Although the reply sent in Roosevelt's name by his aides hotly denied any real divergence, it angered Churchill by playing for time in seeking a truce between Poland's political groups. That proposition he was not prepared to support because he believed that it would allow Russia to make all the rules, deciding what was a breach of the truce and what was not. At last Roosevelt – or his staff handling the correspondence – accepted that it was time for the United States and Britain to express concern directly to Stalin and demand that the Polish problem be settled fairly and speedily. A telegram on 11 April from the White House to Churchill agreed to assess Stalin's attitude carefully and pledged to 'take no action of any kind nor make any statement without consulting you'.

That was the last pledge of the partnership. On the following day, 12 April 1945, Roosevelt collapsed and died at Warm Springs, Georgia. His death was a grievous blow to Churchill since Roosevelt and he had come to personify the Special Relationship. Amid all the eulogies to a President who overcame the enormous handicap of life in a wheelchair to lead his country through traumatic experiences in peace and war, Churchill confessed the depth of his own sadness to Harry Hopkins: 'We have lost one of the greatest friends and one of the most valiant champions of the causes for which we fight. I feel a very painful loss, quite apart from the ties of public action which bound us so closely. I had a true affection for Franklin.'

Inevitably, the character of the relationship changed. Roosevelt once sent a telegram to Churchill saying: 'It's fun being in the same decade with you.' That familiarity vanished at a stroke. When former Senator Harry S. Truman of Kansas City, Missouri, was sworn in as President, he had been Vice-President for only 82 days and, apart from attending Cabinet meetings, had met Roosevelt only twice in that period. On neither occasion, apparently, was there any serious discussion of international affairs. Until he became President, Truman had shown no interest in foreign policy. He did not know Churchill, and as his biographer David McCullough disclosed, 'He didn't know his own Secretary of State more than to say Hello.' It was not until his twelfth day as President, when General Groves came secretly to the White House with Secretary of War Henry Stimson, that he became aware of the Manhattan Project and that its outcome, the atomic bomb, would be ready within four months. But Truman began learning about the problems of the world quickly, principally from Averell Harriman who had been Ambassador to Russia since 1943 and who flew home immediately on Roosevelt's death to warn the new President of the Communist threat in a phrase that stuck in Truman's mind: 'a barbarian invasion' of Europe.

Truman's enthusiasm to make his mark vigorously with the Russians right from the start caught Foreign Minister Vyacheslav Molotov off-guard at their first meeting on 23 April 1945. Cutting short the Soviet minister's ritual diatribe on Poland, Truman said that he was not interested in propaganda and sent him away with instructions to inform Stalin that the United States Government was concerned at the Soviet Government's failure to abide by its commitments at Yalta. Molotov turned ashen. According to David McCullough, Truman's recollection was that Molotov responded: 'I have never been talked to like that in my life.' 'Carry out your agreements,' Truman told him, 'and you won't get talked to like that.' Impressive though it was, Truman had still to win his spurs in Churchill's eyes.

That Churchill's early exchanges with Truman were not marked with the cordiality expected of the transatlantic partnership may well have been partly due to a misjudgement by the Prime Minister in not going to the United States for Roosevelt's funeral. Most experienced politicians recognize that State funerals provide some of the best opportunities to pave the way for future political dividends. Prime Minister Margaret Thatcher needed no convincing about that. Her attendance in Moscow for the funeral of President Andropov in February 1984 enabled her to have 40 minutes alone with his successor President Chernenko – 15 minutes more than George Bush was accorded in deputizing for President Reagan – and ultimately gave her a head start to be the first to 'do business with' Mikhail Gorbachev. The chance to do business with Truman was given to Churchill as the funeral arrangements for Roosevelt were being discussed. The new President let it be known he would appreciate an early meeting and that he could set aside two or three days for talks if Churchill chose to attend the funeral. It was taken for granted that Churchill would go, especially since less than a month before he had written to Roosevelt saying: 'Our friendship is the rock on which I build for the future of the world.' But he decided to stay in London for a memorial service for Roosevelt attended by King George VI and have Sir Anthony

Eden represent him in the United States. Afterwards, when he realized that Roosevelt had not brought Truman into the decision-making process, he acknowledged that there was a gap he could have filled at a critical stage.

An edginess began to cause ripples in the relationship. Three days after the war ended in Europe on 8 May Churchill proposed to Truman that they should meet Stalin, but the new President insisted that nothing should be done which might give the impression that they were ganging up. He wanted the invitation to come from Stalin. Yet a fortnight later Truman sent a special envoy to London, Joseph Davies, a former American Ambassador in Moscow, with a proposition which appeared to relegate Churchill to the status of junior partner. Truman was proposing to meet Stalin alone somewhere in Europe before opening up the sessions as a tripartite meeting. Churchill was furious. In a long, stiff note presented to the hapless Mr Davies to take back to Washington, he was emphatic: 'It must be understood that the representatives of His Majesty's Government would not be able to attend any meeting except as equal partners from its opening.' The underlying implication that Truman saw himself as a mediator in disputes between Britain and Russia caused further resentment: 'The Prime Minister cannot readily bring himself to accept the idea that the position of the United States is that Britain and Soviet Russia are just two foreign powers, six of one and half a dozen of the other, with whom the troubles of the late war have to be adjusted.'

Despite his anger, Churchill diplomatically left room to start the relationship afresh on a better footing, saying that he 'indulged the hope that he might have some private talks with the President before the general sittings commence'. Truman accepted the suggestion and invited Churchill for their first meeting in the 'little White House' at 2 Kaiserstrasse in the Berlin suburb of Babelsberg beside Lake Grieb-nitz, three miles from Potsdam, on 16 July 1945. After their two-hour talk, Churchill's assessment to Lord Moran seemed couched for quotation to the American Press: 'He seems a man of exceptional charm and ability, with an outlook exactly along the lines of Anglo-American relationships as they have developed. He has a direct method of speech and a great deal of self-confidence and resolution.' Years later, Churchill admitted that his private assessment was somewhat different. Aboard the presidential yacht he began a toast by looking back to their first meeting and saying: 'I must confess, Sir, I held you in very low regard. I loathed your taking the place of Franklin

Roosevelt.' Truman was more circumspect in recording his first impressions to his wife: 'He gave me a lot of hooey about how great my country is and how he loved Roosevelt and how he intended to love me etc., etc. Well ... I am sure we can get along if he doesn't try to give me too much soft soap.'

That evening Secretary of War Stimson handed Truman a telegram which stated: 'Operated on this morning. Diagnosis not yet complete but results seem satisfactory and already exceed expectations.' Truman went to bed knowing that a test explosion of the atomic bomb had taken place successfully in the New Mexico desert. On the following day, in accordance with the agreement on consultation, Stimson went to Churchill with the same message in a different code: 'Babies satisfactorily born.' Throughout that week there were complex discussions between Truman and Churchill about what to say to Stalin and how to do so, what terms should be imposed in an ultimatum to Japan and what sort of warning to give the Japanese people. Neither side questioned whether an atomic bomb should be dropped. With the prospect of shortening the war by several months and saving a quarter of a million American casualties, according to General Marshall's calculations, Truman had no doubts. It was basically just a matter of timing and that was left to Truman to decide. The decision was formally endorsed on 24 July when Truman and Churchill met at 2 Kaiserstrasse with the Combined Chiefs of Staff. In the afternoon Truman casually told Stalin about having a new weapon, but the Russian leader did not seem interested enough to ask any questions.

The decision on the atomic bomb was the last wartime consultation that Churchill had with his American allies. He flew back from Berlin to London on 25 July. The ultimatum, which the Japanese instantly rejected, was issued on 26 July, the day the British general election results announced Churchill's defeat. He handed the baton for the Special Relationship to Clement Attlee who took Churchill's seat at the Potsdam Conference with the end of the war only 19 days away. Following Churchill onto the world stage as Britain's leader at such a moment was a daunting challenge for any politician, but the prospects of fresh faces creating new cordiality in the transatlantic relationship were not highly rated, according to Truman's first impressions. His assessment of Attlee and Foreign Secretary Ernest Bevin, written down at the time, was far from flattering:

Mr Attlee is not so keen as old fat Winston and Mr Bevin looks rather

31

rotund to be a Foreign Minister. Seems Bevin is a sort of John L. Lewis type. Eden was a perfect striped pants boy. I wasn't fond of Eden – he is a much overrated man; and he didn't play fair with his boss. I did like old Churchill. He was as windy as Langer [Senator William Langer of North Dakota] but he knew his English language and after he'd talked half an hour there'd be at least one gem of a sentence and two thoughts maybe which could have been expressed in four minutes. But if we ever got him on record he stayed put. Anyway he is a likeable person and these other two are sourpusses.

Nonetheless, Truman appeared ready to keep an open mind about the partnership when he wrote to his wife, Bess, saying: 'We shall see what we shall see.'

III

The Partners Drift Apart

*'Of course a unique relation existed between Britain and America –
our common language and history ensured that. But unique did
not mean affectionate. We had fought England as an enemy as
often as we had fought by her side as an ally.'*

Dean Acheson: 1970

*'The United States administration often behaves insufferably to
its allies. Americans are apt to behave insufferably to each other.
Their natural characteristics and their constitutional processes are
what they are, and it does little good to get angry about them.'*

Lord Strang: 1951

Wartime comradeship, however 'righteous', can sometimes be very
vulnerable to the different demands of peacetime. Those who waited
patiently, as Truman suggested, to 'see what we shall see' were shocked
by the abruptness of the changes announced on 21 August 1945. On
that day, only seven days after final victory in the six-year struggle
against the dictators, Britain received a crushing diktat from Washington. It came in a document placed before the President at the
White House by Leo Crowley, Director of the Foreign Economic
Administration. On signing it, Truman put Britain into a financial
straitjacket since it ended the 1941 Lend-Lease Act instantly. Thereafter
the British Government's credit facilities dried up. Everything imported
from the United States required payment in cash. It was a devastating
blow for Attlee because the country's economy was in a state of
exhaustion after the war, and all the Socialist dreams of building a
better Britain depended on having a breathing space in which to pay
the bills. It was the first warning sign for the new Prime Minister that
the wartime partners were drifting apart.

The crux of the problem in terms of Anglo-American relations was the failure of the Americans to comprehend the vast difference in the legacy of the war on the other side of the Atlantic. In the United States, the end of the war simply meant a return to normal at once. Although billions of dollars in war contracts came to an end, that did not dampen the new prosperity across the country. Manufacturing totals were more than twice the 1939 figure. Prices in the shops had gone up by 30 per cent, but there were no serious shortages and the average working wage had doubled. Wartime controls were cancelled and the go-ahead given for full-scale peacetime production.

In Britain the drain on the nation's resources left the country debilitated, facing austerity on every front. Having been forced to liquidate £2 billion in foreign assets during the war and having accumulated undischarged obligations totalling £3.5 billion to Commonwealth countries, Britain was in the humiliating position of being a debtor nation. People shuddered at the prospect of a hard winter with shortages of food and fuel. Pre-war imports of food and other supplies from the United States at a rate of 22 million tons a year had been halved. Clothes rationing was even stricter than in wartime. Vast numbers were homeless after air raids and V2 rockets left 4 million houses damaged. Coal output dropped from 231 million tons in 1939 to 176 million tons in 1945, with the number of miners down from 782,000 to 712,000. Merchant shipping was reduced to less than half its pre-war strength as a result of German U-boats. Factories suffered from lack of raw materials, outdated equipment and a labour force reduced by one million, since the old men and married women who augmented wartime production were no longer available. Even the Royal Mint was in trouble as the coins of the realm were dependent on American supplies. From 1941 almost all the silver required for Britain's currency came from the United States – under Lend-Lease – at an average of 27 million ounces a year.

What really incensed the British about the end of Lend-Lease was the way it was done. The day before the announcement Winthrop Aldrich, the President of the International Chamber of Commerce, told a luncheon in London of the American Chamber: 'The economic welfare of Britain is inseparably bound up with the economic welfare of the United States. Everyone is agreed that it is no more possible for each to go their separate ways in peace than in war.' Yet there was no consultation over the revocation of the Lend-Lease Act and the consequences of cutting off the flow of goods – civilian as well as military supplies – to allied nations which amounted to £10 billion since 1941. The first that the British heard of it was in a letter on 20 August – the day before the announcement – to the Embassy in Washington stating that the measures became effective on receipt of the letter. Prime Minister Attlee did not get the courtesy of a message from President Truman. Crowley was adamant that no advance warning was required because the beneficiaries should have been aware that, under the terms of the Act, Lend-Lease ended with the surrender of Japan.

Attlee, a man who rarely lost his equanimity, found it hard to contain his anger. He readily acknowledged that no one expected the system to be continued for any length of time, but he told Parliament bluntly: 'We had hoped that the sudden cessation of this great mutual effort, which has contributed so much to victory, would not have been effected without consultation and prior discussion of the different problems involved in the disappearance of a system of so great a range and complication.' Churchill endorsed Attlee's feelings with his own anguish. He found it difficult to believe that 'so great a nation, whose Lend-Lease policy was characterized by me as the most unsordid act in the history of the world, would proceed in such a rough and harsh manner as to hamper a faithful ally'.

The impact of the cut-off was all the more dramatic because it applied immediately not only to goods awaiting dispatch from America but also to supplies on their way to Britain and even to some stocks already there. It put Britain in what Attlee described as 'a very serious financial position'. On the eve of the Japanese surrender, the cost of bringing essential food and non-munitions supplies to Britain was running at the rate of £2 billion a year. Offset against that were exports averaging £350 million a year and reimbursements of around £450 million from the Commonwealth for expenditure incurred on their behalf. That meant that the Exchequer faced a gap of £1.2 billion. To make that up by expanded production would have required a Herculean effort beyond the country's capacity, since the annual amount of Lend-Lease supplies was the equivalent of the output of 1,820,000 people or 11 per cent of Britain's work force. Chancellor Hugh Dalton admitted that the way the Treasury coffers were left so depleted by the American decision was a 'strange and ironical reward' for what the British people had endured for a common cause.

Attlee was constrained from speaking his mind frankly about the blow to the Special Relationship since Britain had to become a suppliant seeking a US loan on the best possible terms. However, the negotiating team he sent to Washington under the leadership of Lord Keynes did not go cap in hand. They reminded the Americans that Lend-Lease was a two-way process and that Britain's help to the United States had been far from negligible. The actual value of reverse Lend-Lease from Britain to the United States was calculated at £949,222,000, but there were many unquantifiable elements such as the British invention of the Pluto pipeline under the English Channel which was important for General Eisenhower's Normandy landings in June 1944. Other dividends for the Americans were the British advances in the development of radar technology and the usefulness of Fido, the fog dispersal system. Even the stately British liners, *Queen Mary* and *Queen Elizabeth*, made a substantial contribution to reverse Lend-Lease by transporting one million American troops back to the United States.

One of the most potent arguments made by Lord Keynes was a ten-point document comparing the burdens borne by Britain and the United States in the course of the war:

1. British casualties were well over twice the American figure, with losses killed and missing three times more.
2. Members of the British forces gave twice as much in man-years as Americans.
3. The proportion of Britons mobilized in the Services or war production was 55 per cent as against 40 per cent in the United States.
4. Industrial plant not in war production deteriorated in Britain by more than twice the extent it did in the United States.
5. Britain's losses in external investment were 35 times greater than those of America.
6. American consumption rose by 16 per cent while Britain's dropped by 16 per cent.
7. British taxpayers paid 53.3 per cent of the cost of the war as against 46.7 per cent by Americans.
8. Britain's total expenditure in the war was 50 per cent greater than the United States'.
9. National debt in Britain rose to a total 40 per cent above America's.
10. British shipping went down through sinkings from 40 million deadweight tons to 19.5 million tons while America's quadrupled to 50 million tons.

Before Lord Keynes left for Washington, Attlee told him to remind the Americans that British people had had to endure one extra burden not experienced in the United States – the blackout. Lord Keynes was optimistic that the Americans would repent their rashness over Lend-

Lease and come up with a deal to get Britain out of its financial problems. Certainly, Truman had second thoughts and admitted afterwards: 'Crowley taught me this lesson early in my Administration – that I must always know what is in the documents I sign.' But any fond illusions Keynes may have had about securing an interest-free loan of the order of £1.5 billion were soon shattered. Within 24 hours of his arrival in Washington, he was made aware that the US Treasury was not in the business of advancing loans without strict conditions. The quick in-and-out visit he envisaged with an agreement worked out in three days was a forlorn hope. It took three months of tough bargaining to get a loan agreement – and that was hedged around with terms that aroused resentment and fierce criticism back in London.

Despite the fury of the Bevanites in the Labour Party that Britain was now beholden to 'American capitalists', Attlee and his Chancellor, Dalton, were realistic enough to accept that their negotiating leverage was minimal and that in the end they had no alternative but to take what the Americans decided to give. It was the first demonstration of the theorem – and there were a number of others in the subsequent decades – that the closeness of the transatlantic relationship was in direct proportion to the usefulness of the British to the Americans at any particular time in the international political and economic arenas. That usefulness was generally determined by the interplay of international forces, but it was also governed by the status which the British Government could claim to have through its political and economic standing in the world. In the immediate post-war situation Attlee knew that he was doomed to hold yarboroughs at the diplomatic bridge table and that he could not command respect as a powerful partner until he had a stronger economic hand.

Attlee also felt that he suffered a disadvantage because many Americans who saw Churchill as the epitome of the fine old English gentleman were fearful about his successor being the leader of a Socialist government, which they saw as just one step short of Communism. The warmth of affection for Churchill was not there for Attlee, especially when Americans heard him announce plans for nationalization. In an attempt to raise his own stock in the United States, Attlee tackled the prejudices against him when he addressed a joint session of Congress during his visit to Washington on 13 November 1945: 'I think that some people over here imagine that the Socialists are out to destroy freedom – freedom of the individual, freedom of speech, freedom of religion and the freedom of the Press. They are wrong. . . . We in the Labour Party declare that we are in line with those who fought for Magna Carta and habeas corpus, with the Pilgrim Fathers and the signatories of the Declaration of Independence.' To disabuse Congressmen of the idea that most of Labour Party MPs were drawn from the struggling wage-earning class, Attlee insisted that, although many of his ministers had worked with their hands, the Party also attracted professional men, businessmen and 'what are sometimes called the privileged classes'. It was an earnest, well-argued case, but not many Americans were prepared to change their views of Socialist Britain or its leader on the strength of one speech.

The loan agreement announced on 6 December which resulted in the United States putting a total of £1.1 billion at Britain's disposal looked impressive in the headlines. It was made up of a credit amounting to £937.5 million and a loan of £162.5 million to cover the cost of the Lend-Lease supplies in the pipeline when the cut-off took place. It was the small print which stuck in the throats of many in Britain. First, the credit had to be repaid over 50 years at 2 per cent – an exaction that Churchill found exorbitant in the circumstances which caused Britain to fall into debt. Secondly, there was the requirement that sterling should become convertible in a year, which even Keynes, a staunch supporter of convertible currency, regarded as a dangerously short timescale. Thirdly, by making the loan a corollary to the ratification of the Bretton Woods agreement, not only was convertibility essential but it required totally free trade unfettered by restrictions such as Imperial Preference, tariffs and subsidies. America's priorities were not disguised. As *The Times* acidly commented: 'Like greyhounds in the slips, their salesmen are ready. The loan to Britain will open a capacious door.'

Attlee and Dalton had a hard time trying to convince MPs – their own supporters on the Left as well as Conservatives – that the terms dictated by the Americans were the best possible deal and that turning one's back on it was not an option, since there were no others capable of offering a rescue package. Sir John Anderson, the leading Conservative spokesman, served notice that the process of lending dollars and then exporting from the dollar area could become a crude device for one-way trade. The maverick Tory Robert Boothby branded the deal an 'economic Munich' and moved an amendment to reject it. A similar amendment for rejection came from Michael Foot; even Churchill urged the Conservatives to abstain. In the end the deal was approved by 345 votes to 98 with a large number of abstentions and over 20 Labour MPs voting against it. However, the strength of feeling registered against the terms imposed by the Americans testified to the disappointment at the way the transatlantic partners had drifted apart so soon after the war.

Dean Acheson, who became Under-Secretary at the State Department a week after Lend-Lease was terminated, insisted afterwards that the action was unnecessary and simply due to a new and inexperienced President accepting the wrong advice. Truman's explanation – that as the bill passed by Congress defined Lend-Lease as a weapon of war it had to be revoked immediately the war ended – was wrong, in Acheson's view, and the decision 'disastrous'. Acheson in his memoirs revealed his leader's remorse: 'In later years President Truman said to me that he had come to think of this action as a grave mistake.'

While the negotiations over the loan were taking place, there was increasing evidence that the closeness of the wartime collaboration was being steadily eroded in another important sphere – atomic energy. As each day passed, it became more obvious that the pledges made in the Hyde Park Aide-Mémoire by Roosevelt and Churchill in September 1944 for full collaboration indefinitely in developments for 'military and commercial purposes' were not being upheld. Even though that agreement was a closely guarded secret – and it was subsequently disclosed that the American copy had been mislaid – the provision for complete collaboration had also been established in the Quebec Agreement of August 1943. Clearly the British members of the Anglo-American Combined Policy Committee were not being accorded what the Committee was set up in August 1943 to ensure: 'full and effective interchange of information and ideas.'

Attlee's anxieties over atomic energy were a confused mixture of conscience – how to place international control over the power of nuclear destruction – and of the practical political importance of reasserting the obligations of collaboration. There was uncertainty in Washington as well, since one of Henry Stimson's last contributions to the debate before retiring as Secretary of War at the age of 78 on 21 September 1945 was to suggest that the United States should share its knowledge of the bomb with Russia. The hubbub created in Congress not only undermined Attlee's suggestion that the United States should hand over its nuclear monopoly to the United Nations, but it also aroused strong feelings on Capitol Hill against passing nuclear information to any foreign government. When Attlee flew to Washington on 9 November with Sir John Anderson, the former Conservative minister whom he had appointed to head his Atomic Energy Committee for the sake of continuity from the wartime period, he found Truman hemmed in by his commitment to await the outcome of the Joint Committee on Atomic Energy set up under the chairmanship of Brien McMahon, the Democratic Senator from Connecticut.

Talks between Truman, Attlee and the Canadian Prime Minister, Mackenzie King, produced the Washington Declaration on 15 November which enunciated the pious proposal of scientific interchange 'for peaceful ends with any nation that will fully reciprocate'. The reassertion of Anglo-American co-operation which Attlee sought was sidetracked to a secret memorandum in order not to have it submitted to Congress, since Congress was unaware of the wartime Roosevelt–Churchill pact. The memorandum drafted by General Groves and Sir John Anderson on 16 November watered down the commitments which Churchill had secured from Roosevelt. According to the Quebec Agreement, atomic weapons were not to be used against third parties 'without each other's consent'. Under the memorandum Britain's right of veto was cancelled and substituted with merely the right of consultation. While the memorandum pledged 'full and effective co-operation in the field of basic scientific research', there were restrictions imposed on co-operation in development, design, construction and operation. Such co-operation had to be approved by the Anglo-American Combined Policy Committee as 'mutually advantageous'.

At first Attlee appeared satisfied that the transatlantic nuclear partnership was back on course, but within a few months it became obvious that Dr Vannevar Bush, the Director of the Office of Scientific Research and Development, was not prepared to see co-operation with the British as 'mutually advantageous'. In this he had the full support of Secretary of State James Byrnes. When Attlee remonstrated with Truman, there was little attempt to acknowledge that he had any grounds for complaint since, it was maintained, supplying information for the construction of a British atomic plant was not in conformity with the Washington Declaration. A further 2,000-word cogently argued appeal to Truman to reconsider America's obligations was ignored. The arrest in Canada of Allan Nunn May, the British scientist who was rewarded with a bottle of whisky and £50 for passing nuclear secrets to the Russians, convinced the Americans that they were wise not to trust the British with any more information.

After the fiasco of the cut-off of Lend-Lease and the deception over nuclear collaboration Attlee felt shabbily treated. If formal proof were needed that the Special Relationship had hit the bottom it came with the enactment of the McMahon Act on 1 August 1946. As a result, Britain had no special status in nuclear matters. The Act banned the transfer of 'restricted data' in the scientific field to any foreign country. It pushed Britain into the cold for a decade in terms of exchange of information and ideas with American nuclear scientists. Looking back on the decision, many American politicians had regrets. As McGeorge Bundy observed: 'If members of Congress had understood that without British help the bomb would probably not have been available in 1945, it is not hard to suppose that the language of the McMahon Act would have been very different.' Dean Rusk, later Secretary of State under Kennedy and Johnson, blamed the United States for withdrawing into a cocoon on nuclear matters: 'The British felt they had been short-changed by the McMahon Act, and I don't blame them.'

The outcome did not leave British scientists marking time for long. Had the Government taken the McMahon Act as the final word, Britain would have been obliged to accept second division status. Attlee secretly summoned an inner Cabinet to assess the situation. Of the six men round the table in Downing Street – Attlee, Foreign Secretary Ernest Bevin, Defence Secretary A. V. Alexander, Leader of the House Herbert Morrison, Minister of Supply John Wilmot and Dominions Secretary Lord Addison – one bludgeoned the doubts out of any waverers wondering whether it was wise for Britain to go ahead with her own atomic bomb. Bevin thumped the table: 'We've got to have this. I don't mind for myself, but I don't want any other Foreign Secretary to be talked at, or to, by a Secretary of State in the United States as I have just had in my discussions with Mr Byrnes. We have got to have this thing over here whatever it costs. We've got to have the bloody Union Jack flying on top of it.'

Attlee, a major who had commanded a company of the South Lancashire Regiment in World War I, was anything but jingoistic, but he never had any hesitation over the question. Without an atomic bomb of her own, he believed, Britain would be totally dependent on the Americans and his recent experiences of being ditched by them convinced him that such a position would be humiliating. There was also an element of pride in wanting to show that British scientists who had played an important role in the Manhattan Project could be successful on their own. Although he gave the formal go-ahead in January 1947 for an atomic bomb to be produced, he did not disclose the decision to Parliament for almost 18 months. Even the rest of the

Cabinet was left in ignorance. To avoid any disclosure in the Defence Estimates, the allocation of funds – almost £100 million – was hidden under innocuous headings. This secrecy was to rebound on him later in strong criticism from the left wing of the Labour Party.

Attlee's resort to going it alone was the result of a combination of many factors, not just frustration over the McMahon Act. He often felt that he had never enjoyed the cordiality and trust which had been extended to Churchill. On the other hand, Attlee did not have strong emotional ties to America like Churchill, who would proudly emphasize the unbroken descent via his American mother, who was born in Spencer, Indiana, through five generations back to a lieutenant who served in George Washington's forces. Truman did not have any real bonds with England. When Attlee flew to Washington for their first summit meeting, the only direct knowledge Truman had of England was a six-hour stopover when he could not spare the time to visit London and King George VI went to Plymouth to give him luncheon aboard the battleship *Renown*. A Missouri farmer's son who became a bank clerk at the age of 19, Truman was very much a homespun politician. Attlee, an Oxford-educated barrister, had a more inter-national outlook, having travelled on missions to India, Russia, Spain and France before becoming Prime Minister. On their initial encounter at Potsdam, Attlee made ritual tributes: 'We talked the same language. We became friends.' But there was little evidence of any personal chemistry between them. Nor was there any between Bevin and Byrnes. There was no attempt at friendship. Byrnes behaved as if he were a cut above other foreign ministers and was better equipped to be President than Truman. The verdict of the President's Chief of Staff, Admiral William Leahy, that Byrnes was 'a horse's ass' was one that Bevin readily endorsed.

This lack of warmth at the top percolated down through the lower echelons. Everyday dealings lost their casual camaraderie for a time. Diplomats in the British Embassy who had become accustomed during the war to an open-hearted approach from the Americans with whom they had to do business found the atmosphere suddenly changed in the early Truman years. One shrewd observation of this change came later from Lord Gore-Booth:

There was an almost morbid fear of upsetting third countries by appearing too friendly with Britain. The consequence in some crucial years between the end of the war and the mid-fifties was a curious aridity of the heart as opposed to head of this side of American affairs. For the first time in two hundred years a tired and battered Britain could have done with an occasional pat on the shoulder from Britain's closest wartime associate which had so outgrown the British in wealth and power.

Ironically, it was an invitation from Truman which gave Churchill, now out of office, the opportunity to issue a call for the transatlantic partnership to be re-established with the special attributes of the wartime association – and afterwards Truman was so embarrassed that he tried to distance himself from it. Truman commandeered what used to be Roosevelt's armoured train, the Ferdinand Magellan, to escort Churchill to his home state for what became the historic Fulton speech on 5 March 1946 at the small Presbyterian Westminster College. Although it subsequently became known as the 'Iron Curtain' speech from the passage in which Churchill said 'From Stettin in the Baltic to Trieste in the Adriatic, an iron curtain has descended across the Continent', it was not the first time that he had used the phrase to describe how Communist control from Moscow had sealed off a large slice of Europe. It had been employed by Churchill once in 1944 and again in 1945. But credit for coining the phrase belongs elsewhere. It was first used in print by Ethel Snowden, the wife of the Labour leader Philip Snowden, in 1920 when describing her arrival in Petrograd in her book *Through Bolshevik Russia*: 'We were behind the "Iron Curtain" at last!'

The dangers of the Iron Curtain were not, however, the central theme of Churchill's Fulton speech. His theme was the means of combating them. He left no one in any doubt about 'the crux of what I have travelled here to say'. He set it out in principle and in detail:

Neither the sure prevention of war, nor the continuous rise of world organization will be gained without what I have called the fraternal association of the English-speaking peoples. This means a special relationship between the British Commonwealth and Empire and the United States. This is no time for generalities, and I will venture to be precise. Fraternal association requires not only the growing friendship and mutual understanding between our two vast but kindred systems of society, but the continuance of the intimate relationship between our military advisers, leading to common study of potential dangers, the similarity of weapons and manuals of instructions, and to the interchange of officers and cadets at technical colleges. It should carry with it the continuance of the present facilities for mutual security by the joint use of all Naval and Air Force bases in the possession of either country all over the world. This would perhaps double the mobility of the American Navy and Air Force. It would greatly expand that of the British Empire Forces and it might well lead, if and as the world calms down, to important financial savings. Already we use together a large number of islands; more may well be entrusted to our joint care in the near future. ... Eventually there may come – I feel eventually there will come – the principle of joint citizenship, but that we may be content to leave to destiny, whose outstretched arm many of us can already clearly see.

Subsequent generations have hailed it as the first warning signal of the 'Evil Empire' of the Soviet Union and a signpost of the coming need for the United States and Britain to weld themselves into a close new alliance. At the time, however, despite praise in some quarters for Churchill's frankness, the speech drew vehement criticism for projecting the concept of confrontation and for arousing suspicions of a new form of Anglo-American imperialism. Many politicians criticized it as a body blow to the newly created United Nations. Several Congressmen were worried by its impact on Russia and feared it would force 'the Russians into counter-alliances'. Republican Senator Owen Brewster from Maine warned that a military alliance between the United States and Britain could 'precipitate the world against us'. Republican Representative Frederick Smith of Ohio insisted: 'An outright British–American alliance would mean a third world war, with the United States carrying most of the burden as usual.'

The speech had a hostile reception in many sections of the Press which did not want what was seen as a link with a new form of British imperialism. The *Boston Globe* condemned the new proposition of partnership since it invited the United States to 'become heir to the evils of a collapsing colonialism, and inevitably their defender all the way from North Africa to the China Sea'. The *Chicago Sun* believed that Churchill was trying to reconstitute a world that no longer existed: 'To follow the standard raised by this great blinded aristocrat would be to march to the world's most ghastly war.' The *New York Post* criticized it as a high-risk policy: 'Churchill offers Americans a false choice between Communism and the defence of the British Empire: democracy has a better alternative.' The *Detroit Free Press* echoed that warning: 'Anglo-American co-operation is one thing; the re-entry of the United States into the British Empire is quite another.'

The torrent of criticism caused Truman to make a hurried retreat from the stance he had taken on welcoming Churchill to his home state. Churchill, always careful in matters of protocol, had not only informed Attlee about his theme at Fulton but had flown from a holiday in Florida in February to Washington to let Truman know in advance about it since he intended it to be a blockbuster of an address. The President's Chief of Staff, Admiral Leahy, who spent time at the British Embassy going over the draft with Churchill, conveyed to Truman that the Fulton speech would call for a full-scale alliance between the United States and Britain to preserve world peace. Secretary of State Byrnes was given a draft and discussed it with Truman before the President and his guest boarded the overnight train from Washington to Jefferson City, Missouri, a 30-minute drive from Fulton. At that stage Truman did not intend to read the full text so that he could claim he had not given it his blessing. On the train, however, Truman took the opportunity to read it and complimented Churchill on it, saying that he thought it would 'create quite a stir'.

In fact, it was a much bigger stir than Truman had bargained for, since few Americans were as clear-eyed as Churchill at the time in realizing that the build-up of Communism would inevitably lead to what became known as the Cold War. Alarmed at criticism that he had been inept in endorsing the speech, Truman denied to reporters on the train journey back to Washington that he had seen the speech before it was delivered and claimed that Churchill had 'put him on the spot'. He was so worried at the impression which might be formed in Moscow that he wrote to Stalin assuring him that the United States wanted good relations with Russia. To placate the Soviet leader, Truman sent him an invitation for equal time and 'exactly the same kind of reception' if he cared to come to Missouri to deliver a speech. Stalin did not deign to reply but used the occasion to denounce Churchill as a warmonger.

In the context of transatlantic relations it was yet another example of the gulf that separated the two sides so soon after the war. It demonstrated Truman's uncertainty over how to handle the Russians and his prevarication over how far he wanted to trust the British. Despite the famous 'Long Telegram', the 8,000-word analysis from the redoubtable George F. Kennan in Moscow warning of the dangers threatened by Russia, which fully endorsed Churchill's assessment, Truman was reluctant to give up the Roosevelt-style hope of doing a deal with Stalin. Byrnes was eager to come to an agreement with the Russians, and Truman was anxious not to make any move that would expose him to blame for creating an unfavourable climate. It took him a year – and a change of Secretary of State – to realize the risks of clinging to a dream about a tranquil post-war world. By then the first *frissons* of the Cold War were requiring him to make a comprehensive reassessment of American policies on Russia – and on Britain.

One major international problem during that period caused serious ructions on both sides of the Atlantic and exacerbated the tensions in the transatlantic partnership: Palestine. It was the first international issue thrust in front of Truman. On 20 April 1945 – only a week after Truman had been sworn in as President – Rabbi Stephen Wise, head of the American Zionist Emergency Council, got into the White House ahead of the State Department experts with a plea for the doors of Palestine to be opened to Jewish refugees from the Nazi concentration camps. Truman responded with an appeal to Britain to lift the restrictions on Jewish immigration under the 1939 White Paper and allow 100,000 refugees into Palestine. Attlee's firm stand against an open-door policy soured Anglo-American relations on Palestine from the outset. A long message from Downing Street to the White House on 31 August 1945 stressed the need for even-handedness between Arabs and Jews under the British mandate held since the end of World War I. Jews were not the only victims of the Nazis, Attlee pointed out, and there was no reason why they should be placed 'at the head of the queue'. Truman was furious.

It was an issue highly charged with emotion on both sides. Each government faced fierce criticism of its policy within its own ranks. Ernest Bevin, the Foreign Secretary, saw the problem in the perspective of Britain's traditional interest in the Arab world and the importance of Middle East oil and trade. For him the Jews were to be dealt with in terms of 'a religion, not a race or a nation'. While Attlee supported the pro-Arab policy of the Foreign Office – even when it led Bevin to excessive partisanship – there was strong opposition to it not only from Jewish MPs and Zionist supporters in the Labour Party but also from within the Cabinet voiced by ministers such as Hugh Dalton and Aneurin Bevan.

In Washington the clashes were less open, but the White House and the State Department were often at odds with each other. Truman, who was a vigorous advocate of a homeland for the Jews, had his Zionist sympathies sustained by one of his oldest friends, Eddie

Jacobson. He was a former business partner from 1919 when they had set up Truman & Jacobson, a shirt shop in Kansas City, and he was to play a key role at a critical point in the final stages of the tense diplomatic manoeuvres over Palestine by getting Chaim Weizmann, the Jewish leader, secretly into the White House to see the President. While Truman's pro-Jewish policy was supported by Presidential aides Clark Clifford and David Niles, it was under fire from some of the big guns in his Administration such as George Marshall, Robert Lovett and James Forrestal.

Bevin sought to turn down the heat through the appointment of an Anglo-American Committee of Inquiry on Palestine on 13 November 1945. Even if it did not diminish the tension, the initiative appeared to offer two dividends: it provided a breathing space and it enabled the United States to move from exhortation on the sidelines to direct involvement in the search for a solution. But the Committee's verdict, announced on 1 May 1946, was a mishmash of recommendations which fell far short of the wishes of all parties. Instead of partition into separate states, it proposed that Palestine should be bicommunal – 'neither a Jewish state nor an Arab state' – while staying under the British mandate. It called for 100,000 entry certificates for Jewish refugees and the disbandment of all illegal forces.

Immediately, Anglo-American relations became edgy again. Truman announced his approval of the extra immigration quota without consulting Attlee. In retaliation, Attlee, not disguising his annoyance at what Dean Acheson described as 'Mr Truman's taking the plum from the pudding', stated two conditions: the United States would have to share the financial and military burden of carrying out the recommendations of the Anglo-American report; and any enlarged quota of refugees would have to await the removal of underground armies. Bevin stoked the transatlantic bitterness by telling the Labour Party conference in June that the Americans were pressing for Jews to be allowed into Palestine because they did not want 'too many of them in New York'.

Four months later the fraternal association was sent plummeting to what Attlee's biographer Kenneth Harris called 'the lowest point ever reached in the personal relationship'. That was the result of a decision by Truman to ignore Attlee and issue a major policy statement on Palestine on Yom Kippur – the Day of Atonement – on 4 October 1946, a month before the mid-term Congressional elections when the Jewish votes in New York, Pennsylvania, Illinois and Ohio were reckoned to be crucial. Its key points were a pledge to continue pressing for 100,000 Jewish refugees to be given entry permits and the assertion that some form of partition of Palestine would attract support in the United States. When Attlee was tipped off about the statement's impending release, he sent a message to Truman urging him to suspend it while Bevin was in discussions with Jewish leaders. Truman's rejection left their personal relations in tatters. In a rare flash of anger Attlee disclosed his feelings to the President: 'I have received with great regret your letter refusing even a few hours' grace to the Prime Minister of the country which has the actual responsibility for the government of Palestine, in order that he may acquaint you with the actual situation and the probable result of your action.'

It was by no means the end of their disagreements. With Truman pro-Jew and Attlee pro-Arab it could not be otherwise. There was constant friction over the boatloads of Jewish immigrants trying to land illegally in Palestine. The British protested over American army trucks being used in an attempt to transport Jews from the Black Sea coast into Palestine. The Americans were enraged at the British for intercepting the American-funded Chesapeake Bay ferry called *Exodus– 1947* and forcing the 4,500 Jewish migrants back to Europe where they were dumped into camps in Germany. When it was announced that British troops would be withdrawn from Palestine with the ending of the mandate at midnight on 14 May 1948, a free-for-all was made inevitable – on the ground between Jews and Arabs, in the corridors of diplomacy with the Americans and the British going their own way, often without consulting each other. Clashes continued right to the day that the state of Israel was declared, none more vehement than over the question of diplomatic recognition.

The fact that priorities were different sharpened the disagreements. Attlee had a high regard for Bevin, giving him a free hand in Middle East affairs. Even if the Foreign Secretary's policy on Palestine was often bitterly attacked for misunderstanding the claims of Zionism, it was Attlee's view that the Prime Minister's priority was to stand by the Foreign Office. Truman had no such sense of priority towards the State Department. Irrespective of what the foreign policy experts said was in the interests of the Middle East, Truman insisted on deciding what was in America's best interests – and those of his Administration facing a presidential election in six months' time. In the end, against all the advice of the State Department not to rush in with recognition of the Jewish state, Truman manoeuvred against them through Clark

Clifford and had an announcement of United States recognition – the first of any country – made at 6 p.m. in Washington, midnight in Jerusalem, on 14 May 1948. Dean Rusk, then Director of United Nations Affairs at the State Department, was not told of the decision until a telephone call from Clifford at 5.45 p.m.

The British were aghast, not consulted or even informed in advance. They learned about it from a news agency bulletin – ironically, while watching the American Ambassador to the United Nations, Warren Austin, unaware of his President's decision, trying to gather votes in the General Assembly for a resolution proposing United Nations trusteeship of Palestine. This lack of Anglo-American consultation contrasted with the diplomatic correctness of the British Government 18 months later. When Britain announced diplomatic recognition of Communist China on 5 January 1950, the State Department – although known to be strongly opposed to it – had been given notice three weeks earlier, the day after Bevin secured approval in Cabinet.

The differences over Palestine, however, had been isolated in a separate compartment of the Anglo-American relationship long before the last chapter of the drama. That was the result of an awareness on both sides of the need for close co-operation in tackling economic and political problems of immense importance for the survival of the democratic system in Western Europe. It led to a revival of interest in the Special Relationship which was largely due to the foresight of two outstanding statesmen – one on each side of the Atlantic – and was facilitated, through a quirk of circumstance, by the perceptiveness and persistence of a distinguished BBC correspondent.

IV

Cold War Brings Back Transatlantic Warmth

'It would probably have died in the aftermath of the 1939–45 war had not Stalin's Russia maintained it. Without the spectre of Soviet expansion seemingly ever present, as it was in the late 1940s and early 1950s, the Anglo-American relationship might have taken quite a different course.'

Professor Richard Ullman: 1986

'Though the Americans often behave as though our views and interest were of little regard to them, in the last resort they know they must rely on us. This strengthens our position in dealing with them.'

Lord Strang: 1951

What became known as the Marshall Plan, hailed by Churchill as a 'turning point in the history of the world' for saving 300 million people in Europe from economic and political chaos, was also the catalyst which revived the Special Relationship. However, what appeared to be a carefully timed and organized political initiative was, in fact, more the result of an extraordinary series of coincidences in the summer of 1947, none more so than that Ernest Bevin, who was not notified in advance that Secretary of State George Marshall was delivering an epoch-making speech, happened to turn on his radio late one night. Had he not done so, Bevin would not have been in a position to make the immediate response which enabled the European Recovery Programme to be launched so quickly.

Bevin had only recently moved into the Foreign Secretary's new official residence at 1 Carlton Gardens – the house built between the Mall and Pall Mall by Nash for the Prince Regent in 1836 and subsequently the home of the newspaper magnate Lord Northcliffe –

and enjoyed the comfort of listening in bed to his radio. On the night of 5 June 1947 he switched on the set expecting to hear an assessment of the international situation by an American correspondent in the programme *American Commentary*, made famous by Raymond Gramm Swing. The scheduled talk was to have been made by the *Christian Science Monitor* correspondent Joseph Harsh, but at the last moment he was sent from Washington on an assignment to Paris. In his place, giving the first *American Commentary* ever broadcast by an Englishman, was the BBC's distinguished Washington correspondent Leonard Miall. It was this historic broadcast which alerted Bevin to the tremendous opportunity being given by the United States to put Europe back on its feet again.

Foreign correspondents at their best are skilled in assessing situations and evaluating them as episodes of history in the making. It is rare for them to play a role in the actual making of history. But Leonard Miall was no mere door-stepper jotting down quotes with an eye to a lead item for a news bulletin. He had a flair for sensing the importance of each political development in Washington and seeing whether it fitted into a pattern for a new policy. In such a mood of expectation that something unusual was going on at the State Department, Miall found his attention gripped when Dean Acheson gave a speech indicating America's concern at the dangerous deterioration of Europe's economic plight two years after the war.

It was just by chance that Acheson, as Under-Secretary of State, made the speech on 8 May 1947 at the World Affairs Forum at Delta State Teachers' College in Cleveland, Mississippi. This was to have been an engagement undertaken by Truman. But after promising friends of his wife, Bess, that he would make a speech there, Truman was advised that with Senator Theodore Bilbo in political trouble in Cleveland it would not be wise to be seen intruding into Democratic politics in Mississippi. So with Marshall unavailable, Acheson was assigned the role of speechmaker. He realized that Congress would require strong arguments to be convinced that Europe's needs were desperate and that only a bold plan for the whole continent would solve them. He knew that he had to awaken the American people to the stark alternative of leaving Western European nations vulnerable to Communism. Consequently, his address had a political impact and alarmed some Congressmen at the prospect of being asked to dig deep into the coffers to finance Europe. However, although there was a stir for a time, interest in it soon subsided – but not Miall's.

His next move was to invite Acheson to lunch on 2 June together with two other British correspondents – Malcolm Muggeridge of the *Daily Telegraph* and Rene MacColl of the *Daily Express* – to probe what was to follow the Cleveland speech, since Miall was certain that it was not just a one-off performance. It was left to Muggeridge to make the arrangements, and he decided on a table at the United Nations Club in Washington on Dupont Circle so that they could have what he knew would be 'a decent glass of sherry and a good wine' with their meal. Before setting off for the United Nations Club, Acheson, still feeling the after-effects of a very convivial dinner the previous evening, confided to the State Department Press Officer Lincoln White: 'If these Limeys offer me sherry, I'll fall over.' However, he survived the sherry and the grilling over lunch, leaving them in no doubt – although he did not mention Marshall's imminent speech – that they should 'watch this space' and that Europe would be expected to respond.

After his Cleveland speech Acheson reported to Marshall, saying: 'I've kicked a fairly important ball pretty high in the air but it's falling rapidly – it's time you caught it and ran with it.' Behind the scenes, State Department experts started preparing material for the follow-through speech, but, once again, it was just another coincidence that Marshall delivered it at Harvard. At one stage Clark Clifford thought it would be best coming from the President so that it could be launched with fanfares as the Truman Plan. But the President's shrewd political nose sniffed trouble ahead in a Congress with Republicans holding a majority in both Houses and told Clifford: 'Anything going up there bearing my name will quiver a couple of times, turn belly up, and die.' Even the timing of Marshall's speech, which was in the end carefully crafted by Charles Bohlen from memoranda by George Kennan and William Clayton, was left until the last moment.

Marshall had a long-standing invitation to accept an honorary degree from Harvard. However, when he notified his readiness to have it conferred Marshall informed the university that he did not regard the occasion as one for a formal address. Eventually, a letter to Dr James Conant, President of Harvard, on 28 May 1947 confirming his attendance on 5 June stated that Marshall would 'make a few remarks of appreciation of the honour and perhaps a little more'. The decision to go beyond 'a little more' was not taken until 30 May when Marshall instructed his assistant, General Marshall 'Pat' Carter, to have a text for a 'less than ten-minute talk' ready for the Commencement Day ceremony at Harvard.

On the day, Marshall eschewed the big blockbuster style of launching his dramatic new programme for Europe, telling the audience of 7,000 that the introduction comparing him to George Washington made him 'fearful of my inability to maintain such a high rating'. He sombrely set out the challenge of the situation: 'The truth of the matter is that Europe's requirements for the next three or four years of foreign food and other essential products – principally from America – are so much greater than her present ability to pay that she must have substantial additional help or face economic, social and political deterioration of a very grave character.' Significantly, he never mentioned figures, dollars or the amount of aid required from the United States. But it was clearly intended to be a recovery operation on a grand scale: 'Any assistance that this Government may render in the future should provide a cure rather than a mere palliative.' It was projected as an integrated transatlantic programme, not as a solution imposed by America: 'It would be neither fitting nor efficacious for this Government to draw up unilaterally a programme designed to put Europe on its feet economically. This is the business of the Europeans. The initiative, I think, must come from Europe.'

Although advance texts of the speech were made available by Charles Kindenbergh at the State Department under embargo 24 hours before delivery, the speech was once more the victim of circumstances. It coincided with the Communist *coup d'état* in Hungary and that became the main headline news. Even so, the initial British response was barely credible. In the absence of the British Ambassador, Lord Inverchapel, his deputy, John Balfour, flicked through the text and decided that it was a routine university address. Since the Embassy had recently received instructions from the Foreign Office to cut down on cabling costs, Balfour consigned the speech to the slow route to London via the next diplomatic bag. In London the next day the Foreign Office, without any guidance telegram on the Marshall speech from Washington, turned to its other two main sources, *The Times* and the *Guardian*. However, *The Times* totally misjudged the importance of Marshall's offer and the *Guardian* completely misunderstood it. *The Times* carried a single-column report on page 4 under the yawning headline 'Basis of American Aid'. In its three-paragraph account, it quoted only 17 words from Marshall's text. Readers of the paper's foreign coverage that day were expected to be more interested in a much longer report of bakery workers on strike in Paris. The *Guardian* did not have a report from its Washington correspondent. It published seven paragraphs from the Reuter news agency report under the headline 'Better Use of US Aid to Europe'. When the *Guardian* got round to analysing the speech a day later, it was dismissive of the value of the Marshall Plan. It said: 'In the present state of American opinion the aid would then seem to be mainly a subsidy to an anti-Russia group. This would make it politically impossible, the Americans realize, for some of the governments of Western and Central Europe to take part. An attempt should be made to carry out the reconstruction programme through the United Nations European Economic Commission of which Russia is a member. If this is done Europe will respond to Mr Marshall's suggestion with enthusiasm yet not with confidence.'

Fortunately, the British Foreign Secretary tuned into the BBC and heard a comprehensive account of the speech's significance by Leonard Miall on *American Commentary*. Bevin's attention was seized from Miall's opening sentence: 'Within the last hour and a half an exceptionally important speech has been made by the American Secretary of State.' Miall justified his judgment with carefully chosen quotations from the Marshall text: 'Our policy is directed not against any country or doctrine but against hunger, poverty, desperation and chaos.' Stressing Marshall's emphasis on cure rather than palliative, Miall caught the mood of the moment with fine phrase-making of his own: 'The emaciated European body needs a dollar blood transfusion which will circulate throughout its lengths. It's true that America has more dollars than it needs. It's like a man with high blood pressure who would benefit considerably by contributing a pint or two. But it's the sick patient whose need is paramount.'

Miall's focus on Marshall's insistence that the initiative had to come from Europe fired up Bevin for action. He stormed into the Foreign Office early next morning, demanding to see the telegram from Washington. When he was told that there wasn't one, Lord Strang, then Deputy Under-Secretary of State, suggested checking with the British Embassy for clarification. Bevin snorted that he did not need anyone else to tell him what he had heard and that he trusted Miall to have got it right. Two years later he paid Miall a public tribute in a speech to the National Press Club in Washington. 'I remember with a little wireless set alongside the bed just turning on the news and there came this report of the Harvard speech. I assure you, gentlemen, it was like a lifeline to sinking men. It seemed to bring hope where there was none. The generosity of it was beyond our belief. It expressed a mutual thing. It said: "Try and help yourselves and we will try to see what we can do. Try and do the thing collectively, and we will see what we can put into the pool." I think you understand why, therefore, we responded with such alacrity, and why we grabbed the lifeline with both hands.'

Bevin's alacrity in immediately contacting the French Foreign Minister, Georges Bidault, and then flying to Paris to work out joint action as an assurance that the Marshall Plan was taken seriously put the transatlantic partnership back on cordial terms again. Alan Bullock in his magisterial biography of Bevin was emphatic: 'It is arguable that Bevin's action in the next few days was his most decisive personal contribution as Foreign Secretary to the history of his times.' In seizing the diplomatic initiative ahead of the French, Bevin saw himself as America's broker rounding up the Europeans to negotiate the terms of the recovery programme. It was part of his strategy to reinforce his claim that Britain should have a place alongside the United States in the Big Power league. However, the run-down of Britain's dollar reserves at a time when sterling convertibility was required under the US loan agreement undermined Bevin's aspirations to some form of 'financial partnership' with America which would elevate Britain above the others in Europe. Ten months later, however, after hard-fought negotiations in Europe and Washington, Congress voted aid worth $5.3 billion for the European Recovery Programme for 12 months. Britain's share was $1.263 billion. Overall, Britain received a bigger slice of Marshall Aid than any other country – $3.2 billion out of a total of $13 billion – and unlike the American loan after Lend-Lease ended, which required repayment at 2 per cent, Marshall Aid was a free gift.

One of the underlying concerns of the US Government was to provide economic stability in Europe so that countries would be politically stable enough not to succumb to internal subversion through national Communist parties. At the same time, the United States wanted Western Europe strong enough to hold the line against Communist pressures from outside as well as inside. Britain had been the bulwark for shoring up the weaker nations, Greece and Turkey, until her economic problems forced her to tell the United States on 21 February 1947 that the burden could no longer be borne. This first admission that Britain's global power was waning paved the way for what was called the Truman Doctrine. Picking up the bill of $400 million for aiding Greece and Turkey, Truman set out his doctrine to a joint session of Congress on 12 March in these terms: 'I believe that it must be the policy of the United States to support free peoples who are resisting attempted subjugation by armed minorities or by outside pressures.'

It took another year, however, before the United States saw the Soviet threat to the West in as menacing terms as Bevin perceived it. But Bevin kept warning of the need to prepare a shield against the Communists as they strengthened their forces in Hungary and Czechoslovakia. Undaunted by attacks from the 'Keep Left' group in the Labour Party who branded him subservient to the United States, Bevin persisted in alliance-building in Europe as a stepping stone to a transatlantic security system. The Treaty of Dunkirk with France in May 1947 was followed by the Brussels Treaty linking Britain, France and the Benelux countries on 17 March 1948. On the strength of that link, Bevin convinced Marshall that it was only logical to broaden the concept of Western security to include the North Atlantic area. Almost the entire planning at political and military levels was in the hands of the Americans and the British for the next 12 months. Bevin's persistence was rewarded with the establishment of NATO on 4 April 1949 as a 12-nation alliance which was subsequently extended to 16 with Greece and Turkey joining in 1952, Germany in 1955 and Spain in 1982.

If there was one event which signalled the necessity for the Special Relationship to be strengthened, it was the challenge of Russia's Marshal Vasily Sokolovsky at the meeting of the Allied Control Council in Berlin on 20 March 1948. As the rotating president in charge of the meeting, he accused the Western Powers of violating the Quadripartite Agreement, pronounced that the Allied Control Council could not therefore continue to exist, and walked out. It marked the intensification of the East–West confrontation into the Cold War only ten days after Jan Masaryk, the last non-Communist with any authority in Czechoslovakia, was found dead on the pavement under the open window of his Prague apartment. The first stage of the Berlin blockade was announced by Sokolovsky's deputy, Lieutenant-General M. Dratvin, on 30 March with the imposition of restrictions on military traffic by road and rail through the Soviet zone to the Allied sectors. It was ratcheted up until June when the issue of a new Deutschmark in the Western zones to replace the discredited Reichsmark was used by the Russians as the excuse for sealing off Berlin from a currency they refused to accept. By 24 June, they had imposed a total blockade of the city.

Discussions between Bevin and Marshall on how to handle a crisis over Berlin had taken place since December 1947. They had an agreed position that the United States and Britain would stand fast in Berlin, firm in the belief that any compromise would undermine the security of Western Europe as a whole. They knew that in numbers the odds were against them: 6,500 Allied troops – 3,000 Americans, 2,000 British and 1,500 French – facing 18,000 Russian troops who could call on 300,000 more in East Germany. What they had not worked out was how to succour the 2.5 million Germans in Berlin who were left with food for 36 days and fuel for 45 days. The answer of an airlift for civilians and not just for the Allied garrisons came from the British. A plan was drawn up by Commodore Reginald Waite of the Royal Air Force for a minimum of 4,000 tons of food to be airlifted each day. US General Lucius D. Clay was persuaded that it was feasible since an airlift on a small scale had ferried supplies to American forces when the first road restrictions were imposed.

The Berlin airlift was an Anglo-American partnership from the first flight on 25 June, because the French did not have the transport planes for the operation. French authority was further weakened by the collapse of the Government in July, leaving it politically in limbo for two months. Britain was therefore the only reliable partner the Americans had during that early testing period. Operationally, the Americans had the major role since they had far more planes: first of all they used 100 C-47s, each able to transport two-and-a-half tons of supplies, but later they brought in 160 C-54s with a capacity of ten tons. When the blockade ended 14 months later on 12 May 1949, there had been 277,804 flights with a total airlift of 2,325,809 tons. The airlift coincided with the Allied decision – which was the main reason for the Russians trying to seal off Berlin completely – to establish a new German federal republic running its own affairs from Bonn.

The airlift not only saved Berlin; it re-established Anglo-American air force links with the same closeness they had enjoyed in wartime. America's Secretary of Defence, James Forrestal, realized that sending two squadrons of B-29 Superfortresses to Germany was not enough. The Americans needed extra facilities within a short flying distance, and Britain was the obvious supplier. Bevin did not hesitate over the proposition. He had it approved by the Berlin Crisis group of ministers in the Cabinet, which Attlee chaired, on 28 June. Preparations were made at three Royal Air Force stations in East Anglia to enable 60 Superfortresses to arrive on 17 July. Although described as 'Atomic Bombers', since it had been a B-29 which dropped the first atomic bomb, none of the planes which landed at the RAF bases had been converted to carry the bomb. Three months later a further 30 Superfortresses had joined them, bringing to 90 the number of planes spread over seven RAF stations and the American wartime supply base at Burtonwood, Lancashire, made available again to service them.

The establishment of American bases in Britain was carried out without any formal treaty being signed. When the planes arrived, it was stated that they would be in England 'for a short period of temporary duty'. The uniqueness of the occasion was described by US Force Commander Lieutenant-General John K. Cannon: 'Never before in history has one first-class power gone into another first-class power's country without any agreement. We were just told to come over and "We shall be pleased to have you".' Parliament was told that they had come 'under informal and long-standing arrangements between the two air forces for visits of goodwill and training purposes'. As the 'temporary' nature of the US Air Force bases became accepted as a fixture, they symbolized one important aspect of the Special Relationship: an American commitment to stand alongside Britain in the defence of Western interests in Europe. The precise terms of the commitment, however, were left vague even when the Truman–Attlee Understanding on the use of the bases was worked out in October 1951. There was a general acknowledgement that in times of emergency there had to be consultation and a joint decision, but this was never fully spelled out.

British attempts to extend this new cordiality to closer co-operation on atomic energy swiftly followed. The decision by Attlee to go ahead with a British bomb after the McMahon Act cut off the flow of scientific information strengthened the British negotiating position in the review of Anglo-American atomic collaboration. It was argued that information which would be passed to Britain in future might well not be any more important than what the United States might receive from Britain, and that in any case the British were on course to produce their own atomic weapons. Dean Acheson, who succeeded Marshall as Secretary of State in January 1949 and was appointed Chairman of the Special Committee of the National Security Council, was more sympathetic than others in the Administration towards co-operation with Britain. However, Senator Arthur Vandenberg swung substantial

Congressional opinion behind him with powerful arguments for keeping the United States in a dominant position in production, research and storage of atomic raw materials.

During negotiations with Under-Secretary James Webb, the concept of American domination was set aside by the Russian explosion of an atomic device in October 1949. Progress was being made on the basis of atomic weapon production being concentrated in America, but with a reasonable allocation to Britain, when a spy scandal brought negotiations to an end. The Americans lost faith in the British as reliable energy partners on 2 February 1950 when Klaus Fuchs, a naturalized British scientist who had worked on the Manhattan Project at Los Alamos and subsequently at Harwell, was arrested for passing secrets to the Russians. The furore over Fuchs and the opening of Senator Joseph McCarthy's campaign against the State Department for 'sheltering Commies' put paid to any prospects of Britain negotiating a deal on atomic co-operation during the rest of the time that Bevin and Acheson held office.

It was a blow much regretted by both statesmen who found – at times to each other's profound surprise – an amazing degree of companionship and identity of view despite their vastly different backgrounds. Socially and intellectually, they were poles apart: Bevin, born in poverty, whose schooling ended at the age of 11, clawed his way up from a £2-a-week trade union official to become Minister of Labour and National Service in Churchill's War Cabinet; and Acheson, son of the English-born Bishop of Connecticut, who moved elegantly from Groton to Yale and Harvard to become the archetypical striped pants diplomat. Minister-to-minister relations, which had been cold and formal – sometimes even bitter – during the Byrnes–Bevin era, improved substantially when Marshall took over at the State Department, but while each had great respect for the other there never was any familiarity between them. Although Acheson was once berated by General MacArthur as a 'pompous diplomat with a phoney British accent', Bevin and Acheson hit it off well together. It was 'Ernie' from Acheson but never 'Dean' from Bevin, who preferred to address him as 'me lad'. None of the arrogance for which Acheson was renowned was ever directed at Bevin, for whom he admitted there was a very great affection. Reminiscing in his memoirs, Acheson warmly recalled their partnership: 'Life with Ernie was gay and turbulent for his temper could build up as suddenly as a summer storm and could flash and thunder as noisily, then disappear as the sun broke through it. ... His mind was not closed. It was tough and often stubborn but always open to arguments strongly and honestly presented.'

The rock-like reliability each recognized in the other was assessed as a highly significant element in the partnership of that period by Alan Bullock: 'The friendship of Bevin and Acheson, perhaps closer than of any other Foreign Secretary and Secretary of State, was founded on the belief that there was a greater degree of identity than of conflict between the interests of the two countries and that much depended for the Western world upon acting on that belief. It could be argued that in 1949, with Bevin and Acheson in office, the Special Relationship between the United States of America and Britain counted for more in the policies of the two countries than at any other time apart from the Second World War.'

Whether Acheson would have endorsed that assessment so fulsomely is questionable, if only because he found the phrase distasteful and rarely used it. When he came across officials at the State Department working on a policy paper defining the 'Special Relationship', Acheson became very angry and warned them not to waste their time on such an exercise. He commandeered all copies of what he termed 'the wretched paper' and had them destroyed. Yet he took the initiative to encourage his own special relationship in discreet diplomacy with the British in Washington. Lord Inverchapel was not an ambassador Acheson trusted; he was written off as too eccentric and unpredictable. But Acheson formed a very high opinion of his successor, Sir Oliver Franks, and a strong bond of friendship was established. They met regularly, alone without note-takers, either at the Embassy residence or at Acheson's home, sometimes after dinner or during the cocktail hour. Their discussions ranged over all current international topics with each feeling free to assess the attitudes of various political figures in each capital. They talked about the likeliest options for each government and how the various priorities on each side could be accommodated. It was acknowledged as a unique form of confidentiality which the Secretary of State did not extend to any other ambassador. It was also a relationship that carried risks, as Acheson subsequently admitted: 'The dangers and difficulties of such a relationship were obvious but its usefulness proved so great that we continued it for four years.'

The arrangement was particularly valuable during the last two years of the Labour Government when Bevin's failing health, which led to his resignation as Foreign Secretary on 9 March 1951, made him progressively unable to give sufficient attention to detail. Although Attlee was often mistrustful of Foreign Office mandarins' 'expertise', he had a high regard for the judgement of Franks and of Sir Gladwyn Jebb who became the man of the hour as Ambassador to the United Nations in the stormy days of 1950. Attlee was more attentive to the telegrams from Washington and New York when it was obvious that he had to take a more active role in handling foreign affairs. Dealing with the boxes of telegrams was never a chore for Attlee, since he recognized the importance of keeping a close watch on matters affecting Anglo-American relations.

The Prime Minister's personal involvement in international developments on a day-to-day – sometimes hour-by-hour – basis was made inevitable when the North Korean army invaded South Korea on 25 June 1950. Attlee was in no doubt about its significance. He recognized at once that the Korean crisis reaffirmed the need for the sort of Anglo-American collaboration which had been successfully undertaken during the Berlin blockade, but before long it gave rise to so many divergences over policy, strategy and diplomatic manoeuvres that the overall relationship became soured. At the outset, however, there was a common assessment of the way the danger should be tackled despite a difference of view as to what lay behind it.

Although the British, like the Americans, were caught off-balance by the invasion, Attlee immediately ordered Britain's Far Eastern Fleet under Admiral Sir Patrick Brind to be put 'at the disposal of the United States authorities to operate on behalf of the Security Council in support of South Korea'. This was a much larger naval commitment than any other country provided – an aircraft carrier, an aircraft maintenance ship, three cruisers, seven destroyers, eight frigates and a hospital ship. Attlee had more trouble over sending troops. The Chiefs of Staff as well as a number of Cabinet ministers felt that the Army was already overstretched with its commitments in Malaysia, Hong Kong, Cyprus and Europe. But Attlee recognized that it would have been damaging to Anglo-American relations to deny Truman's request and authorized two infantry battalions with support units to be sent to Korea.

Political differences emerged at the start when the British bridled at the American assessment that Russia was orchestrating the Korean offensive as part of 'centrally-directed Communist imperialism'. There was concern from the very beginning on the British side that the crisis over Korea might be used by the Americans to extend the confrontation which could result in a challenge to China and Russia that could escalate to global war. There was anxiety in Downing Street that America's military energies might be so closely focused on Korea and the Far East that Western defences in Europe might become vulnerable to the Russians who had 80 divisions lined up against the West's mere ten divisions.

British manoeuvres to promote peace negotiations caused endless friction between Washington and London. Only a few weeks after the invasion, the United States slapped down a proposal from Attlee that approaches should be made to Russia for ending the conflict in Korea through an agreement to discuss all outstanding Far East issues such as Formosa and the entry of Communist China into the United Nations. Acheson instructed America's London Ambassador, Lewis Douglas, to leave the British Government in no doubt that if they pursued such a policy 'its possible consequences between your country and mine might be very serious indeed'. Although British concern over the possible use of atomic weapons by the Americans did not hit the headlines until December, the issue had been raised secretly five months earlier. The first alarm bells were rung by Deputy Under-Secretary Sir Pierson Dixon in a memorandum on 1 July which was sent to Bevin and studied also by Attlee. Dixon put down a marker in a significantly perceptive warning: 'The Americans may, if the military situation becomes desperate, contemplate using atomic weapons, and I feel that at the appropriate moment we ought to obtain an assurance from them that these weapons will not be used without prior consultation with us.'

Dixon's prediction came perilously close to being proved right on 24 November 1950. That day, Truman admitted, brought him the worst news since he became President: a massive invasion across the Yalu river by 260,000 Chinese troops. Within days General Douglas MacArthur's forces, which had moved into North Korea, were driven back humiliated across the 38th parallel. In the rapidly escalating crisis, Attlee feared that he was being confronted with a double danger of alarming proportions: first, that the Americans would embark on a war against China, and second, that they might in desperation resort to an atomic bomb. That anxiety reached fever pitch with a news agency bulletin transmitted on 30 November by United Press International at 10.47 a.m. Washington time, 2.47 p.m. London time: 'President Truman said today that the United States has under consideration use of the atomic bomb in connection with the war in Korea.'

It was the result of what must surely rank as one of the most disastrous Press Conferences given in the White House. Had Truman been in office for only six days or even six months it might have been excused as the ineptness of a political novice. But for Truman to have behaved the way he did after six years in the White House indicated a dangerous level of incompetence. Having been questioned about how the Chinese aggression could be halted, Truman should have confined himself to his general statement that all necessary measures would be taken. Instead, he allowed himself to be drawn into answering a series of supplementary questions with the admission that these measures included 'every weapon we have'. From there he was trapped into admitting there was always 'active consideration' of the use of the atomic bomb and that the military commander in the field would be in charge of weapons.

Dean Acheson immediately sensed the panic escalating round the world and set about instant damage limitation with a 'clarification' which a clearly rattled Truman was only too relieved to have issued within an hour. It emphasized that what had been said at the Press Conference did not represent any change: 'By law only the President can authorize the use of the atomic bomb and no such authorization has been given.' This did not make Attlee cancel his decision to go for crisis talks with Truman. Politically, he could not ignore the consternation created in Parliament, where 100 Labour MPs signed a letter calling for action to get assurances from the Americans of more responsible behaviour. Attlee flew to Washington on 3 December – without Bevin who was too ill to travel but with his Service chiefs, Field Marshal Sir William Slim and Air Marshal Lord Tedder. He told the Cabinet that the decision on using the atomic bomb could not be left to the United States alone and he would seek agreement that it would not be used without prior consultation with Britain.

It was, inevitably, a forlorn bid to re-establish equal status for Britain which time and the economy had made a very junior partner in the Special Relationship. Nonetheless, the diplomatic drafting talents of Ambassador Franks salvaged more than even Attlee could have privately expected of Britain's diminished status. In the words of the communiqué: 'The President stated that it was his hope that world conditions would never call for the use of the atomic bomb. The President also told the Prime Minister that it was also his desire to keep the Prime Minister at all times informed of developments which might bring about a change in the situation.' Attlee reported to the

Cabinet that he was 'entirely satisfied'. However, it was far short of the right of consultation, let alone the right of veto. His one consolation was that the right to be kept informed at least put Britain one step ahead of the rest, but this proved only a temporary respite from disagreements over basic political strategy. While there was continued irritation in Washington over what the Americans regarded as a British predilection for appeasement in order to reach a settlement with China, the British were alarmed at the way the Americans risked enlarging the war. Two days before going into hospital on 22 January 1951, Bevin sent a message to Jebb in New York about his worries that America's attitude could lead to war with China. This divergence of approach reached a climax in clashes over a United States resolution to have the UN condemn China's aggression. At one stage – largely due to vigorous arguments from Kenneth Younger, the Foreign Office Minister of State deputizing for the ailing Bevin – the Cabinet was about to authorize Jebb to vote against the resolution. It was only the intervention of Chancellor Hugh Gaitskell, who was concerned about the repercussions such a vote might have on America rescuing Britain from its sterling problems, that the Cabinet consensus was moderated first to abstention and ultimately to a supporting vote.

Even though the political differences were less prominent throughout the subsequent twists and turns of the war, from then until the armistice three years after the invasion was a period of uneasiness for the partnership. There was constant concern at the way MacArthur acted as if he were a law unto himself, taking military decisions and making political statements without regard to anyone else. Although he was appointed Commander of United Nations forces under Security Council Resolution 1588 of 7 July 1950, neither the British nor any other government contributing forces had any say in the way the war was waged. Until Truman finally summoned up the courage to dismiss the man he called 'Mr Prima Donna, Brass Hat' on 11 April 1951, there were many anxious moments over the way MacArthur defied the President, used South Korean troops across the 38th parallel and threatened to bomb Chinese cities. The widespread fear that MacArthur might drag everyone into a much wider conflict than was authorized under the Security Council resolutions stoked up the growing resentment in Britain against the Americans. Even Gaitskell admitted that he was worried at the anti-American feelings of his ministerial colleagues during the Cabinet debate on the UN resolution to condemn China's aggression.

Differences between the two governments were exacerbated by the strong emotional currents in public opinion on both sides of the Atlantic. At times the British felt that the tide of anti-Communist feeling was running so strongly among Americans that they were liable to seize any pretext for a fight with China. It drove Younger, deputizing for Bevin hospital, to warn Jebb at the UN on 23 January 1951: 'It must be brought home to the United States that it is not the rest of the world which is out of step with them but their own public opinion which is out on a limb by itself.' But British public opinion was regarded in Washington as being responsible for pressures from the Foreign Office to keep the door open to negotiations for a peaceful settlement, with provisions for a review of the problems of Formosa and the admission of China to the UN. There were occasions when the US Embassy warned Downing Street of the strong anti-British feeling over what was seen as a lack of resolution in pursuing the war and a tendency to prefer talking to action.

Throughout the war there were complaints on the American side that the British were not pulling their weight which gave rise to further discord in the Anglo-American relationship. The British, however, claimed that proportionate to their resources they were taking their fair share of the burdens. In the first year of the Korean War America's defence expenditure was 6.9 per cent of national income compared to Britain's 7.7 per cent. At that time 6.6 per cent of British men aged between 18 and 44 were in the armed forces compared to 4.8 per cent in the United States. How seriously these burdens were taken in Britain was underlined to the Americans by the resignation of Aneurin Bevan from the Government on 23 April 1951 over health charges brought about by a Budget which, he claimed, was a 'grave extravagance' in military expenditure. Where the Americans undeniably took the biggest share was in casualties. By the end of the war American casualties totalled 141,648 including 33,629 killed, 103,284 wounded and 4,735 missing presumed dead; British casualties were 3,514 including 749 killed, 2,556 wounded and 209 missing presumed dead. This serious cost in lives weighed heavily in the minds of the American people and made them resentful of criticism from the junior partner on how the problems of the war should be tackled. But the British could point to the fact that, small though their casualty figures were in comparison to America's, they were larger than any other ally of the United States in the 16-nation UN command.

Another factor which weakened the Anglo-American relationship

was the departure from the Foreign Office of Ernest Bevin on 9 March
with the illness which caused his death five weeks later. He had been
a pillar of the partnership. Despite his more frequent criticism of
American policy during the Korean War, he always regarded the
Americans as Britain's best friends and won immense respect from
Acheson at the State Department and Marshall, both at the State
Department and subsequently at the Defence Department. Bevin was
a realist. He knew how far he should go in criticizing American policy
in the Far East because he was well aware that going too far could
jeopardize American support for what mattered to Britain in Europe.
For Bevin – and Attlee strongly supported him in this instance –
Russia was the biggest threat to the security of Britain, not China.
Therefore Britain could not afford to antagonize the United States
over China to the point where the shield against Communist aggression
in Europe might be undermined.

Bevin's successor, Herbert Morrison, carried little weight in Washington. Attlee's choice was dictated by Morrison's seniority in the
Party plus the fact that Morrison was eager to have the job and the
status that went with it. Attlee had to decide quickly. He had to go
into hospital for treatment of duodenal problems less than a fortnight
after Bevin resigned and felt that he needed a senior politician in
charge during his absence. The trouble was that Morrison had no
diplomatic skills and no feel for foreign affairs, as one of his first jovial
observations about the job revealed: 'Foreign policy would be OK
except for the bloody foreigners.' Morrison never had anything like
the close working relationship with Attlee which Bevin had from the
first day he entered the Foreign Office, and this was a factor which
affected Morrison's standing in the United States. Morrison's attitude
to international issues struck Attlee as far too jingoistic with the result
that Attlee had none of the confidence he used to have in 'leaving it
to Ernie'.

One of the surprises for Morrison about the state of Anglo–American
relations was the way the United States went ahead with the ANZUS
Treaty of Mutual Security signed in September 1951 without any
regard for Britain. He was taken aback that the United States had
decided to link itself in an alliance with two Commonwealth countries,
Australia and New Zealand, without discussing the possibility of British
membership. There was not even provision for the British to have an
observer attached to the ANZUS headquarters at Canberra. Behind
the ritual British welcome for the treaty there was no doubting the

double anguish in Downing Street that the Americans did not see a role for Britain in the defence of an area where the interests of her two old Dominions lay, and that Britain's most loyal Commonwealth partners did not push to have her included.

In his seven months at the Foreign Office handling Korean War issues Morrison irritated the Americans with his attempts to gain international credit for generating peace moves. Much of his diplomatic energy was directed at securing a declaration by all 16 nations with units in the UN command urging ceasefire talks as a means of convincing China that they genuinely wanted peace. Despite strong resistance from Acheson, who regarded it as gesture politics, Morrison persisted with his lost cause. When it came to direct talks between the Americans and the Russians, and subsequently to ceasefire negotiations involving both Chinese and North Korean delegations, the United States conducted the moves without allowing Britain any meaningful role. That demonstrated more than anything else the decline in the status of the British Foreign Secretary in the big league of international diplomacy in the Far East.

By the time of Attlee's defeat at the general election on 25 October 1951, some of the eidetic aspects of the Anglo-American relationship resulting from their co-operation on the Marshall Plan, the Berlin blockade, the creation of NATO and the strengthening of the West in facing the Cold War had been dulled by the divergences over Korea. The closeness of co-operation in Europe was not matched in the Far East, and Attlee, showing signs of exhaustion from his long stint in Downing Street, did not seem to have the energy to inject fresh dynamism into the partnership. Yet only a month after the end of the Korean War – with Eisenhower in the White House and Churchill at 10 Downing Street – one of the most remarkable examples of how special the relationship could become occurred in circumstances normally only found in paperback thrillers.

V

Churchill Lights the Torch Again

'Our strongest resolve is to keep our two countries bound together in their sacred brotherhood.'

Churchill, in a letter to Eisenhower: February 1955

'We clearly recognize the great importance to the security of the free world of our two governments achieving a step-by-step progress both in policy and action.'

Eisenhower, in a letter to Churchill: February 1955

It was the advice of a woman which resulted in Britain and the United States undertaking a joint venture unique in the annals of the Special Relationship – the overthrow of another government. Eisenhower and Churchill personally committed themselves to a course of action which neither had ever authorized before or would ever do so again. It was a form of co-operation that could never be publicly acknowledged. Each government had its own reasons for wanting a change; each had its own plan. Circumstances brought America's Central Intelligence Agency and Britain's MI6 together to organize an operation neither had previously attempted on its own nor would ever do in partnership again. That the idea of toppling a government in an exclusively male regime should have come from the mind of a woman caused no surprise in Downing Street, for hers was no ordinary mind and she was no ordinary woman. What she set in train by her forthright analysis has been kept in the secret records of the Foreign Office for 40 years, so it is appropriate now to disclose the consequences in detail as an example of the extraordinary extent to which the Special Relationship was taken to meet Anglo-American objectives in another country.

Professor Ann (Nancy) Lambton was recognized as a virtually unrivalled expert on Iran. She knew the people, their language, their history, their religious beliefs and their mentality better than almost anyone else in Britain. She had spent almost the entire of World War II working in the British Embassy at Ferdowsi Avenue in Teheran as Press Attaché. As a member of Sir Reader Bullard's staff, she met the high standards he set: fluent in Farsi and interested in meeting people, travelling all over the country and making contacts at all levels. Like others in the Lambton family, she had boundless energy and played a hard game of squash. After leaving Iran, she was a frequent visitor to the country and had many important Persians from all walks of life call on her in London where she was Reader in Persian at the School of Oriental and African Studies. If anyone wanted to know what was happening under the surface of life in Iran, he was directed to seek out Nancy Lambton.

That was exactly what Sir Eric Berthoud, Assistant Under-Secretary of State at the Foreign Office, did on the evening of 14 June 1951. The Foreign Office was very worried about developments in Iran – and it had good reason for its concern. The first alarm signal was the assassination on 7 March 1951 of General Ali Razmara, the Prime Minister, by the Crusaders of Islam. A week later the Majlis, Iran's parliament, voted overwhelmingly for the nationalization of the oil industry run by the British through the Anglo-Iranian Oil Company. Britain's worst fears were confirmed on 28 April with the appointment of a new Prime Minister, Dr Mohammed Mossadeq. Although originally helped to power by the British who got him the job of governor-general of Fars province, Mossadeq was determined to cut the British down to size and three days after he took office, the nationalization law was passed. It quickly became clear that, even though the British acknowledged the nationalization of oil, they had no prospect of negotiating a 50–50 deal for sharing revenues for refining and marketing it.

When Berthoud asked Nancy Lambton what should be done he got a straight answer which was set down for the Foreign Secretary in a confidential memorandum on 15 June. Her verdict on Mossadeq was blunt: 'It is not possible to do business with him.' The strategy suggested by Nancy Lambton was to strengthen the British Embassy 'with a view by covert means (a) to undermine the position of Mossadeq; and (b) to give encouragement to the substantial body of Persian friends we still have who are unlikely to show their faces and risk being called traitors.' The assessment was not hedged by any qualifications: 'Miss Lambton feels that without a campaign on the above lines it is not possible to create the sort of climate in Teheran which is necessary to change the regime.'

She even suggested 'an ideal man' to pave the way for the overthrow of 'Old Mossy' and the establishment of a new regime in Persia. Nancy Lambton's recommendation was to send out Dr Robin Zaehner, a Swiss-born British lecturer in Persian at Oxford. 'He knows everyone who matters in Teheran and is a man of great subtlety,' she enthused. To emphasize his 'ideal qualifications', Nancy Lambton stressed his experience in covert action during Russia's threat to the north-west province of Azerbaijan in 1945 when he contrived to 'mobilize public opinion from the bazaars upwards about the dangers of Russian infiltration'.

Less than a month later in July Zaehner arrived in Teheran with the rank of counsellor at the British Embassy. The British Ambassador, Sir Frances Shepherd, welcomed the addition to his staff of such a distinguished Persian expert, but he did not know what the new arrival's mandate was – and he was not told. That mandate was simple: to employ whatever means were necessary – 'legal or quasi-legal' – to prepare for the overthrow of Mossadeq. Zaehner was assured of virtually unlimited funds. In the course of his operations, funds in excess of £250,000 were made available to him in Persian rials – big by British standards but not an enormous sum compared to the CIA's budget of $1 billion a year under the Eisenhower Administration. The MI6 funds were to buy the support of politicians, newspaper editors, tribal authorities and influential businessmen. Since Zaehner had previously worked in Iran until 1947, his contacts were still fresh. Persian friends had visited him regularly in the intervening period to keep him abreast of the developments in the power struggles.

For the next 15 months while Zaehner went about his business, two key figures at the British Embassy were in charge of Intelligence operations which were to prove of incalculable importance when the decision was subsequently taken to launch a coup. They were Christopher 'Monty' Woodhouse, who had earned his spurs during the trouble in Greece immediately after the war, and Norman Darbyshire, an enterprising Army officer who had so impressed Ambassador Bullard during the war with his knowledge of Persia and its language that he was posted back afterwards as the SIS co-ordinator with the rank of First Secretary at the Embassy. Woodhouse realized very soon after his arrival in August 1951 that the support of the Americans would be essential for success in securing a change of regime. He also appreciated that the Americans were far more concerned about the Communist threat than about oil since they were not dependent upon Iranian supplies like the British. Therefore he worked on the basis that American support depended upon highlighting the dangers of the Communist Tudeh Party using Mossadeq as a stepping stone to seizing power. Darbyshire, who knew the country well from his time as Vice-Consul in Meshed in north-east Iran before being transferred to Teheran in April 1951, was skilled in building up a network of people whose loyalty to Britain could be trusted in an emergency. These preparations required reliable people to be taught how to act as clandestine radio operators for the time when action had to be mounted.

Month by month the relations between Mossadeq and the British Government became increasingly bitter. A ban on British exports of steel, sugar and iron to Iran was followed by the dismissal of 20,000 Iranian oil workers by the British at Abadan. Mossadeq retaliated by ordering the expulsion of the British staff from Abadan. Their evacuation aboard the British cruiser *Mauritius* on 4 October 1951 led to suggestions in Downing Street for the use of force. Foreign Secretary Herbert Morrison strongly opposed what he castigated as the policy of 'scuttle and surrender', but Truman and Acheson made it clear that such action would be universally condemned and Attlee backed off.

When Churchill was returned to 10 Downing Street on 26 October after the general election, the Americans were still anxious about Iran being destabilized if Mossadeq fell. Sir Anthony Eden, back at the Foreign Office, was left in no doubt at his first meeting with Acheson in Paris on 5 November that the Americans were eager to explore every prospect of a settlement either through negotiation or international arbitration. Various attempts in 1952 came to naught, so Berthoud sought the views of Nancy Lambton again. Her advice, recorded in a confidential memorandum by Berthoud on 13 October 1952, was as firm as before: 'It is still useless to accept any settlement with Dr Mossadeq.' Four days later, Mossadeq broke diplomatic relations with Britain and by the end of the month the British Embassy had been evacuated.

This was the crisis for which MI6 had been waiting. Out of the Top Secret drawer in the office of Major-General Sir John Sinclair, Head of MI6 and directly responsible to the Prime Minister, came the contingency plans for a coup to remove Mossadeq which was to be the climax of all the clandestine activity of Woodhouse, Darbyshire and Zaehner. Woodhouse had given it the codename 'Operation Boot' since its objective was to boot out Mossadeq. The key figures recruited by Zaehner in Teheran were known as the Boot Brothers. They were three members of the Rashidian family: Qudratullah the eldest, Assatullah, the middle brother who was active in politics and had contacts with the Shah, and Saifullah, the youngest and the only one of the three who spoke some English. The family had started its business empire with a chain of cinemas throughout Iran and they had good connections in commerce and politics. All had been brought up to have a high regard for the British after their father had been given refuge in the British Embassy during an earlier constitutional upheaval. They had proved their worth as vigorous anti-Communists. They were experienced in mustering crowds onto the streets, a skill they had acquired during a campaign against Russian-backed moves of the Tudeh Party in 1945–6.

The Director of MI6 – known as 'Sinbad' Sinclair, a nickname derived from his days as a midshipman in World War I before being commissioned into the Royal Artillery – did not waste any time. He put a proposition to Churchill for action against Mossadeq and summoned Woodhouse home from Teheran ahead of the Embassy evacuation. Churchill was always interested in bold initiatives, however irregular they might seem to those steeped in protocol, and suggested that Eden should discuss it with MI6. Woodhouse arrived at the Foreign Office accompanied by Zaehner. Eden, a Farsi speaker himself, had a great respect for the judgement of Nancy Lambton, but he had little of Churchill's enthusiasm for cloak-and-dagger adventures. His response to Woodhouse was extremely cautious, but, being aware that as no Britons were left in Iran any operation there would require full-scale American co-operation, Eden left it to MI6 to see whether they could enlist the support of the CIA.

Sinclair's Deputy Director, Air Commodore Sir James Easton, briefed Woodhouse on the tactics for putting the proposition for a coup to the Americans and sent him to Washington in November. It was not the best timing for such a visit, since it was in between administrations with Truman as caretaker about to hand over to Eisenhower. The State Department was still following the Acheson policy of avoiding the uncertainty of deposing Mossadeq because it was questionable whether his successor could bring stability. But Woodhouse made his mark at the CIA. His ideas for 'Boot' were not set down in the detailed form of an operational manual. They were basically an appetizer for engaging American interest. In the course of several meetings he won a number of senior CIA executives over to the idea of a coup, including the influential Director of Operations, Frank Wisner. In Woodhouse's absence Sinclair seized the opportunity of waylaying the CIA's Director of Middle East Operations on his way through London back to Washington after a visit to Teheran. Sinclair's catch was no run-of-the-mill Intelligence agent. He was Kermit 'Kim' Roosevelt, grandson of the US President from 1901 to 1909, Theodore 'Teddy Bear' Roosevelt, and well disposed to the promotion of the Special Relationship. Something of a maverick, Kim Roosevelt enjoyed coping with situations which were not covered in an agent's rulebook. He had a good knowledge of Iran and after talking to the American Ambassador in Teheran, Loy Henderson, a shrewd analyst of the situation, Roosevelt was concerned about the dangers of the country falling into chaos through Communist intrigue. It did not take him long to become a convert to the idea of 'Boot'. But he rewrote the script, changed the codename to 'Ajax', the Greek hero of the Trojan War, and insisted on keeping it in his pending file until the new Eisenhower Administration had settled down in Washington. He realized that the State Department was in no mood to take risks at that stage.

During this waiting period, MI6 went ahead with co-ordinating their preparations with those of the CIA. It was an unprecedented form of close co-operation in the field. Norman Darbyshire, who had been on leave when Mossadeq ordered the British out of Iran, had flown back to Teheran for the last hectic ten days to co-ordinate Intelligence arrangements in the hands of trusted Persian agents once the Embassy closed down. After leaving the Embassy's road convoy in Baghdad, Darbyshire flew to Beirut for consultations with Woodhouse where it was decided that he would set up an Intelligence command post in Cyprus as the 'Teheran station in exile'. Working from the British Middle East Office in Nicosia, Darbyshire controlled a network of secret radio communications with contacts in Iran. It was all very primitive technically compared with today's satellite communications systems. Darbyshire had to rely upon the old 122 wireless sets with operators tapping out Morse signals at fixed times on a variety of frequencies to be picked up in Iran by the Boot Brothers. CIA agents from Teheran moved back and forwards to Beirut to convey fresh developments about prospects of help from the army.

In the midst of this groundwork Eden began to have doubts about the wisdom of the venture. While he was wavering, he issued instructions to suspend financing the operations. Fortunately, MI6 had more faith in Anglo-American co-operation and delayed carrying out Eden's instructions. When Darbyshire was ordered to inform the Boot Brothers that the organization so carefully built up was to be stood down, he had a hunch that there would be second thoughts so he stalled. He ensured that remittances went as usual to the Boot Brothers' accounts in Paris. A week later the plans for the coup were given the go-ahead in Washington. Kim Roosevelt pulled Ajax out of his pending file and secured the necessary political support for the operation. That was followed by a more detailed planning session in which Secretary of State John Foster Dulles, his brother Allen as Head of the CIA and Under-Secretary General Walter Bedell Smith assessed the problems with Sinclair and Sir Patrick Dean, Assistant Under-Secretary at the Foreign Office.

One problem that caused the British to swallow hard was the proposed successor to be installed after Mossadeq. CIA soundings with the Iranians suggested General Fazlollah Zahedi. He was not the obvious choice for the British. Zahedi was not regarded as a friend of Britain, particularly because of his wartime record. Brigadier Fitzroy Maclean had arrested Zahedi at Isfahan in 1941 on suspicion of working with the Germans and had him interned in Palestine. However, faced with the fact that Zahedi was the most likely candidate to be acceptable to the Shah as Prime Minister, and that there were no others with any charisma or anything like the range of army support that he had, the British had no option.

Even so, despite all the care taken over the logistics and politics of Ajax, it was plagued with a sequence of calamities, uncertainties and misunderstandings which left the operation dangling perilously close to disaster until the last cheer at the overthrow of Old Mossy died away in the streets of Teheran in August 1953. When Eisenhower recalled the confusion of the last 48 hours in the drama he admitted: 'Some reports from observers on the spot in Teheran during the critical days sounded more like a dime novel than historical fact.' Right at the outset Mossadeq delivered a body blow by ordering the arrest of the Boot Brothers. The two elder brothers were caught and jailed. Their detention might well have undermined the entire operation, but the enterprising Saifullah escaped over a wall and survived to play a crucial role. It meant that he had to be on the move all the time to keep one step ahead of Mossadeq's agents, and for six months he slept in a different house every night.

Uncertainty over the Shah's commitment to getting rid of Mossadeq was a constant source of anxiety to the British and United States Governments. Not a man who could make up his mind quickly or be relied upon to stick to any plan, the Shah was beset with suspicions that the British were really plotting to overthrow him. Like many Iranians he believed that if the British set their minds to achieve anything they could do it even if they had been expelled from the country. The Shah called in US Ambassador Loy Henderson to air his doubts to him about the British, saying that they had got rid of the Qajar dynasty, then brought in his father Reza Shah and subsequently deposed him. Following a report from Henderson to the State Department, the British Ambassador in Washington, Sir Roger Makins, sent a 'Priority Top Secret' telegram to Downing Street on 21 May 1953 stating that the Shah had informed Henderson that if the British wished him to go 'he should be told immediately so that he could leave quietly'. The Makins telegram added two other urgent queries from the Imperial Palace in Teheran: 'Did the British wish to substitute another Shah for himself or to abolish the monarchy? Were they behind the present efforts to deprive him of his power and his prestige?'

Churchill sent a reply through the Americans in typical tongue-in-cheek style, stating: 'While we do not interfere in Persian politics we should be very sorry to see the Shah lose his powers or leave his post or be driven out.' Not even that assurance stopped the Shah's shilly-shallying. When Henderson conveyed it to the Shah, he found him still so vacillating that he felt it necessary to tell him that it would be disastrous if he withdrew his support from the forthcoming operation after all the American and British Governments had done to help him. Reports of the Shah's prevarication prompted Churchill to send a sharp message on 5 June for Ambassador Henderson to transmit to the Shah: 'It is the duty of a constitutional monarch or president when faced with a tyrannical action by individuals or a minority party to take the necessary steps to secure the wellbeing of the toiling masses and the continuity of an ordered state.' This advice did not reach the Shah as Henderson had left Teheran before the message arrived, so the final decision to go ahead with the coup was taken on 25 June without any certainty that the Shah would play his part.

By this stage Eden was no longer in charge at the Foreign Office as he was recovering from serious surgery and the reins had been handed to Churchill. This was a matter of great relief to MI6 because while Eisenhower and John Foster Dulles were unswerving in their conviction that Mossadeq had to be ousted in order to forestall a Communist take-over, there were strong doubts about Eden's readiness to give the go-ahead. He had become hesitant about authorizing any drastic intervention and never called in Woodhouse after their initial meeting in October 1951. Churchill had no hesitation. He was enthusiastic from the start and eager to be shoulder-to-shoulder with Eisenhower in the venture. He urged continued efforts to make sure that the Shah was brought firmly into line with the commitments of operation Ajax.

The first attempt was to use the Shah's sister, Princess Asraf, to try to convince her brother that the British and American Governments were totally behind him and wanted stability restored after the removal of Mossadeq. It was an Anglo-American enterprise: Norman Darbyshire, accompanied by a CIA officer, Colonel Steve Meed, flew to Paris to discuss the mission with the Princess. They were authorized to hand over ample expenses for the trip, which they insisted had to be made direct to Teheran. But Princess Asraf said that she would need to buy certain things beforehand: 'I'll just go down to Monte Carlo.' At that remark the sheaf of large dollar bills was drawn back across the table. She was told there was a first-class air ticket for a direct flight from Paris to Teheran and there could be no diversions for shopping expeditions. When she reached the Palace, the Shah behaved in a strained fashion as if he feared that every word was being recorded. Eventually she managed to be alone with him, but it was only for a very brief period. The Princess returned to Paris without any confidence in her brother's determination to fulfil his role in Ajax.

The next envoy sent to the Shah was General H. Norman Schwarzkopf, father of the famous commander of Operation Desert Storm which liberated Kuwait from Saddam Hussein's Iraqi invaders in 1990. Schwarzkopf senior was a highly respected figure in Iran as commander of the Imperial Gendarmerie from 1942 to 1948. His arrival in Teheran was disguised as a short transit stop in the middle of a world tour. When he met the Shah he was furtively led into the gardens of the Palace. Even outdoors the Shah remained highly suspicious about being overheard. He kept the conversation on such general terms that the General was ushered out without having any clear idea about the Shah's willingness to co-operate in the moves leading up to the planned coup.

It was left to Kim Roosevelt as field commander of the planned coup and a friend of the Shah from previous visits to make the last pitch. A clandestine meeting at midnight on 1 August enabled Roosevelt to hammer home the basic point that President Eisenhower and Prime Minister Churchill were each personally authorizing the action being organized in Iran. To remove any lingering doubts that the Shah had it was arranged that Eisenhower would use a coded phrase in a speech at San Francisco to be carried by the news agencies and secondly that the BBC World Service would depart from its usual form of words on the time signal – instead of the announcer saying 'This is the BBC: it is now midnight', it would be 'This is the BBC: it is now ... exactly ... midnight'.

After a further meeting late at night a week later to steady the Shah's nerves and rehearse the details of his role, Roosevelt thought all his worries were over. How mistaken that assumption turned out to be. As he waited in hiding in a house of one of his local agents, playing a record of the *Guys and Dolls* song 'Luck Be a Lady Tonight', his own luck deserted him. The success of Ajax depended upon Mossadeq being deposed by an imperial firman – an edict from the Palace for action to be taken – delivered by Colonel Nematollah Nassiri, Commander of the Imperial Bodyguard. Even getting the Shah to sign the firman was a protracted operation fraught with uncertainty day after day for a fortnight after the original request was put to him. Roosevelt's eventual success was conveyed in a triumphant telegram to Darbyshire in Cyprus: 'Have been holding his feet to the fire and, believe it or not, he has finally signed it.' Then the Shah went off to await events at the imperial hunting lodge of Kelardasht, 100 miles north-west of Teheran.

Like most secrets in Teheran, however, the fact that there was a firman signed by the Shah deposing Mossadeq stayed secret for only half an hour. General Raqi Riahi, Chief of the General Staff, was tipped off about Nassiri's mission and alerted Mossadeq. When Nassiri arrived with a posse of tanks and troops to carry out the coup he was promptly arrested. Instead of returning from the Caspian in triumph, the Shah and Queen Soraya flew via Baghdad to Rome on 18 August prepared for life in exile. Zahedi took refuge in a safe house organized by Roosevelt. It seemed that all the months of careful preparation by the British and the Americans had been brought to naught by Nassiri's bungling. An exultant Mossadeq made a personal broadcast telling the people that a conspiracy fomented by foreign elements to overthrow him had been foiled and he was assuming full powers now that the Shah had fled. Amid the dismay and confusion, Thomas Bromley, the Foreign Office counsellor left behind to look after British interests when diplomatic relations were severed, compounded the bewilderment by reporting: 'It may be argued that the Shah, by running away with so little dignity, must have forfeited any audience his messages may have commanded in Persia. On the other hand we should not entirely discount the Shah as a possible leader of opposition to Mossadeq.' Ambassador Loy Henderson was made of sterner stuff. Having lain low in Switzerland during the Nassiri phase, he returned to Teheran to see what could be retrieved. Kim Roosevelt was not prepared to admit defeat either. The Americans were helped by a crucial tactical error of the Communists. The Tudeh Party tried to cash in on the failure of the move to depose Mossadeq and got the crowds out on the streets to celebrate. Carried away by their enthusiasm, they attacked the mosques – a move which American Intelligence agents exploited by getting rival rent-a-crowd mobs to cause further offence to the religious elements of the population.

Overnight the mood of the people was transformed. Early in the morning of Wednesday, 19 August, the Boot Brothers' organization marshalled their support onto the streets to demonstrate in support of the Shah. They secured the religious support of the influential Ayatollah Mustafa Kashani. This was achieved by one of the Boot Brothers' fixers, Ahmed Aramesh, who handed over $10,000 to Kashani to assemble a crowd of agitators calling for the arrest of Mossadeq. Almost as important, they drew out the crowd-pullers from religious institutions like the Zirkaneh, which specialize in displays of strength and rhythmic dancing. Zirkaneh weightlifters led the parade from the bazaars with religious fervour shouting 'Zindabad Shah' – Long Live the Shah. A few hours later – after angry street fights around Mossadeq's house had left 300 dead – Teheran Radio announced that the 'government of traitors and swindlers' had been overthrown, General Zahedi had taken charge as Prime Minister and the Shah was on his way home. In his memoirs the Shah referred to the overthrow of Mossadeq as being 'inspired by indigenous nationalism' but added: 'I do not deny that payments could in some cases conceivably have been made.' When news of the coup was sent to Eden on a convalescent cruise off the Greek islands, he admitted afterwards: 'I slept happily that night.' Only one person took it with typical sang-froid back in London: MI6 Director 'Sinbad' Sinclair. He did not wait by the phone all day in his office for a progress report on the reorganized coup. He went off to Lords to watch cricket and had one of his men stand by a public telephone kiosk to give him 'the latest score from Teheran'.

On his way back to Washington, Kim Roosevelt had a more enthusiastic audience at 10 Downing Street. Churchill listened avidly to every detail of the days of drama in Teheran and confessed to Roosevelt that he would have enjoyed taking part in the venture had he been a younger man. Woodhouse was saluted in Washington later when Allen Dulles expressed the CIA's appreciation for the 'nice little egg' he had brought when he came over the previous year with his proposition for Operation Boot. Darbyshire was promoted Consul in Geneva and returned to the embassy in Teheran in 1964. Whatever reflected glory there was for Sinclair, he did not last long. He was pensioned off in 1956 after Commander Lionel Crabb's disastrous Intelligence operation in April 1956 against the Russian cruiser which brought Bulganin and Khrushchev to Britain. An economic dividend for the Americans came in the oil settlement. Although their motivation for joining the coup was to block Communist infiltration in Iran, they picked up 40 per cent of the oil. The former British monopoly was cut down to 40 per cent, with the Dutch getting 14 per cent and the French 6 per cent. Iran's immediate bonus was a combination of emergency economic assistance and technical aid programmes amounting to £85 million.

Whether it was worth all the trouble taken by the CIA and MI6 has come to be questioned in recent years. There are analysts who argue that the coup paved the way for the political, social and economic tensions which led to the Khomeini revolution in 1979. They claim that if Mossadeq had not been ousted a more democratic system than the autocracy of the Shah might have emerged and prevented the development of an authoritarian Islamic government hostile to the United States and Britain. Others argue that the coup eliminated a very real danger of the Communists acquiring power via Mossadeq and gave the country a pause from further upheavals for 25 years. The fact that the Shah's regime permitted excessive corruption and savage persecution of opponents through the SAVAK security service was not, they argue, an inevitable consequence of the coup. Irrespective of its outcome in the long run, the joint venture demonstrated an aspect of the unique co-operation in the Anglo-American relationship which Churchill set out to cultivate on his return to power.

However, Churchill's optimism about restoring that close partnership across the board on becoming Prime Minister again in October 1951 had to take some hard knocks in his first year of office. He thought it would not require much effort to do better than Attlee, but he was soon made to realize that nothing could be taken for granted. If proof were needed, he had only to study the secret files on atomic energy co-operation. A request for American facilities to test Britain's first atomic bomb lay unanswered for months before a brusque refusal was delivered in October 1950. After a second rejection the following year, the British test was successfully carried out at Monte Bello in Australia on 3 October 1952 – without any Americans being invited as observers.

Consequently, the first 'My dear Ike – if I may so venture' letter to the newly installed President from Churchill on 7 February 1953 focused on atomic energy co-operation: 'I am hopeful that now that we are making the bomb ourselves we could interchange information to mutual advantage.' Being a member of the club and with British scientists having proved their atomic credentials, Churchill felt that he had a strong case when he raised it at a meeting with Eisenhower. One problem was that the American copy of the 1943 Quebec Agreement – providing for joint consent on the use of the bomb and for the American President to have discretion over sharing information with Britain on peaceful uses – had been mislaid in the wrong file of the US Navy Department. However, once Churchill had shown Eisenhower his copy, the President acknowledged that Britain had been badly treated and deserved a new deal. His message to Congress seeking amendments to the McMahon Act led to the Atomic Energy Act in 1954 which permitted a certain amount of data exchange on weapons. This enabled Britain to get further access under agreements in June 1955 to information on peaceful uses of atomic energy and on military defence. In turn this paved the way for an agreement a year later for the data to be provided on reactors for nuclear submarines. It was well short of full co-operation with an open door for the British to share American secrets. That had to await a deal between Kennedy and Macmillan. But it was a substantial improvement on the exclusion imposed by the McMahon Act.

Yet while the rhetoric made it seem that the close camaraderie of the two wartime leaders had been restored – with Ike's greeting from 'your old friend' answered with 'every good wish from your much older friend' – it was impossible to turn back the clock. It was not for want of trying on Churchill's part. He even went to the length of persuading Eisenhower to sign a new Atlantic Charter at the end of their talks in the White House on 29 June 1954 which echoed the declaration he had made at his first meeting with Roosevelt in 1941. Although the Charter proclaimed that 'in intimate comradeship we will continue our united efforts to secure world peace', it lacked the statesmanlike resonance of the original and was forgotten almost as soon as it was delivered. Before he made his inaugural address, Eisenhower made it clear that for all the closeness of the wartime partnership it could not be re-created in the same terms. Any suggestion of a two-power coalition was out of the question since it would arouse what he regarded as unnecessary jealousies and suspicions in the rest of the world. He emphasized the point by refusing to have an Anglo-American summit in Bermuda in December 1953 unless France's Joseph Laniel was also invited.

Although Eisenhower insisted that his 'affection and respect' for Churchill had not declined and towards the end of their correspondence stressed their 'indestructible personal friendship', the personal chemistry between them had changed. Churchill at the helm again at the age of 77 was a much less dynamic figure than when Eisenhower first met him – and considerably slower and frailer after his stroke on 23 June 1953. Eisenhower would refer jokingly to Churchill's deafness which 'he seemed to turn on and off to suit his purposes', but on occasions Eisenhower became irritated at Churchill's refusal to wear a hearing aid which meant that what were intended to be private conversations became embarrassing shouting sessions for Eisenhower. As a reserved person not given to unfolding his innermost feelings, Eisenhower did not often feel at ease with an outgoing, charismatic character like Churchill. There was almost a shyness between them, as when he confessed that he would like to do a painting of Churchill and wrote asking if it would be 'an intolerable burden on you to allow an artist friend of mine to visit you long enough to take a few photographs and draw a few hasty colour sketches that I could use in such an attempt'.

One of the aspects of Churchill's approach to politics which Eisenhower found increasingly irksome as time passed was his unquenchable enthusiasm for trying to set up summits with the Russians. In the course of the next three decades this eagerness for summits with the Russians as evinced by Churchill and two other flamboyant Conservative Prime Ministers, Macmillan and Thatcher, came to be categorized in Washington as the English diplomatic obsession. Churchill's first bid for a summit with Prime Minister Georgi Malenkov as a 'solitary pilgrimage' was proposed to Eisenhower for his approval in May 1953. It met with sharp advice to drop any idea of 'precipitate initiatives'. Churchill took it badly, telling Eisenhower: 'I find it difficult to believe that we shall gain anything by an attitude of pure negation.'

After Churchill's stroke forced him to abandon an early summit with Malenkov, it was assumed in Washington that his mind would turn to other projects. Not so. Churchill could not resist using the emergence of new men in the Kremlin following the death of Stalin as grounds for launching a fresh attempt at an East–West summit bringing together the leaders from Washington, Moscow and London – and as an afterthought perhaps Paris too. Again, however, Eisenhower was not enthused but declined to deter Churchill from an exploratory mission. With ill-concealed disdain, he told Churchill: 'No one could be happier than I to find that I have been wrong in my conclusion that the men in the Kremlin are not to be trusted no matter how great the solemnity and sincerity with which they might enter into an agreement or an engagement.'

But Churchill refused to be put off. He argued that future generations would be astonished that with so much at stake 'no attempt was made by personal parley between Heads of Government to create a union of consenting minds on broad and simple issues'. He tried to shame Eisenhower into second thoughts: 'Fancy that you and Malenkov should never have met, or that he should never have been outside Russia, when all the time in both countries appalling preparations are being made for measureless mutual destruction. . . . After all, the interest of both sides is survival and, as an additional attraction, measureless material prosperity of the masses. "No," it is said, "The Heads of Government must not ever meet." '

Eisenhower, rigid in his opposition to what he termed 'the evil conspiracy centring in the Kremlin', argued that Western leaders meeting the Russians at a summit would give the captive world the impression that they condoned the way the Communists behaved. His verdict in December 1954 denied Churchill his chance as a peace-broker: 'I cannot see that a top-level meeting is anything which I can inscribe on my schedule for any predictable date.' And when he did see his way to do so six years later alongside Khrushchev, Macmillan and de Gaulle, it was the sort of disaster he had feared would ensue from Churchill's summit obsession.

Differences over policy issues erupted between Downing Street and the White House less than two months after Eisenhower's inauguration. The first of these was over Britain's negotiations with Egypt on the Suez Canal Zone – an ominous early warning of serious trouble to come between London and Washington. Churchill resented American innuendoes about British imperialism dictating policy towards Egypt and felt aggrieved that the United States, far from being on Britain's side, appeared to be taking sides against her. It provoked him to remind Eisenhower of the hunter's plea, 'Oh Lord, if you cannot help me don't help the bear.' He tried to argue that the maintenance of a British base with 80,000 men at a cost of £50 million a year was in the interests of the West as a whole. When President Neguib broke off the Anglo-Egyptian talks, Churchill was annoyed that the Egyptians got the impression that they could turn to the Americans for aid. It resulted in a barbed observation to Eisenhower: 'After all, there are other bases conceded for mutual security in other countries not even established by formal treaty – for instance yours in the United Kingdom.'

The first rumblings of a long-running dispute over trade controls of exports to the Communist bloc – which escalated to angry clashes between Britain and the United States in the 1980s – were recorded during this period. COCOM – the Co-ordinating Committee for export controls concerned with restricting trade with the Communists – emerged as a sort of clandestine appendix to the Marshall Plan and convened its first formal session in Paris in January 1950. In conjunction with it the Americans had their own lists under the Mutual Defence Assistance Control Act – known as the Battle Act from the Foreign Affairs Subcommittee Chairman, Congressman Laurie C. Battle – which came into effect on 24 January 1952 and banned American aid 'to any nation unless it applies an embargo'. Public opinion ran high on both sides of the Atlantic over what was strategic and what was not.

Trade restrictions were a very sensitive element of what became one of the biggest sources of friction in Anglo-American relations – policy towards China. Eisenhower often seemed more concerned by the threat posed by China than by Russia's confrontation with the West in Europe. He was alarmed by Britain's 'soft' attitude and admitted that the differences between the two governments 'puzzles us sorely and constantly'. It came to the point where he set out the gulf between them in these blunt terms: 'Although we seem always to see eye to eye with you when we contemplate any European problem, our respective attitudes towards similar problems in the Orient are frequently so dissimilar as to be almost mutually antagonistic.' He repeatedly warned of Communist expansion in Asia and felt annoyed that the British Government appeared to attach little importance to it despite Chinese intervention in Korea and Indochina. Eisenhower never ceased to wonder why Churchill, who was quick to see the threat of aggression from Hitler, was seemingly so complacent about China's advances in neighbouring territories which the Americans regarded as much faster and more relentless than the expansion of Nazi power in the 1930s. 'I think it is dangerous to dismiss too complacently the risks that the bad faith, bad deportment and greed of Red China pose to our world,' Eisenhower told Churchill.

Alarm over these divergences on the China question reached a climax when the Peking Government launched a massive artillery barrage in September 1954 against the tiny islands of Quemoy and Matsu nestling close to the Chinese mainland with a population of 60,000 and almost the same number of Nationalist Chinese troops. As it was seen as part of the stepped-up Chinese campaign to 'liberate' Nationalist-held Formosa (Taiwan), there was deep concern in Downing Street that it might trigger off a conflict involving the United States, China and possibly Russia and raise the spectre of a nuclear war. Churchill was so worried about Eisenhower's determination to stand by his 'brave ally' Chiang Kai-shek in Formosa that he urged the American President to discourage any revival of Chiang's ambitions to reconquer the mainland – 'he deserves the protection of your shield but not the use of your sword,' he counselled.

This crisis prompted Churchill to make a proposition designed to calm the situation without, as he saw it, any loss of face for the Nationalist Chinese or the Americans. It was a three-point plan for the evacuation of Quemoy and Matsu coupled with a US pledge to defend Formosa and a warning that any attempt to interfere with the withdrawal would be met by the Americans with 'whatever conventional force is required'. It was advanced by Churchill on the grounds that the islands might become the centre of an incident 'which would place the United States before the dilemma either of standing by while their allies were butchered or becoming embroiled in a war for no strategic or political purpose'.

It found no favour with Eisenhower who emphasized that as an ex-soldier 'who may have a bit of competence in the strategic field' he would be unwilling to put so much pressure on Chiang to withdraw from the offshore islands that the Nationalist leader might give up the entire struggle. Eisenhower believed that the loss of Formosa would have a domino effect on the rest of the region. The danger of internal subversion spreading throughout the area would be greatly increased, in Eisenhower's view, if the Americans and their friends were to 'show ourselves fearful of Communistic brigands and create the impression that we are slinking along in the shadows, hoping that the beast will finally be satiated and cease his predatory attacks before he finally devours us'.

It was this sort of stern language over these critical weeks in the spring of 1955 which made Churchill abandon his mediation. He realized that persuading Eisenhower and his Secretary of State, John Foster Dulles, to change their policy over the offshore islands was beyond his power. Continuing to challenge the United States over Formosa was not worth the amount of stress it put on the transatlantic partnership. In reaching this conclusion he was tacitly acknowledging that the Special Relationship had severe limitations in the Pacific area where the Americans continued to act, as they did during World War II, with scant regard for the views of the British.

As he bowed out of 10 Downing Street, however, Churchill could take credit for having restored some of the glow to the fraternal association in other parts of the world and in one part in particular to have acted jointly with Eisenhower in a successful operation demonstrating the uniquely special character of the relationship. And despite the clashes over China in his last few months of office, Churchill could not have foreseen how dangerously close to extinction the Special Relationship came in the year after his departure.

VI

Eden Almost Snuffs It Out

'Americans may think the time past when they need to consider the feelings or difficulties of their allies. It is the conviction that this tendency becomes more pronounced every week that is creating mounting difficulties for anyone in this country who wants to maintain close Anglo-American relations.'

Eden, telegram on Indochina: April 1954

'An alliance in which the members ignore each other's interests or engage in political or economic conflict, or harbour suspicions of each other, cannot be effective.'

NATO report at the time of Suez: December 1956

Historians have been relentlessly harsh on Anthony Eden in their verdicts on the Suez fiasco in 1956. Understandably so. The catalogue of mistakes, misjudgements and misunderstandings is formidable. In consequence, the curse of the albatross was hung on Eden for bringing the Anglo-American relationship to its lowest point in its entire existence or even, in the view of some historians, for torpedoing it for ever. To blame Eden alone for the Special Relationship reaching its nadir during his premiership, however, is unjust. Whatever his prejudices – and Eden had perhaps more than most politicians – he had none against the United States. He was far more of an Atlanticist than a European and, on occasion, turned his back on the European movement. While a politician often insists that his readiness to co-operate is not enough in itself and that it takes two to tango, it has to be recognized that it usually takes the same number, if not more, to rupture a partnership. The attitudes on both sides of the transatlantic partnership in the three crucial years from 1954 to 1956 were often totally selfish; policies were crudely pursued without proper regard for

86

the other's interests. American egocentrism was a contributory factor to the deterioration of the Special Relationship for which Eden is usually held solely responsible.

At the heart of the problem – present long before it turned into a crisis – was the appalling personal relationship between Eden and the American Secretary of State, John Foster Dulles. It is difficult to name two other statesmen from the United States and Britain in the past five decades who had a greater loathing for each other than these two had. Sir Evelyn Shuckburgh, who was Private Secretary to Eden with a tolerance far beyond most of his Foreign Office colleagues, elegantly described the lack of harmony between his master and Dulles: 'They were like two lute strings whose vibrations never coincide.' Churchill, according to his physician Lord Moran, was more down-to-earth about his anxieties over the Dulles–Eden clash of personalities. On one occasion in Washington in June 1954 when Eden was late returning from a meeting with Dulles at the State Department, Churchill emerged from a long soak in the bath, wrapped in a towel, and shouted to his valet, Kirkwood, to find out whether Eden had returned: 'Mr Eden must be back. Oh, go and see. Christ! I hope they haven't quarrelled and killed each other.'

The animosity went back to a time before Eisenhower was elected President and put his trust in Dulles. In May 1952 when Eisenhower was still Allied Supreme Commander at NATO, Eden made a highly unusual request to him. Knowing that Eisenhower was about to leave the US Army to campaign as Republican candidate for the presidency, Eden had a meeting with him and urged him to choose someone other than Dulles as his Secretary of State when he got to the White House. He was unashamedly blunt: 'I do not think I would be able to work with him.' It is hard to imagine that Eden would have kept his temper cool faced with an American request that on becoming Prime Minister he should appoint someone other than Macmillan as Foreign Secretary. Eisenhower took it with astonishing forbearance, although he confessed that had it not been for his wartime association with Eden he would have deeply resented what he regarded as an unwarranted intrusion into American affairs. Churchill had no greater respect for Dulles than Eden had and often made fun of the boring way in which Dulles droned on by saying, 'Dull, Duller, Dulles'. But he valued his partnership with Eisenhower too much to have an open showdown with Dulles. Not so Eden. He had no qualms about having a furious row with Dulles and telling him straight that his ideas were as rabidly anti-Communist as Joseph McCarthy's.

Serious clashes between the two men soured relations for over two years before the final schism over Suez. The first sign of trouble between them came over American anxieties about the state of Europe's defence. Dulles felt that the Europeans were sheltering too much under the American umbrella and not taking a big enough share of the burdens – a theme which led to his famous phrase on 14 December 1953 about the United States having to make an 'agonizing reappraisal' of its policy if the moves towards creating a European Defence Community foundered. It was Eden who came in for most of the criticism from Dulles about the state of defence disarray on the grounds that Eden was not evincing sufficient enthusiasm for EDC and giving a lead to the other Europeans. It reached a point where Dulles hinted at 'a parting of the ways' with Britain. So when the National Assembly in Paris scuppered the EDC in August 1954, it was left to Eden to pick up the pieces and devise a more realistic alternative, resulting in the Western European Union with a rearmed West Germany as a member of NATO plus the commitment that the British Army of the Rhine would maintain four divisions in Germany.

If a date had to be fixed for the start of the deep antagonism between Dulles and Eden it would be 11 April 1954, as the crisis in Indochina over France's difficulties in holding back the tide of Vietminh attacks on Dien Bien Phu reached a climax. Dulles had talks with Eden in London and was annoyed to be told that Britain would not agree under any circumstances to have her troops involved in Indochina. He left, however, with the impression that Britain would support moves to set up a nine-nation South-East Asia Defence Organization. But as soon as Dulles issued invitations for a meeting about such moves Eden forbade Britain's Ambassador, Sir Roger Makins, from attending. Dulles was furious and accused Eden of going back on his word, lying and double-crossing him. Eden was almost equally incensed at Dulles for not inviting India to be present at a meeting concerned with the security of South-East Asia. Regardless of whether the Indians wanted to be bound into defence pacts, Eden insisted that they should have been invited. His anger was conveyed in a telegram to Ambassador Makins inveighing against the Americans for ignoring others' feelings and saying: 'We, at least, have constantly to bear in mind all our Commonwealth partners even if the United States does not like some of them.'

Eden and Dulles continued their angry exchanges in the margin of a NATO meeting in Paris about intervening in Indochina to help the French. Despite Eden's insistence that it was too late to stave off a French defeat at Dien Bien Phu, French Ambassador René Massigli told Eden on 24 April that Dulles had decided to back France with an American air strike and wanted Britain to join the United States in a declaration to use force to end Communist aggression. When Eden clashed with Dulles the following evening, the American Secretary of State claimed he was not in favour of an air strike after all but warned that if they did not support France then Malaya would be the next victim of the Communists. Dulles accused Eden of trying to push everyone blindly into a ceasefire which would be used by the Communists to undermine the whole of Vietnam. Eden still suspected that Dulles was weighing up the prospects of launching bombing raids by Superfortresses based in Manila.

By the time they met in Geneva for the Indochina conference, Dulles and Eden found it hard to be civil to each other. Eden warned that if the Americans joined in the fighting they would soon find themselves taking on the Chinese. Since Mao Tse-tung could call on the Russians to honour their obligations under the Sino-Soviet agreement, Eden believed that the United States risked dragging everyone into World War III. Although Dulles asserted that he was seeking only moral support from Britain, Eden snubbed him with the retort that there could be neither military nor moral support. Dulles left Geneva in high dudgeon on 3 May refusing to speak to Chou En-lai, who was attending his first conference outside China. Under-Secretary of State Walter Bedell Smith was instructed to protect America's interests at the Conference without committing the government to anything. Eden's forecast about the impossibility of defending Dien Bien Phu was proved correct on 7 May when it was overrun by the Vietminh.

Dulles, however, kept sniping at Eden from a distance in the United States, returning to his accusations of duplicity over their 11 April meeting during an address in Los Angeles. When Dulles refused to join the reconvened Indochina conference in July, Eden renewed his efforts for a settlement and found his way to a diplomatic breakthrough after France's Premier Pierre Mendès-France pledged to reach a peace agreement in a month or else resign. With that deadline reached on 21 July, Eden secured a ceasefire and agreement to end the eight-year war in spite of what Macmillan described as 'the elephantine obstinacy of Dulles'. Obstinate to the end, Dulles barred Bedell Smith from signing the peace agreement since he maintained that the American people could not stomach guaranteeing 'the subjection of millions of Vietnamese to Communist rule'. Instead there was an American declaration 'taking note' of the first 12 of the 13 points – ignoring the 13th, requiring countries to consult on any questions submitted by the international supervisory commission. For Eden it was – outside the United States – a much praised triumph of negotiating skills. At least for a time. It did not produce much more than a pause of a few years to enable the Communists to prepare for the next round which brought the Americans into the quagmire despite the warning Eden gave Dulles in a memorandum on 30 April 1954: 'Communism cannot be checked by military means alone.'

Parallel with the Anglo-American divergence over the Far East was the far more damaging gulf between the two governments over the Middle East. Ironically, it developed not long after President Gamal Abdel Nasser proclaimed on 26 July 1954: 'A new era of friendly relations based on trust, confidence and co-operation exists between Egypt, Britain and the Western countries.' That was the day he signed the agreement for the evacuation of all British troops from Egypt after 74 years of military occupation. For Dulles it was a satisfactory conclusion after months of pushing Britain towards a deal. His next push had drastic results. Dulles's obsession with countering Communism drove him to organize a northern tier of Middle East countries into the Central Treaty Organization – CENTO or, more notoriously, the Baghdad Pact – in April 1955. It linked Iraq, Iran, Pakistan and Turkey to Britain, with hopes of persuading Jordan and Syria to widen the membership – but its promoter, the United States, stayed in the background with vague promises of joining later.

Nasser was furious and marshalled the power of Cairo Radio to denounce the pact throughout the Middle East as a new manifestation of British colonialism intent upon dividing the Arab world. Almost overnight the hostility of Arab leaders against the West was focused on Britain. Dulles, anxious to preserve America's good relations with both Israel and Saudi Arabia as well as to avoid offending Egypt, craftily stayed on the fence. Eden was bitter at the duplicity, especially when there were indications from Washington that the Americans were taking credit for not joining the much-abused Pact and for distancing themselves from the Iraqi Premier Nuri es-Said who was fiercely attacked in Cairo. Harold Macmillan was highly critical of the Americans' behaviour and what he termed Dulles's 'vicarious brinkmanship' over the pact: 'They had first led us along this path and then hesitated to follow themselves.' When Eden taxed the Americans about their vacillation, the answer was that Dulles would only consider joining the Pact once a Palestine settlement had been achieved.

The next initiative by Dulles was even more crucial in creating the circumstances which led to a showdown between Eden and Nasser and ultimately brought the Anglo-American partnership to an abrupt halt. It was the decision taken by Dulles on 19 July 1955 to withdraw the offer of a loan for building the Aswan Dam. Eden did not deny Dulles a leading role in this situation since the United States was to put up $56 million and Britain $14 million of the initial $70 million. Following the first announcement of the offer on 16 December 1955, Dulles had become concerned at the way Nasser was playing off East against West with Communist arms deals and barter trade. His tolerance was stretched to the limit on 15 May the following year when Nasser announced a barter arrangement of Egyptian cotton for Chinese steel and capped it by giving diplomatic recognition to China – which US Ambassador Henry Byroade only learned indirectly from the Nationalist Chinese in Cairo. When Egypt's Finance Minister Dr Ahmed Hussein arrived in Washington on 16 July for final talks on the Aswan offer, Dulles informed the British he was disinclined to go ahead. Foreign Secretary Selwyn Lloyd did not indicate any disagreement but made it clear that Eden did not think it wise to rush into an abrupt cut-off. France's Maurice Couve de Murville advised caution with the percipient warning that otherwise the consequence could be the seizure of the Suez Canal by Egypt.

On the day Dr Hussein went to the State Department Dulles's patience snapped at the Egyptian minister's suggestion that if the West did not put up the money for the Aswan Dam then the Russians would. Dulles took it as blackmail and called off the offer. Seven days later on 26 July, as Eden was toasting the health of King Faisal of Iraq alongside his Premier Nuri es-Said at dinner in 10 Downing Street, an official whispered the news: Nasser had announced the nationalization of the Suez Canal. Eden claimed that Dulles's decision – and its consequences – came as a surprise. 'We were informed but not consulted and so had no prior opportunity for criticism or comment,' he maintained. In fact there would have been time for Eden to urge a different course of action or timescale had he wanted to do so. Yet the Downing Street claim was sustained after the event when Sir Harold Caccia, then the new Ambassador in Washington, told Herbert Hoover as Dulles's deputy that 'the whole Suez crisis had started by the way in which the United States had turned down the Aswan Dam project without any consultation'.

At least in the first 24 hours after Nasser's announcement the Americans had no grounds for what subsequently became a source of immense aggravation: being kept in the dark by Eden. America's London Chargé d'Affaires, Andrew Foster, was invited by Eden together with French Ambassador Jean Chauvel to an emergency meeting of ministers after the Downing Street dinner for King Faisal; they remained until after midnight assessing the options for action. After a second emergency session of the Cabinet and Chiefs of Staff on 27 July, Eden set out in a telegram to Eisenhower what he regarded as the priorities for meeting the challenge. In calling for firm action Eden left the Americans in no doubt about the length to which he was prepared to go in these words: 'My colleagues and I believe we must be ready, in the last resort, to use force to bring Nasser to his senses. For my part we are prepared to do so. I have this morning instructed our Chiefs of Staff to prepare a military plan accordingly.'

If Eisenhower had any doubts about Eden's resolve to order British troops into action, they should have been eradicated by a report from Under-Secretary Robert Murphy who was sent to London on 28 July in the absence of Dulles, who was in Lima attending the inauguration of Peruvian President Manuel Prado. After talks with Eden, Macmillan and the Foreign Secretary, Selwyn Lloyd, and with Chargé d'Affaires Andrew Foster for a first-hand account of the midnight Cabinet meeting, Murphy sent back his considered verdict on 30 July that Eden was determined that force was both necessary and inevitable to dislodge Nasser. It was not a politically welcome verdict at a time when Eisenhower's main concern was not to be diverted from the presidential election campaign by any foreign adventures. But it did have a sympathetic hearing from some of the American Service chiefs. One of them, Admiral Arleigh Burke, put the view to Eisenhower that if Nasser's seizure of the Canal could not be reversed by political or economic pressures then the only alternative was to support Britain in the use of force, but this was not a proposition that an electioneering president was prepared to endorse.

If Eden nursed any ideas that Eisenhower might come round to that suggestion or even be willing to acknowledge that the British had a case for using force and there was no good reason for America to discourage them, all the signals from the White House made it clear that these hopes were unrealistic. In Eisenhower's first message on the crisis, delivered to Eden by Dulles on arriving in London on 1 August, he warned: 'Initial military successes might be easy, but the eventual price might become far too heavy.' Even if Eden had imagined that Eisenhower was not totally ruling out force in that message, a further letter to Eden on 3 September was unambiguous: 'I must tell you frankly that American public opinion flatly rejects the thought of using force.' Any final lingering doubts were dispelled by a blunt statement from Dulles on 13 September: 'We do not intend to shoot our way through the Canal.'

While the Americans pursued a settlement through weeks of international diplomacy, conferences and meetings of the Suez Canal Users' Association, they realized that on the British side it was regarded as largely a matter of form while they made their military preparations. But they resented the way the British undertook their diplomatic manoeuvres without any consultation. Dulles was particularly annoyed to discover that Eden and Lloyd had suddenly decided – almost behind his back – on 22 September to have the Suez crisis inscribed on the United Nations Security Council agenda. To emphasize his displeasure, Dulles made a statement on the day Lloyd arrived for the Security Council debate, saying: 'The United States cannot be expected to identify herself 100 per cent either with the colonial powers or the powers uniquely concerned with the problem of getting independence as rapidly and fully as possible.' This barbed reference to Britain and France as 'colonial powers' touched a raw nerve in London.

Although the rhetoric of the Special Relationship continued, with Eden saluting Eisenhower's 66th birthday on 14 October in a telegram stating that their friendship was 'one of my greatest rewards', the reality of the widening gulf was marked by the way Eden left Washington without a British Ambassador for the last four weeks of the Suez crisis. Sir Roger Makins returned to London on 11 October for the senior appointment at the Treasury. His successor, Sir Harold Caccia, did not arrive until 8 November. Diplomatic practice does not permit the outgoing and incoming ambassadors to be in the country at the same time, but in an emergency or period of crisis it is unusual not to have an ambassador with direct access to the head of government. This four-week gap covered the deception of the collusion between Britain, France and Israel for the invasion of Egypt. It signified a formal cut-off in communication between the transatlantic partners.

It also left Downing Street out of touch with the innermost thoughts of the Americans at a crucial time, since Makins was held in high regard in Washington and was respected for his shrewd reading of the minds of America's leaders. While Dulles admitted to Eisenhower ten days before Israel launched the war that he was baffled about what the objectives of the British and French really were, Eden and his closest colleagues were unaware of how strong the American reaction to the Anglo-French invasion might be. At worst Eden imagined that Eisenhower would take up an attitude of pained neutrality. It never seemed to occur to him that his action might arouse moral outrage in Washington which would drive the United States to oppose the use of force vehemently. Eden's misjudgement was buttressed by Macmillan's gross miscalculation of Eisenhower's attitude. After meeting Eisenhower on 25 September, Macmillan came away with the impression that 'Ike will lie doggo until after the election'. He persisted in that advice to Eden in the weeks leading to the invasion.

When Britain and France issued an ultimatum on 30 October to Egypt and Israel to withdraw as the precursor to the Anglo-French invasion, tempers in Washington became incandescent. With good reason, too. Eden committed the cardinal error of not giving Eisenhower any advance notice of the ultimatum. The first that Eisenhower knew about it was from an Associated Press bulletin and he felt that he had enough to handle without a Suez showdown. The presidential election was only a week away and the White House already had one major crisis on its hands over the Russian moves to crush the Hungarian uprising. The Americans were enraged when the British – and the French – at the UN Security Council vetoed an American resolution for an Israeli withdrawal which would have removed the technical *casus belli* for the invasion. Eisenhower fumed over the phone to Downing Street and, according to one version, shouted: 'Anthony, have you gone out of your mind?' Before realizing that his telephone call had been answered by Eden's Press Secretary, William Clark, the President exclaimed: 'You've deceived me.' Even America's London Ambassador, Winthrop Aldrich, admitted that he was surprised 'at the vitriolic nature of Eisenhower's reaction'.

From that moment onwards the Americans took the gloves off: for the next week there was nothing special about the relationship. It was not Dulles's revenge. He was out of action from 2 to 18 November undergoing the first of his cancer operations and did not assume full command again in Washington until 3 December. Eisenhower took charge with a tough team around him: Treasury Secretary George

Humphrey, the toughest, but vigorously aided by Herbert Hoover, Acting Secretary of State, and Henry Cabot Lodge at the United Nations. Mustering all the pressures of a superpower – diplomatic, economic and financial – the United States cornered Britain and her partner France into throwing in the towel. Chancellor Macmillan watched powerless and friendless as the sterling crisis mounted with reserves drained in the first week of November by $279 million. Sterling difficulties in New York were compounded by the US Federal Reserve Bank selling large blocks of its sterling holdings. Not only was there no chance of a US loan but any prospects of getting funds from the International Monetary Fund were blocked by the Americans. Two days after British paratroopers landed at Suez on 5 November, Eden bowed to the American pressure and accepted a ceasefire.

Transatlantic relations were not thawed out immediately. At first Eden thought that they had when he telephoned Eisenhower on 7 November to congratulate him on his re-election and asked if he could fly with French Premier Guy Mollet for talks at the White House on the following day. Eisenhower on the spur of the moment agreed, but he had second thoughts when he discussed it with Hoover and Humphrey who pointed out that the Arab world might take it as a sign of approval for the Suez invasion after all. To Eden's chagrin, the invitation was cancelled just before he was about to announce it triumphantly to the House of Commons. Thereafter Eisenhower kept the British at a distance for weeks. When Lloyd went to the United Nations he was frozen out by Eisenhower. Cabot Lodge was branded hostile and highly emotional. Most difficult of all, in British eyes, was Humphrey whom Ambassador Caccia classified as 'the most intransigent member of the Administration about our actions at Suez, and he is most vindictive'.

With heavy selling of sterling and oil supplies difficult to obtain and pay for, the British Government was in no position to resist America's terms: no financial or economic help unless and until there was total withdrawal of British troops. When Caccia went to see Humphrey on 27 November about American support for access to the IMF he received a stony response in these reported terms: 'You will not get a dime from the United States Government if I can stop it until you have gotten out of Suez. You are like burglars who have broken into someone else's house. So get out. When you do, and not until then, you'll get help.' There was no escaping the leverage the Americans had over Britain. From the United Nations Sir Pierson Dixon gave his verdict: 'The past weeks have shown that those directing United States policy are impervious to arguments and appeals to sentimental ties.'

One week later – in the absence of Eden who flew to Jamaica on doctor's orders to recuperate on 23 November – the British Government accepted the inevitable and decided on 3 December to order the withdrawal of all British troops. Humphrey kept his word. The US put no obstacle in the way of Britain being able to draw $561 million from the IMF on 10 December, followed by a loan of $500 million from the American Export-Import Bank. But when Dulles met Macmillan in London on 13 December after a NATO meeting, the atmosphere remained chilly. Macmillan described it as 'a rather painful discussion', with Dulles in a 'querulous and unhappy mood'. From their talks he was left in no doubt that Eisenhower was 'wounded and rather mystified'.

It was not a one-sided change of mood. While the Americans did not hide their anguish over the deception, their behaviour aroused resentment in many quarters in Britain. After the high moral tones used in the United Nations to denounce Britain as an aggressor there was a surge of anti-American feeling. More than 100 Conservative MPs were so angry at the Security Council resolution calling for the immediate withdrawal of troops from Egypt that they tabled a Commons motion accusing the United States of 'gravely endangering the Atlantic alliance'. As it was backed by many eminent Tories such as Angus Maude, Viscount Hinchingbrooke and Sir Ian Horobin, the American Embassy in London alerted the State Department to the strong feelings in the Conservative Party against further bowing to US pressure. However, the main question mark over continuing the transatlantic partnership on the basis of trust was posed in the United States. So long as Eden remained Prime Minister it was not seriously addressed; when he resigned on 9 January 1957 it had to be faced.

All the Jeremiahs of Academia had their funeral orations prepared for the Special Relationship. It was finished beyond reviving, they proclaimed. No nation with aspirations to Big Power status could, in their view, survive the humiliation of defeat over attempting to impose its will on a minor Third World country. Britain's status in the eyes of many Americans was almost completely undermined and in consequence the relationship with Britain was devalued. But politicians are pragmatists, loath to break a mould just because the pattern of partnership has lost its popularity. One politician taking the long view was Churchill, who bypassed Downing Street and sent a letter to the American Embassy in London for transmission to President Eisenhower. His basic advice was contained in one sentence: 'Whatever the arguments adduced here and in the United States for or against Anthony's action in Egypt, it will now be an act of folly, on which our whole civilization may founder, to let events in the Middle East come between us.'

His counsel was well received at the White House and at Downing Street when Macmillan succeeded to the premiership on 13 January 1957. The familiar rhetoric was restored in the letters exchanged on 14 January, with Eisenhower warmly recalling his wartime association with Macmillan in North Africa and Macmillan stressing his personal links with America – having only the previous year in the midst of the Suez crisis visited the town of Spencer in Indiana where his mother was brought up and where his grandfather, Dr Joshua Belles, was buried in the Methodist Church graveyard. Eisenhower ended the freeze by welcoming the new Minister of Defence, Duncan Sandys, to the White House on 27 January. After talks with Defence Secretary Charles Wilson, who was authorized to discuss co-operation on guided missiles, Sandys came back to London with almost Churchillian hype about how he had been left 'in no doubt that they, like us, wish to re-establish fully and at once the special and intimate relationship between our two countries which was momentarily interrupted by recent events'.

But the resurrection of the Special Relationship was really Macmillan's own doing. He made it his top priority. What astonished even the sceptics was not just that he restored so much of the glow that many feared had been lost in the bitter clashes on the road to Suez but that he accomplished it so quickly. Most of the political pundits took the view that whatever was retrieved from the old relationship would have to be put together again slowly and carefully in stages over years, not months. Macmillan did not want to be seen rushing the refurbishment, but he was equally determined not to let slip any opportunity to wipe the slate clean and get back to business as usual. He was realistic enough to accept that he could not project a Britain so discredited in the Arab world after Suez as being on a par with the United States in global terms, but he was aware of the strong card he could play on the European scene where the Americans wanted an effective junior partner at a time when they remained dubious about the place of France and Germany on the international stage.

Macmillan, however, did not relish going cap in hand to Washington and he was much relieved when circumstances ensured that he did not have to do so. Eisenhower took the initiative only nine days after

Macmillan became Prime Minister by sending his London Ambassador, Winthrop Aldrich, round to 10 Downing Street on 22 January with an invitation for a meeting – and, shrewdly, offered to have it on British territory at Bermuda. Macmillan was delighted at the chance to mend fences so quickly. As he loved putting on a show there was a razzle-dazzle welcome for Eisenhower when he landed at the island's capital, Hamilton, on 20 March. The Governor, Lieutenant-General Sir John Woodall, had every Union Jack and Stars and Stripes in the government stores flying and everyone in the town on parade waving flags. The garrison band saluted the American President twice with the 'Star-Spangled Banner' – the extra time by mistake – and the guns fired 84 rounds in his honour which even a military man like Eisenhower admitted was 'a lot of explosions in the cause of peace'. Later in the year there was more pageantry when the Queen played her part in reviving the warmth of the Anglo-American relationship during her visit in October to mark the 350th anniversary of the founding of Jamestown, Virginia. Having been concerned at the damage to the partnership emphasized in the letter to Eisenhower which Churchill had also sent to the Queen, she used the occasion to exorcise the ghost of George III.

After the razzmatazz of the reception in Bermuda, Macmillan secured more substantive dividends than even his Cabinet colleagues expected. The biggest was the American agreement to supply Britain with 60 Thor guided missiles. No other ally at that time would have been considered for such a deal. It was presented as an indication of the importance attached to Britain in defence strategy that intermediate-range ballistic missiles were assigned to her for targeting at 'the heartland of the Soviet Union'. Under the arrangements the Americans retained negative control by having the warheads stored under their authority. Once the missiles were deployed in East Anglia and manned by units of the RAF, they were stated to be under the two-key system whereby they could not be fired without 'a joint positive decision of both governments'.

However, on 24 February 1958, 48 hours after the terms of the missile agreement were published, MPs prepared for a showdown with Macmillan over whose finger was really on the firing button. A furore erupted at Westminster over a statement by a US Air Force officer, Colonel Zinc, claiming that on taking over command at missile bases in England he would have 'full operational control'. When Macmillan was alerted to reports of the statement he telephoned Ambassador

Caccia at 6 a.m. Washington time to get the Americans to straighten out the Colonel for 'putting his foot in it on a grand scale'. A State Department denial of Colonel Zinc's claim was issued immediately to the news agencies in time for a statement in the Commons to calm MPs' anxieties. How effective the 'two-key system' would be in a crisis was fortunately never put to the test, but there were apparently several false alarms over 'clarifications of the command procedures' to judge from Macmillan's comment: 'The American alliance is continually being put in jeopardy by the folly of American officers, in all ranks.'

Macmillan set great store by another agreement at Bermuda under which the Americans committed themselves to joining the military committee of the Baghdad Pact. That, however, was much overrated – a gesture doomed to be short-lived. What was more useful from Macmillan's point of view was a personal arrangement made with Eisenhower at the island's Mid-Ocean Club to write regularly to each other, as Churchill used to do, with the freedom and confidentiality to raise issues which it might be awkward to discuss through diplomatic channels. Eisenhower left as delighted as Macmillan: 'The meeting was by far the most successful international conference that I have attended since the close of World War II.' The follow-through from Bermuda on the exchange of information on atomic research and development was even more significant in the long term. An agreement was reached on 5 June between Sir Edwin Plowden, Chairman of the UK Atomic Energy Authority, and Rear-Admiral Lewis Strauss, Chairman of the US Atomic Energy Commission, over a wide range of matters on the peaceful use of atomic energy. For a change it was the Americans who complained about not getting a fair share. The British side put the brakes on the sharing because they were not convinced that their highly sought-after information on Calder Hall designs would not be secretly passed on to commercial companies in the United States. With this sort of leverage it was not surprising that after the Bermuda meeting there was a readiness on the American side to discuss classified data on nuclear-powered submarines. One bonus was a visit to England by Rear-Admiral Hyman G. Rickover, a key influence in the design of the US atomic submarine *Nautilus*. His time spent with Rear-Admiral Guy Wilson is reckoned to have greatly accelerated the construction of the first British atomic submarine, HMS *Dreadnought*.

Macmillan was so buoyed by his progress with the Americans that he seized the opportunity created by their anxiety over the growth of the Russian challenge – highlighted by the launch of the Soviet

Sputnik on 4 October 1958 – to propose a Washington summit to assess closer co-operation to meet it. His main aim was to push for the repeal of the McMahon Act so that there could be uninhibited co-operation between British scientists, technicians and defence experts and their American counterparts. He took a full team to the White House for his three-day visit from 23 to 25 October, including Sir Edwin Plowden, but to his surprise he found that he was pushing on an open door with Eisenhower describing the McMahon Act as 'one of the most deplorable incidents in American history'. Two working groups were established: one under Plowden and Strauss on nuclear co-operation; and the other under Sir Richard Powell, Permanent Secretary at the Ministry of Defence, and Donald Quarles, US Deputy Defence Secretary, on missiles and rocketry.

The outcome was proclaimed in a further flourish of traditional rhetoric called the Declaration of Inter-dependence or alternatively the Declaration of Common Purpose. The third article of the nine-point declaration gave Macmillan what he most wanted: a commitment by Eisenhower to request Congress to amend the McMahon Act to permit 'close and fruitful collaboration of scientists and engineers of Great Britain, the United States and other friendly countries'. In theory, all America's European allies were equal in the 'friendly countries' category, but one was much more equal than the others. This was for Macmillan 'the great prize' and he returned to tell the House of Commons proudly that there had been 'a new start' in Anglo-American relations. Congress duly responded to enable the Agreement for Co-operation on the Uses of Atomic Energy for Mutual Defence Purposes to be signed on 3 July 1958.

At the first meeting Duncan Sandys had with the new US Defence Secretary, Neil McElroy, after the McMahon Act was amended he noted that 'no topics are now barred and all the cupboards are open'. One of the most important immediate gains was that under Article III of the new agreement a complete nuclear propulsion plant was made available by the United States for the British submarine *Dreadnought*. It also enabled Britain to obtain enriched uranium from America to fuel the plant. British scientists and engineers obtained access to information on research, development and design of military reactors and to advances made in delivery systems for atomic weapons. With the provision of training for British personnel in the use of atomic weapons under Article II, there was the acknowledgement that Britain was being given the basis for continuous advancement in the evolution of nuclear strategy.

What Macmillan achieved, however, was more than the keys to greater knowledge and new techniques. It was formal recognition that Britain was accorded a nuclear status which, though well short of the two superpowers, was far beyond the reach of any other medium-scale power. Only 18 months after the doldrums of the Suez disaster, Britain was back in a pivotal position on the international stage. That the Americans saw it as important to have Britain in such a key role was not a matter of sentiment but self-interest. It was deemed necessary to have one signal standard-bearer in Europe in the front line of Western defence with nuclear know-how and access to the means of combating the threat from Russia. It was also a realistic assessment: with Britain prepared to go it alone with her own deterrent programme, it was wise to spare the British the cost of duplicated research and development by making available America's expertise. By putting the partnership on an evolutionary path as nuclear science progressed, the Americans were providing a new foundation for continuing the Special Relationship as long as confrontation lasted.

Significant as that was, it did not mean that consultation and co-operation operated smoothly across the board or that the two countries were less likely to be at odds with each other on political issues. There were still moments of anguish in Washington over Britain's refusal to abide by the trade embargoes which the United States imposed on China. The State Department declared that it was 'most disappointed' that Britain did not bar 50 items for China in the same category as for Russia but allowed trading on 207 items. Senator William Knowland, Republican leader in the Senate, condemned the British decision as liable to strengthen 'the common enemies of the Western allies'. The Baghdad coup on 14 July 1958, in which King Faisal was assassinated, caught both governments totally off guard with no contingency planning on either side for joint consultation, let alone joint action. Eisenhower did not concert policy with Macmillan; he just telephoned to say that he was sending troops into Lebanon. Macmillan agonized long and hard over what to do about helping King Hussein of Jordan. He tried to get Eisenhower to join him in a combined operation but ended up having to send 2,200 paratroopers on their own to Jordan.

On summitry with Khrushchev, both sides played their hand surreptitiously. Macmillan could not resist seeking an excuse to be the first peacetime Prime Minister to visit Moscow even though the

Americans were highly dubious about the value of making the journey. His visit from 21 February to 3 March 1959 provided many photo-opportunities for him in his white fur hat – a purchase in Finland which it might have been more diplomatic to replace – but did little to ease the current crisis over Berlin. In turn, Eisenhower took a decision on his own to invite Khrushchev to visit America which, again, was interesting for its photographs – taken in Washington, New York, Los Angeles, Des Moines, Pittsburgh and Eisenhower's farm at Gettysburg – but not noteworthy for lessening East–West tension.

Anglo-American plans for a joint summit with Khrushchev were frustrated at the last moment when an American U-2 reconnaissance plane was shot down on 1 May 1960 near Sverdlovsk in the Urals after an incursion 1,250 miles inside Soviet territory. Macmillan was as crestfallen as Eisenhower; he had always been the more eager summiteer and made valiant efforts to rescue it at the eleventh hour. On 15 May – the day before the summit was due to open in Paris – following a long meeting with Eisenhower, de Gaulle and Germany's Dr Adenauer at the Elysée Palace, Macmillan volunteered to tackle Khrushchev on his own. For one and a half hours he employed all his diplomatic skills in an attempt to argue Khrushchev out of forcing a breakdown of the summit. He even resorted to repeating de Gaulle's disdainful obser-vation that discussing 'the peccadilloes of Intelligence services' was not worthy of the attention of heads of government, but Khrushchev responded with a six-page statement requiring inordinate amounts of humble pie to be eaten by Eisenhower with a promise to call off all spy flights.

Even when the summit was virtually beyond saving Macmillan did not give up. He had Selwyn Lloyd spend an hour with Foreign Minister Andrei Gromyko at the British Embassy in a last-ditch effort to end the deadlock. Knowing how damaging it was publicly for Eisenhower to be so humiliated in Paris, Macmillan felt it his duty to demonstrate Anglo-American solidarity. He suggested a show of defiance by driving round the French capital in an open car with Eisenhower and accepted a working breakfast with him despite a firm conviction that no Englishman should have to face grilled chops and marmalade at that time of day.

Privately, Macmillan was disappointed that Eisenhower was so naive in his handling of the U-2 crisis as to make the summit an inevitable fiasco. He felt that Eisenhower would have benefited from more resolute strategy if there had been a stronger figure at his side than Christian

Herter as his Secretary of State (Dulles having died the previous year). There was surprise in London Intelligence circles that the U-2 flights had not been suspended once the Paris summit had been fixed, if only because of the suspicions of significant improvements in Soviet missile technology. Between 5 May when Khrushchev disclosed the shooting down of the plane to the Supreme Soviet and 15 May when Eisenhower arrived in Paris for the summit there was a series of contradictory statements issued in Washington which seriously damaged the President's room for manoeuvre. This puzzled those involved in Paris and London with the summit preparations.

Equally worrying, the White House persisted with its lame cover-up – that the pilot Gary Powers had been on a weather reconnaissance flight to gather data on air turbulence and had come down after experiencing oxygen problems – long after this was discredited. There was no attempt to discuss with Macmillan how the summit might be saved by some form of oblique apology and an 'out' for Khrushchev if he could be persuaded that the summit could be worthwhile for him. Macmillan had hoped for some less rigid stance by Eisenhower than a blunt refusal to apologize for action which was deemed necessary for the security of the United States. Even the host, President de Gaulle, thought the best tactic would have been to bluff it out by suggesting that the spy plane was not on an offensive mission and that everyone was engaged in some form of espionage, not least the Russians. Macmillan kept his thoughts about Eisenhower's conduct to himself until the verdict in his memoirs: 'When the moment came he was too honourable to rely upon a diplomatic white lie and too conscious of his position as Commander-in-Chief to throw responsibility upon a subordinate.' It was also a comment on his own set of values, since Macmillan was not totally averse to a white lie if there was a good diplomatic or political reason for being less than 100 per cent honest.

Huge though the headlines were throughout the 13 days of May on the summit crisis in Paris, there was one event which attracted much less coverage at the time but which kept creating political trouble and public demonstrations in the United Kingdom for three decades thereafter. That was the agreement made public on 1 November 1960 for the Americans to have facilities for Polaris nuclear submarines at Holy Loch on Clydeside. Macmillan acknowledged that it was a matter over which he pondered for a long time and only gave his consent after 'grave thought'. There were many Opposition voices warning that allowing an anchorage for American nuclear submarines in Scotland exposed the country to a much higher level of danger of a pre-emptive strike by Russian rockets. Although there had been left-wing criticism of the close co-ordination of the Royal Air Force with the US Strategic Air Command at air bases in Britain, it was argued that the Holy Loch agreement added a much more perilous dimension on the risk-taking scale. Macmillan answered these fears in the House of Commons by asserting: 'This arrangement does not add to the risks to which we are all inevitably exposed in this nuclear age.' However, although he did not admit it at that stage, he was very much aware of the link in American minds between Britain granting facilities at Holy Loch and the negotiations undertaken by Minister of Defence Harold Watkinson with American Defence Secretary Thomas Gates for an agreement to get the Skybolt missile on favourable terms. It was this linkage which Macmillan was to use in reverse to the Americans two years later when the Skybolt crisis brought the two countries to a head-on collision at the Nassau summit.

With that challenge still beyond his political horizon, Macmillan was entitled to feel well satisfied with his salvage operation on Anglo-American relations. As the Eisenhower–Macmillan era of the trans-atlantic partnership came to a close on 20 January 1961 with the inauguration of President John F. Kennedy, much of the damage done three years earlier in the fateful last days of the Eden Government had been repaired. Khrushchev had played his part by the way he sustained and intensified the East–West confrontation, thus making the Americans more anxious to have Britain as a reinvigorated partner. Britain's steady stance against Khrushchev's blusterings won fresh support in the final months of the Eisenhower Administration when Macmillan treated with a fine blend of sang-froid and disdain the raucous interruption of his address at the United Nations General Assembly by the Russian leader. It was for Eisenhower – and many other Americans watching on television as Macmillan paused momentarily to make a mannered request for a translation of the Russian abuse – 'British reserve in its finest flower'. Macmillan may well have thought that he had reached the highest peak possible in the relationship since the days of Churchill and Roosevelt, but he was to discover that the best was yet to come when Khrushchev took Russia's brinkmanship to the edge with his nuclear challenge to Kennedy over Cuba.

VII

The Golden Days of Mac and Jack

'No differences of opinion or age prevented the two leaders from getting along famously. ... A fondness developed between them which went beyond the necessities of alliance.'

Theodore Sorensen: 1965

'In nearly three years of co-operation, we have worked together on great and small issues, and we have never had a failure of understanding or of mutual trust.'

Kennedy's last letter to Macmillan: October 1963

The moment that the British delegation arrived at the Langley head-quarters of the Central Intelligence Agency on the outskirts of Washington on the morning of Monday, 15 October 1962, they sensed that something unusual was going on. None of the big black limousines of the CIA chiefs was in the parking lot. Their suspicions were confirmed when they were shown into the CIA conference room. The three other 'old Dominions' teams' were there at full strength – senior Intelligence officials from Canada, Australia and New Zealand. But their hosts were absent: CIA Director John McCone and his Deputy Director, General Marshall 'Pat' Carter. No explanation was given for the unprecedentedly low-level welcome at the annual review of Western Intelligence leaders.

So the high-powered British representatives sat through a dull routine meeting in increasing bewilderment: Sir Burke Trend, designated Cabinet Secretary about to succeed Lord Normanbrook, Sir Hugh Stephenson, Deputy Under-Secretary of State at the Foreign Office, Major-General Sir Kenneth Strong, Head of the Joint Intelligence Bureau at the Ministry of Defence, and Thomas Brimelow, Russian-speaking Counsellor at the Embassy whose sharp analytical mind took him ten years later to be Head of the Foreign Office. On their return to the Embassy in Massachusetts Avenue a telephone call came to Sir Kenneth Strong from an old friend at the CIA which was to solve the mystery and prove the incomparable importance of the Special Relationship. It was an invitation for the British team to return on their own on Tuesday, 16 October, before the general meeting resumed.

Few British Intelligence experts have been held in such high esteem in the United States as Strong. Son of the rector of Montrose Academy on Scotland's east coast, he made his mark as a military attaché in Germany, France, Italy and Spain with the rare ability of being a skilled interpreter in all four languages. As Head of General Eisenhower's Intelligence Staff in 1943, Strong was sent to negotiate an armistice with Italy in Sicily, then negotiated the surrender of the Germans in Berlin. After the war, having been awarded America's Distinguished Service Medal and the Legion of Merit – as well as Russia's Order of the Red Banner – Strong kept in regular contact with the Americans as Director-General of Intelligence at the Foreign Office before becoming the first Director of the Joint Intelligence Bureau at the Ministry of Defence in 1948.

When Strong – out of uniform, wearing a dark blue suit with the regimental tie of the Royal Scots Fusiliers – walked back into the conference room at CIA headquarters at 9.30 a.m. on Tuesday with the British team there was only one person to greet them. The handshake at the end of the table was from Dr Ray S. Cline, CIA Deputy Director of Intelligence, a former London agent who had enjoyed a close working relationship with Strong during the years 1951–3. What Dr Cline had to say left Strong – a man not unaccustomed to having alarming information conveyed to him in unexpected circumstances – totally incredulous.

The same eight-word message had been conveyed to President Kennedy only an hour earlier at the White House: *The Russians have sited offensive missiles in Cuba.* For General Strong, who had faced all the fears of war right up to the last days of the fighting against the Nazis when he arrested Field Marshal Wilhelm Keitel, who was to sign the German surrender, this was the ultimate uncertainty: were the superpowers now set on a course that would bring nuclear devastation to the world? The British delegation around him had realized something extraordinary was happening when they arrived. That message gave them the answer but it had to stay a secret.

Until now all the accounts of the Cuban missile crisis have assumed that the British were kept in the dark until the official communication from Kennedy to Macmillan six days later. Not so, as this disclosure of the meeting in the CIA conference room reveals. It was explained that Major Rudolph Anderson, a US Air Force officer seconded to the CIA, had returned to McCoy Air Force Base in Florida on Sunday, 14 October, with film taken on a U-2 reconnaissance flight 12 miles above Cuba. This was the first direct evidence of intermediate-range ballistic missiles having been installed on transporter-erectors at San Cristobal. To make absolutely sure that there was no misunderstanding over what had been photographed, since they were on the brink of what the CIA called a five-star crisis, photoanalysts spent several hours on Monday, 15 October, checking every frame.

Although it was not admitted at the time, accurate identification of the missile sites was greatly facilitated by the espionage of Colonel Olev Penkovsky, the key Western agent inside the GRU – Soviet Military Intelligence. Secret film taken by Penkovsky's camera of confidential documents at the Soviet missile headquarters enabled Arthur Lundahl, the Head of the National Photographic Intelligence Centre, to confirm to Dr Cline that the U-2 flight had produced irrefutable evidence. It was obtained just in time, since the CIA was to learn a fortnight afterwards on 2 November that Penkovsky had been arrested in preparation for a show trial which ended with his execution by firing squad in May 1963.

President Kennedy was not the first in his Administration to know what the CIA had discovered about the Cuban missiles. Dr Cline's first call at 8.30 p.m. on Monday was to McGeorge Bundy, the National Security Adviser, who was in the middle of a dinner party at his home. Bundy took the decision that it would be unwise to be seen panicking in late-night meetings since it would be difficult to conceal emergency White House sessions from the Press. He was also swayed by the fact that the President had just returned from an exhausting election campaign trip to Niagara Falls and would benefit from a good night's rest before becoming immersed in crisis talks. Cline was advised to stand by at the White House at 8.30 a.m. on Tuesday. His next call was to CIA Deputy Director General Carter, who promised to pass on the information to General Maxwell Taylor, Chairman of the Joint Chiefs of Staff, whom he was meeting that evening. One further call was made – to Roger Hilsman, Director of Intelligence and Research at the State Department, who passed the information to Secretary of State Dean Rusk. Although others got to know through discreet

Intelligence whispers, these were the main people with inside knowledge of the burgeoning crisis while the President slept.

Early on Tuesday morning the photographs, enlarged and given caption labels, were delivered to Cline who took them to the White House where he met Bundy and Attorney-General Robert Kennedy. Cline briefed the two of them. Bobby Kennedy went upstairs with Bundy to have the first crisis session with the President who then summoned a meeting of the 15 members of the Executive Committee of the National Security Council – EXCOMM – in the Cabinet Room at 11.45 a.m. It was straight after his briefing with Bundy and Bobby Kennedy that Cline drove back to Langley for his meeting with the British.

Having left all his prints of the missile sites at the White House, Cline could not offer Strong incontrovertible evidence and the General took some convincing. Strong found it difficult to believe that Khrushchev could have taken such a high risk of being found out so quickly with 24 missiles – having the explosive capacity of 20 Hiroshima bombs – targeted on the United States and only 90 miles off the American coast. However, the graphic description given to the British left them no alternative but to swallow hard and accept that the West was facing a horrendous test of will and nerve. Since Bobby Kennedy went into talks with his brother determined not to rush into a response to Khrushchev before all the options were carefully weighed, it was laid down at the White House that no information should be given to anyone outside the trusted circle. That Strong was considered worthy of exemption from this high-security edict is proof that in times of crisis in the Cold War, whatever the cynics said about Britain as a hapless bystander, the British were not left on the outside.

Because of the security strictures, the British delegation were warned not to mention a word to anyone else at the conference. Strong was advised to go back to London at once and tell Macmillan. No telephone calls to be made; not even a message in diplomatic cipher from the British Embassy. Strong went to London on the first available plane while the other three members of the delegation carried on with the conference agenda, including a boat trip on the Potomac which the CIA had organized with fleets of cars discreetly available at every landing stage in case the Cuban crisis suddenly came out into the open.

Despite the fact that Macmillan, alone among America's Western partners, had been alerted to the Cuban crisis on Wednesday, 17 October, he never gave any hint of having such advance information.

Cabinet records made available under the 30-year rule in January 1993 show that the first mention in Cabinet of the crisis was at a meeting convened at 10.30 a.m. on Tuesday, 23 October, the day after President Kennedy made his broadcast revealing that Russia had installed offensive missiles in Cuba. In the absence of the Cabinet Secretary, Sir Norman Brook, who was ill, his deputy recorded as the third item of the meeting: 'The Prime Minister said that on the evening of Sunday 20th October [the date was left uncorrected: it should have been the 21st] he had been warned by the US Ambassador in London [in fact the British Ambassador in Washington] to expect a personal message from President Kennedy. *This was the first intimation to him of the chain of events which had led to the imposition of the US blockade on Cuba'* [author's italics]. As the Prime Minister usually has to approve the record of the meeting it is strange that this section was left unamended.

Even in the volume of his memoirs published in 1973 Macmillan preserved the fiction of not having had any substantial advance knowledge. He merely referred vaguely to indications of a missile crisis from Sir David Ormsby-Gore, the British Ambassador in Washington, on Friday, 19 October. Recalling the quickening pace of events on the Sunday he stated: 'We had already received, two days before, some warning from the British Ambassador, to whom the President had spoken in guarded terms.' In fact, the Ambassador had been fully informed of the disclosures given to the British delegation at CIA headquarters before Strong left for London to report to Macmillan at Admiralty House – where the Prime Minister's office was temporarily housed during repairs to 10 Downing Street. Coded confirmation of this is given in a Top Secret telegram from the Ambassador to Sir Harold Caccia, by now the Permanent Under-Secretary of State at the Foreign Office, on Saturday, 20 October. Referring to American concern at the build-up of Soviet arms in Cuba, Ormsby-Gore stated that reports suggested 'that the types of arms may not be entirely defensive. ... Sir Hugh Stephenson will give a full report to the Secretary of State when he returns to London' – a cryptic reference to the startling disclosures by Cline at Langley which Strong, as a senior figure at the Ministry of Defence, would not have reported directly to the Foreign Office.

Cabinet telegrams now available at the Public Record Office indicate that Macmillan knew what to expect when he was warned to be ready for a communication from Kennedy. A telegram from Washington, No. 2630, at 7.31 on Sunday evening marked 'Emergency Top Secret:

Personal for PM from Ambassador' stated: 'I have just come from seeing the President. He will be sending you an extremely important message on Cuba by teletype machine to Admiralty House at about 10 p.m. London time. I think it essential that you should be there to receive it immediately. The President particularly stressed that not only are the contents of the message confidential in the highest degree but that the fact that you are receiving the message at this time should on no account become known.' That Macmillan did not take the Ambassador's advice points to the conclusion that he was well aware of what was at issue.

An 'Explanatory Note' from Timothy Bligh, the Prime Minister's Private Secretary, was attached to the secret file: 'After reading Washington 2630 the PM decided to stay at Chequers and not come up to London until after lunch on Monday, 22 October. Subsequently after reading the President's personal message the PM said he would come up to meet the American Ambassador at noon on Monday.' Significantly, too, Macmillan did not think it necessary to share his knowledge that evening – or on the days after Strong returned with his exclusive news – with his Foreign Secretary. He did not alert Lord Home until after the American Ambassador's visit on Monday, when Macmillan telephoned Home and asked him to come over to Admiralty House to help draft the first reply to Kennedy. At that stage, when it was clear that a crisis of horrendous potential was evolving, Lord Home was the only Cabinet minister informed by Macmillan.

Kennedy's message to Macmillan on the Sunday evening – before informing any other Western leader – underlined the importance he attached to close co-operation with Britain. While the full details were to be conveyed by America's London Ambassador, David Bruce, on Monday, the priority attached to British views was underlined: 'I want you to have this message tonight so that you may have as much time as possible to consider the dangers we will now have to face together.' While he explained that for reasons of secrecy and speed he had to take the first decision on a response to Khrushchev on his own, Kennedy stressed that from that moment onwards they should stay 'in the closest touch'.

To appreciate fully how close that was it is essential to take account of the role of Lord Harlech, or Sir David Ormsby-Gore as he then was, at the Washington Embassy. His appointment as Ambassador was an inspired choice by Macmillan. Not only did Ormsby-Gore know the workings of the Foreign Office and the political system as Minister

of State from 1957 to 1959 handling East–West questions and disarmament, but he had the inestimable advantage of being a member of
the Kennedy clan. A cousin of Kathleen Kennedy's husband, who was
killed in World War II, he was a frequent weekend guest at Hyannis
Port or Cape Cod and a regular golfing partner of the President with
usually the added responsibility of calculating what players owed each
other under the complex betting system which the President enjoyed
devising. When the Kennedys went to Camp David, to the rented
estate Glenora in Virginia, or in winter to Palm Beach they had the
Ormsby-Gores with them. The British Embassy staff, who always had
to have means of contacting the Ambassador in an emergency, reckoned
that apart from the time when the President was out of the country
there were only three or four weekends when the Ormsby-Gores were
not with the Kennedys. Although the French Ambassador, Hervé
Alphand, was a senior figure with the ear of de Gaulle, and Germany's
Wilhelm Grewe was well respected too, neither had anything like the
access of David Ormsby-Gore. Kennedy would often say: 'I would
trust David as I would trust my own Cabinet – after all, he's Bobby's
best friend.'

Another highly confidential enterprise in Anglo-American co-operation – this time solely to the advantage of the United States – was
the service British diplomats provided as the Intelligence eyes and ears
for the Americans through the British Embassy in Havana. The CIA
listed their Intelligence collection requirements every day to Thomas
Brimelow at the Washington Embassy. As a result Sir Herbert Mar-
chant, the Ambassador in Havana, reported to the Foreign Office in
London on 23 October for onward transmission to the Americans that
two Russian ships had arrived that morning and that one of them, the
Volgoles, had a cargo of military vehicles. Before the crisis became
public knowledge the CIA was anxious to find out about work on the
missile sites and asked the British if they could spot any 'cherry
pickers' – the American term for arc lights on a swivel enabling night-
shift engineers to work in badly-lit areas where the missiles were sited.
However, despite several excursions by members of the Embassy staff
driving along the roads of San Cristobal they failed in their mission
since the missiles were hidden in a valley with the road sealed to
unauthorized vehicles.

On the Sunday, 24 hours before the Presidential broadcast revealed
the crisis to the world, Kennedy called in Ormsby-Gore to discuss
the situation. In a personal telegram to Macmillan afterwards

Ormsby-Gore explained: 'He asked me to come unseen to the White House just before lunch. We were quite alone and he told me that no one else outside the United States Government was being informed of what was going on.' In an amazingly frank review Kennedy said that he had two choices – an all-out air strike the following morning on Cuba or an immediate blockade which would stop further supplies by sea. The President candidly admitted to Ormsby-Gore the disadvantages of an air strike in not offering total elimination: 'The military authorities estimated that such a strike would eliminate at least 50 per cent of the Cuban missile potential but it would inevitably cause a large number of casualties to Russians as well as Cubans.' He stressed the weakness of relying solely on a blockade: 'This would mean leaving the Cubans with their present offensive capacity, such as it was.'

The total frankness of their discussions was exemplified by Kennedy asking Ormsby-Gore which course of action he should choose. When Ormsby-Gore warned that an air strike would be too drastic a response and advised the more gradual approach of a blockade Kennedy was pleased since that was his own conclusion. At a later meeting Kennedy discussed with him the crucial question of where the interception point should be for US warships to stop Russian ships. Ormsby-Gore argued that Khrushchev was faced with difficult decisions and, since he had to be given a chance to climb down without too obvious humiliation, every additional hour would help to avoid an escalation of the crisis. Kennedy accepted his suggestion for reducing the blockade interception distance from 800 miles off the coast of Cuba to 500 miles in order to give the Russians more time for second thoughts about a confrontation and the opportunity to turn back.

He acted at once, telephoning Secretary of Defence Robert McNamara to issue instructions, and then returned to continue the discussion with Ormsby-Gore. It was a private conversation in a corner between him and Kennedy after a small White House dinner party on the Tuesday which resulted in the decision to make some of the U-2 pictures of the missile sites available to the Press – in Europe simultaneously with the United States. Ormsby-Gore urged the President to do so partly because some people in Britain were not convinced that missiles had been put in place in Cuba. Kennedy ordered an aide to bring him a stack of aerial photographs and then went through them with Ormsby-Gore to pick out the best of the low-level shots. Having agreed the selection, he instructed them to be given world-wide publicity to demonstrate the threat to peace posed by Khrushchev's gamble.

There were several occasions during the crisis when, if they could not meet, Bobby Kennedy and Ormsby-Gore had long discussions by telephone. The President's brother relied on the Ambassador to assess European reaction to each stage of the crisis. No one else in Washington's diplomatic colony could imagine himself being invited as Ormsby-Gore was to sit alongside McNamara with the President in the Situation Room at the White House scanning the tracking of Russia's ships on an operations board. When reporting on the highly confidential observations made to him by Kennedy, he told Macmillan in one telegram: 'I had previously hesitated to report these remarks because in some instances they were so frank that I doubt whether he would repeat them to any of his Administration except his brother Bobby. You will realize how important it is that no knowledge of them is disclosed to any American including the President himself.'

Yet in spite of all the inside information – from Strong and Ormsby-Gore – Macmillan remained hesitant about taking it at its face value even when Ambassador Bruce arrived to see him just after noon on Monday, 22 October. A further message from Kennedy delivered by Bruce emphasized the special position Macmillan had in the President's priorities. It informed him that letters would be going to Canada's John Diefenbaker, France's General de Gaulle, Germany's Konrad Adenauer and Italy's Amintore Fanfani. 'However, I wanted you to be the first to be informed of this grave development in order that we should have the opportunity, should you wish it, to discuss the situation between ourselves by means of our private channel of communication.' Acknowledging European anxieties of a possible backlash by Khrushchev against Berlin where the simmering crisis had caused deep concern for the past year, Kennedy stressed the importance of Anglo-American relations: 'We must together be prepared for a time of testing. It is a source of great personal satisfaction to me that you and I can keep in close touch with each other by rapid and secure means at a time like this, and I intend to keep you fully informed of my thinking as the situation evolves.'

Alongside Bruce at the meeting with Macmillan that day was a CIA agent specially chosen by Cline for the assignment, Chet Cooper. As someone who had worked in the American Embassy in London and had an importance well above his ranking in the CIA, Chet Cooper was thought to be the best person to handle Macmillan if the Prime Minister were in a querulous mood since Cooper was well liked in

British circles and had a way of being at ease with them. Cooper supplied fresh material on the missiles and presented a new set of photographs of the sites to Macmillan. They were studied closely by Macmillan who gave the impression that he was not entirely convinced that the CIA had got it right in assessing the sort of threat apparently indicated by the pictures. Macmillan insisted on keeping the pictures and sending them to his own MI6 experts for a second opinion. His attitude contrasted sharply with the manner in which General de Gaulle subsequently behaved when Dean Acheson arrived at the Elysée Palace in Paris on a similar mission. The General listened very attentively to all the details of the missile build-up in Cuba, but when Acheson was about to open his dossier of photographs de Gaulle made a dismissive gesture with his hands indicating that he had no need to see them in order to be convinced. 'No, Mr Acheson. The President of the United States of America would not deceive me on a question of such importance.'

Macmillan's hesitations about the crisis rarely surfaced in the official communications between him and Kennedy since he was anxious to preserve their close working relationship. However, recently released Foreign Office documents reveal that reservations over the way the Americans were behaving towards Cuba were being underlined in communications from Macmillan and Foreign Secretary Lord Home in the six months leading to the missile crisis. Differences emerged over American pressure on its allies to impose credit controls and trade restrictions on Cuba which were tantamount to putting Cuba in the same economic straitjacket as the East European Communist countries suffered under the COCOM regulations. Over dinner with Dean Rusk at the Foreign Secretary's residence at 1 Carlton Gardens on 24 June, Lord Home acknowledged that Britain was in a minority of one in the Atlantic Council over a trade embargo against Cuba but insisted that sanctions would have no effect just as they had failed against Mossadeq in Iran and Nasser in Egypt.

In Cabinet when Lord Home appeared to waver and see a case for some compromise, the President of the Board of Trade, Frederick Erroll, vigorously opposed any extension of trade restrictions regardless of the Foreign Secretary's argument that it would 'cause a major row with the Americans'. Macmillan backed Erroll against Home and re-emphasized his reservations about America's strategy when the Foreign Secretary was in New York on 1 October at the United Nations. He cited his suspicions over an American missile deal with Israel as a reason for doubting that the United States was playing straight over Cuba. In a blunt telegram to Home he stated: 'It is only a quibble for the State Department to say no negotiations have been undertaken but admit it is quite definite that the Israelis will take up the American offer. I am afraid I cannot alter the view that the Americans have deceived us all through. We must always have this in mind in discussing other subjects with them.' On Cuba Macmillan was emphatic in his instructions to Lord Home to withhold agreement to impose COCOM restrictions: *'There is no reason for us to help the Americans on Cuba'* [author's italics].

These reservations before the missile crisis about isolating Cuba re-emerged in determining Britain's role at the United Nations Security Council. Macmillan was concerned that by pushing too hard against Cuba the United States might undermine European solidarity. In his first message to Kennedy after the meeting with Ambassador Bruce on Monday, 22 October, Macmillan underlined that danger in shrewdly worded terms: 'While you know how deeply I sympathize with your difficulty and how much we will do to help in every way, it would only be right to tell you that there are two aspects which give me concern. Many of us in Europe have lived so long in close proximity to the enemy's nuclear weapons of the most devastating kind that we have got accustomed to it. So European opinion will need attention. The second, which is more worrying, is that if Khrushchev comes to a conference he will of course try to trade his Cuba position against his ambitions in Berlin and elsewhere. This we must avoid at all costs as it will endanger the unity of the alliance.'

Despite the unique advance notice about the build-up of the missile crisis, Macmillan admitted privately in a telegram to Ormsby-Gore that he was puzzled about what the President was trying to do. He confided his rather bewildered first impressions to the Ambassador: 'Since it seemed impossible to stop his action I did not make the effort, although in the course of the day I was of a mind to do so. I feel sure that a long period of blockade, and possible Russian reaction in the Caribbean or elsewhere, will lead us nowhere. Therefore he must decide whether he wants a *coup de main*, which will at least put one card in his hands, or face a conference where Berlin, nuclear disarmament and many other issues will have to be discussed.'

There were other dilemmas for Macmillan raised by the crisis. Difficult legal questions threatened to disturb Anglo-American relations at the Security Council when Cuba's Ambassador, Dr Mario Garcia

Inchaustegui, accused the United States of an act of war by imposing
a blockade. In response to urgent pleas from Sir Patrick Dean, Britain's
UN Ambassador, for guidance on the legalities of America's action Sir
Nicolas Cheetham, Assistant Under-Secretary of State, sent back this
typically diplomatic advice: 'In view of the difficulty of the legal case
you should leave it to the Americans to defend the legality of the
blockade. For your own information, while it may be possible to justify
action against Cuban and possibly against Soviet ships, it is very
difficult to justify action against ships of third countries.' There was
also great reluctance to support America over the claim made in the
Kennedy broadcast that Khrushchev's action had caused a 'secret
disturbance in the balance of power'. Cheetham's advice was to dodge
answering that question: 'While the presence of Soviet missiles no
doubt greatly increases Soviet striking power, it could still be argued
that the total American strength was still ahead of Soviet nuclear
strength.'

Macmillan's anxiety over the legalities led him to ask for a considered
opinion from the Lord Chancellor, Lord Dilhorne. That stated: 'In
our view the imposition of "quarantine" cannot be justified as a "pacific
blockade" under international law. In fact, the United States' conduct
is not in conformity with international law.' But Lord Home intervened
with Macmillan to advise silence on this point: 'I am very anxious that
we should not take sides against the United States by saying Her
Majesty's Government doubt whether the blockade is legally justified.'
Sir Patrick Dean was instructed to offer America's UN Ambassador,
Adlai Stevenson, general support but to keep quiet on matters of
international law.

There was a further alarm, however, over the blockade when a
suggestion surfaced of extending it to cover tankers. Lord Home was
adamant that oil could not be construed as an offensive weapon under
the terms of Kennedy's original statement. He sent a telegram to
Ormsby-Gore to feed into EXCOMM's deliberations this discreet
warning: 'Interdiction of oil supplies to Cuba could strike at the moral
basis of the American action and convert a purely military blockade
into an economic blockade.' His continuing concern about the freedom
of navigation resulted in a further warning, sent in a telegram on 25
October, for the Ambassador to register with the Americans: 'Drastic
enforcement of the blockade measures against British shipping could
cause acute difficulties for us in Parliament and outside and would be
liable to alienate much of the present public sympathy with, and

support for, Her Majesty's Government's stand behind the United States.'

During the tense period when Khrushchev appeared unwilling to budge, Macmillan was eager to find a role as a peace-broker and told the Cabinet on Thursday, 25 October, that he was ready to take 'any opportunity of intervening if he felt that by doing so the prospect of a settlement could be advanced'. It was a notion he nursed from the very outset. He disclosed it in a telegram to Ormsby-Gore on Sunday, 21 October, among his first thoughts after Kennedy's message: 'You will realize, for your personal information only, that I could not allow a situation in Europe or in the world to develop which looks like escalating into a war without trying some action or calling a conference on my own, or something of the kind, to stop it.' That option was given even greater urgency in Macmillan's view on Friday, 26 October, when speculation rose that the United States might launch an air strike against Cuba in the absence of any moves by Russia to withdraw the missiles. It led to an anguished secret debate between Macmillan and Lord Home about a British intervention and its consequences for Anglo-American relations. As what the Americans would call the 'faithful moderator' in this debate, Caccia wrote a summation in a confidential memorandum to Lord Home on 27 October – also passed to Macmillan – which has now been released from the secret files of the Foreign Office (FO 371/162384).

Since it is such a fascinating analysis of the trials and temptations confronting the Prime Minister as he awaited the outcome of the President's test of nerve, Caccia's hitherto secret memorandum is worth detailed examination:

1. Yesterday evening [October 26] the President assured the Prime Minister that he would not act under 48 hours [24 scored out by hand] and that he would not take any drastic action, which presumably means bombardment or invasion, without telling the Prime Minister in advance. This does not mean that we shall be consulted, but, as the Prime Minister is aware, that deals with the formalities not the realities of the situation.

2. The reality then would in all probability be that the President had already taken the decision to act. Thus at that time it would likely be too late for any other initiative. If the Prime Minister were to ask for more time, in order for instance to summon a meeting of Heads of State, the result could hardly change things at that stage. It would

only have the consequence that the President would conclude that when it came to the crunch Britain wanted to chicken out.

3. If this is right we would not have been able to alter events and we would have done lasting damage to our relations with the United States.

4. On this reasoning the time for any useful initiative may be within the next 24 hours, if during that time the build-up on the missile sites in Cuba continues and U Thant gets nowhere. An independent British initiative should not cross the wires of what is now being attempted. What is wanted is something if U Thant, during the next hours, appears to be failing in his task.

5. This does not suggest that an initiative by us to call a conference would be the best method. It might only muddle things at a critical stage. But it does reinforce the possibility of U Thant himself deciding to do something on his own authority if his present efforts seem to be failing.

6. I would therefore suggest that the telegram which was sent to HM Ambassador in Washington last night should be repeated to Sir Patrick Dean and that he should be given discretion to put the idea to U Thant after telling Mr Stevenson what he intends to do before he does it. HM Ambassador in Washington should simultaneously be instructed to tell the United States Government of the discretion which we have given to Sir Patrick Dean.

7. In view of the time factor I should recommend that the Secretary of State should summon the Soviet Representative this morning and tell him not as a threat but as a fact that the chance of negotiation hangs on the immobilization of the missile bases in Cuba.

In the last days of the crisis Macmillan made two dramatic interventions. His first attempt was to give Khrushchev a way out by what he called 'the idea of reciprocity'. This was a proposition offering to balance Russian missiles being withdrawn from Cuba by having Britain's Thor missiles immobilized along with the American missiles in Turkey, thus avoiding the Turks feeling that they were expendable elements in a barter. Kennedy made it clear at once that he was 'not happy with this initiative'. Even more opposed were the Turks. Foreign Minister Feridun Erkin ruled out any proposition which would make Turkey a victim of international bargaining with the Communists behind her back. Macmillan's second bid was a letter to Khrushchev offering a summit once the Cuban crisis was resolved so that they could 'work towards a more general arrangement regarding armaments including banning tests on nuclear weapons'. Before it could be delivered, however, Khrushchev backed down with an announcement that the missiles would be withdrawn from Cuba. The turning point was when Soviet ships carrying more missiles to Cuba stopped dead in the ocean and sailed back to the Black Sea. In the classic phrase of Dean Rusk who recalled a childhood game in Georgia when two boys would stand two feet apart and try to stare each other out: 'We are eyeball to eyeball, and the other fellow just blinked.' That blink took the two superpowers back from the brink without the frightening death toll everyone feared. Instead there was only one casualty – tragically, the death of the man who gave the first warning of the missiles in Cuba. The day before Khrushchev's climbdown, Major Rudolph Anderson died when his U-2 was hit by a Soviet missile in eastern Cuba.

Reporting to the Cabinet on the following day, 29 October, Macmillan complained that, while he had played what he called 'an active and helpful part' in the outcome, Britain's role had not been properly appreciated. 'In public little had been said and the impression had been created that we had been playing a purely passive role,' the Cabinet record stated. To some extent Macmillan had only himself to blame after being given advance knowledge of the impending crisis from Strong and Ormsby-Gore which any other ally of America would have felt amazingly fortunate to have received. For a natural showman he was uncharacteristically reticent about the information given to him ahead of all other Western leaders.

On the day of the first Cabinet meeting on the crisis, the Cabinet files reveal a handwritten note by Timothy Bligh to Macmillan which stated: 'The Lobby will ask questions about the amount or degree of prior consultation or informing. The argument is that because Kennedy has said that he would regard an attack from Cuba as an attack from Russia, the UK are now involved in the affairs of Cuba, whether we like it or not, and were we consulted. I have talked to Harold Evans [the Prime Minister's Press Secretary] and he will stick to the line that we were informed when Ambassador Bruce called to see you (not consulted).' Bligh knew that there had been earlier contacts with the White House – hence his note about Macmillan not taking Ormsby-Gore's advice and staying at Chequers on Sunday after receiving Kennedy's first official message. Clearly, Macmillan went along with the bland line taken with the Press, otherwise he would have instructed Evans to be more forthright. Even at the last Cabinet discussion of

Cuba after the crisis subsided, his attitude remained the same: 'There might be no harm in leaving somewhat vague the degree of consultation which had taken place.'

One of the consequences has been that it has become fashionable to write off Macmillan as a mere witness to history during the Cuban crisis, without any influence on the outcome. That verdict is discredited by the disclosure that Macmillan was given the secret information by Sir Kenneth Strong which is revealed at the beginning of this chapter and by the contents of Cabinet documents and Foreign Office telegrams made available 30 years later. These show that Macmillan was closer to the evolution of policy than the American Congress. The first information they got was a briefing from Kennedy to 30 Congressional leaders two hours before his broadcast – which was eight days after the U-2 plane brought back the first pictures of the missiles.

Every night Kennedy and Macmillan had long discussions on the telephone about the day's developments. It might have been assumed that Kennedy would have turned to his neighbour, John Diefenbaker, since Canada was in more direct danger than any country in Europe. The explanation may lie in the comment made by Bobby Kennedy to Ormsby-Gore that 'the only half-hearted response to his actions that the President had received was from Canada'. If any doubts about Macmillan's role remained, the telegrams and telephone calls between Washington and London, as revealed in the documents now made public, show them to have been totally misguided. Although, naturally, it was the President alone who took decisions, the Prime Minister's input – directly to Kennedy and via Ormsby-Gore – justified to some extent Macmillan's pride in being part of the process when he observed: 'We in Admiralty House felt as if we were in the battle HQ.'

Transcripts of the conversations at last made available at the Public Record Office indicate Kennedy's eagerness to discuss the problems of the blockade and his readiness to have Macmillan's views. While the form of address on the telephone did not give the impression of two close friends talking – it was not Harold to Jack but Prime Minister to President – the relaxed interplay of ideas demonstrated a depth of trust rare in world statesmen. It continued throughout the difficult days of the slow implementation of the Russian withdrawal of bombers from Cuba with Kennedy discussing the situation with Macmillan in these terms: 'We do not want to crank up the quarantine again over the bombers. The only question is whether we should do that or take some other action. For example, we might say the whole deal is off and withdraw our "No invasion" pledge and harass them generally. I think what I will do, Prime Minister, is to send you a message about what we propose to do in Cuba. I should be grateful for your judgement.' When the two leaders could not converse on the telephone it was left to Macmillan's Principal Private Secretary, Philip de Zulueta, and Kennedy's National Security Adviser, McGeorge Bundy, to convey their masters' ideas and make arrangements for propositions to be considered.

Three messages at the end inevitably reflected the rhetoric of a diplomatic triumph but also underlined the substance of each other's regard. Macmillan's to Kennedy said: 'It was a trial of wills and yours prevailed. Whatever dangers and difficulties we may have to face in the future I am proud to feel that I have so resourceful and firm a comrade.' Kennedy's to Macmillan said: 'Your heartening support publicly expressed and our daily conversations have been of inestimable value in these past days.' Macmillan's to Ormsby-Gore stated: 'I am glad that the crisis leaves us with strengthened ties with the Administration.'

If proof of that were needed it came more quickly than anyone expected, just two months later. Had there not been 'strengthened ties' it is highly doubtful whether the Special Relationship could have survived what turned out to be one of the toughest Anglo-American confrontations ever to take place between an American President and a British Prime Minister. Even the mild-mannered Dean Rusk admitted that it was 'a painful, regrettable – and temporary – disturbance in US–British relations'. The contest took place in the balmiest of settings – Nassau in the Bahamas – from 18 to 21 December 1962. Once again it was a missile crisis; not in an East–West context like the Cuban crisis but a West–West one over the ill-fated Skybolt air-to-ground missile.

It was a crisis which could not have occurred at a worse time for Macmillan. Only a few hours before flying from London to the Bahamas, he had returned from talks with de Gaulle at Rambouillet with what he described as 'rather heavy hearts' after finding the General completely intransigent on the deadlocked negotiations for British membership of the European Community. Nothing seemed to be going right for Macmillan. The Government still looked shaky and uncertain following the savage reshuffle of the Cabinet in July which removed six leading ministers, including the faithful Selwyn Lloyd as Chancellor of the Exchequer who was told 'Enough is enough'. No longer

'SuperMac' but caricatured as 'Mac the Knife', Macmillan had to face a vote of no confidence in the House of Commons with Opposition leader Hugh Gaitskell accusing him of 'a conspiracy to retain power'. The Government's handling of the economy was assailed on all sides; after the failure of the Pay Pause, Macmillan was struggling to introduce an effective incomes policy with a National Incomes Commission. Overseas he had his problems, too, with the Central African Federation breaking down.

On the British side the Skybolt crisis was portrayed in one of Whitehall's less imaginative phrases as a 'bolt out of the blue'. After spending about $350 million on developing Skybolt and a series of test failures, the Americans came to the conclusion they would be better off concentrating on Polaris and Minutemen missiles. Shadow Labour Minister George Brown maintained there was never any secret about 'the speculative nature or the uncertain future of Skybolt'. But Harold Watkinson, who had been Minister of Defence for three years until the July reshuffle, claimed that the last time he met US Defence Secretary Robert McNamara the main concern of the Americans was to know how many Skybolts the British wanted to order. On the American side there seemed to be a lack of basic political awareness, since both Rusk and McNamara believed that it was 'primarily a military matter with only incidental political overtones'.

The issue came to a head only one week before the Nassau summit when McNamara flew to London on 11 December to discuss with the new Minister of Defence, Peter Thorneycroft, the 'technical problem' of the United States cancelling the Skybolt project. It was a double-edged blow for the British Government: having abandoned their own Blue Streak missile and placed their nuclear future on Skybolt, they faced not only the dilemma of having to rethink their defence strategy but also the pressures of an American lobby seeking to discourage the US Government from helping Britain to remain a nuclear power. McNamara himself had strengthened the case of the non-proliferation advocates in a speech in June warning that independent nuclear forces could be dangerous and 'lacking in credibility as a deterrent'. Leaks from the London talks between McNamara and Thorneycroft triggered reports in the British newspapers of outrage in Whitehall which the Americans suspected – not without some justification – as having been inspired to prepare the battle lines for a showdown in the Bahamas.

Despite the seriousness of the occasion – particularly in view of the threat to Britain's continued membership of the Nuclear Club – it was one which Macmillan approached with a certain amount of relish. There was no doubting what was at stake: it was summed up in the headline over the article written by Vincent Ryder, the *Daily Telegraph*'s Washington Correspondent: Special Relationship on Trial. As one summit sherpa saw it, Macmillan appeared determined as he strode into the Villa Bali Hai in Nassau for his opening meeting with Kennedy that if there were to be any nominations for a Diplomatic Oscar his performance would put him top of the list. He admitted as much in his memoirs: 'I had to pull out all the stops – adjourn, reconsider; refuse one draft and demand another, etc., etc.'

Macmillan knew that there was no better way of presenting his case than by recalling the days of Churchill and Roosevelt when Britain's scientists had been the pacemakers in the Tube Alloys project. After the difficulties Britain had experienced under the McMahon Act her scientists had made progress on their own until they resumed Anglo-American co-operation after it was amended, he reminded Kennedy. The commitment to Skybolt was such, Macmillan argued, that he had been given an assurance by Eisenhower that if the missile failed then Britain could have Polaris instead. That enabled him to reject Kennedy's suggestion that Britain should carry on with Skybolt with America paying half the development costs or, alternatively, take the Hound Dog missile for the Royal Air Force. There was no question of his accepting a cobbled-up compromise. He made it clear that if the tactics were to freeze out Britain as a nuclear power then the response could be so fierce as to bring down the government and create a prolonged period of anti-American resentment in Britain. Macmillan left Kennedy in no doubt that the Western alliance could not last if the United States were to insist on being the West's 'sole authority' in nuclear defence. He rested his case on one final point: we must remain allies but we must not become satellites. His vehemence resulted, he admitted, in 'much discussion, often rather heated'.

Kennedy was in a difficult position, too. It was awkward for him to argue that Skybolt was too expensive and not reliable enough for the United States and at the same time try to persuade Macmillan that it might well be made to work for Britain. While he wanted a solution to meet what he called 'our obligation to the British', he did not wish to jeopardize moves to limit nuclear proliferation and annoy other European allies by agreeing to a purely bilateral deal for Britain to get Polaris missiles. The argument that an American deal giving Polaris missiles to Britain would be enough to turn de Gaulle against Britain's bid for European Community membership was met with the conviction that if the General was going to say 'No' – as he was expected to do – then that would only be a superficial reason. The last of the three days of intense discussion was the toughest of all – 'an exhausting experience', even a veteran negotiator like Macmillan acknowledged. It ended with a ten-point Statement on Nuclear Defence Systems which was a masterly facing-both-ways communiqué satisfying the requirements of both sides.

For the British Government, it was almost the bargain of the century. The key provision under Article 8 stated: 'The President and the Prime Minister agreed that the United States will make available on a continuing basis Polaris missiles (less warheads) for British submarines.' It was an extraordinary coup for Macmillan, because it meant that for the next three decades at least Britain was assured of its place – however secondary – as a nuclear power. Instead of a dubious air-to-ground missile there was provision of a weapon much more appropriate to an island nation. A seaborne missile is much more flexible than a weapon fired from a fixed site on land; by being in a submarine it has a second-strike capacity; and by being so elusive underwater it is the most difficult target for retaliation. Financially, it was an exceptional deal. The submarine and the nuclear warheads were to be totally British-made. The rockets and their accessories were to be bought from the Americans as in the Skybolt agreement. None of America's £700 million research and development costs for Polaris had to be borne by Britain. Instead, the British government was required to pay 5 per cent on the purchase price – only £50,000 for every £1 million worth of rockets.

America's interests were satisfied by the arrangement under Article 7 that 'the provision of the Polaris missiles must be for the development of a multilateral NATO force in the closest consultation with other NATO allies'. To make this look more convincing, it was stated that 'a start could be made by subscribing part of the NATO force already in existence'. That meant allocating units from United States strategic services and RAF Bomber Command to a NATO nuclear force and having them targeted to meet the requirements of NATO plans. There was an additional assurance by the British Government, updating a previous pledge, 'not to use nuclear weapons anywhere in the world without prior consultation with each other, if circumstances permit'.

Macmillan, however, secured one crucial exception clause which preserved Britain's independence of action: 'The Prime Minister made it clear that, except where Her Majesty's Government may decide that her supreme national interests are at stake, these British forces will be used for the purposes of international defence of the Western alliance in all circumstances.' This was a shrewd provision inserted by Macmillan to cover the sort of situation where the interests of Britain could be legitimately judged more important by a British Government than by another government. As he subsequently explained to the House of Commons: 'It is right that a British Government, whatever the conditions and principles under dispute, should be able to make its own decision without fear of nuclear blackmail.'

When the treaty was signed on 6 April 1963 by Dean Rusk and David Ormsby-Gore there were significant extra advantages for Britain in the small print. Article 3 of the 16-chapter treaty stipulated that Britain should be provided with not only the Polaris missiles plus launching and handling systems but all the supporting services. Britain was assured of all the latest technical documentation – royalty-free and under irrevocable licence – to enable engineers in the UK to manufacture whatever was necessary for repair and modification. There were also arrangements for the Americans to supply technical assistance for British production projects with either engineers or training.

Macmillan's success at Nassau had its penalties. It meant the end of his attempt to join the European Community. De Gaulle announced his veto at a Press Conference on 14 January 1963 and the negotiations in Brussels came to an end a fortnight later. Premier Pompidou used the Nassau agreement to justify slamming the door on Macmillan: 'Britain has shown that she is tied first of all to the United States, which is not in Europe.' In fact, Agriculture Minister Christopher Soames believed that he got the real reason from an observation to him by a French minister: 'Maintenant, avec les Six, il y a cinq poules et un coq. Si vous joignez (avec les autres pays) il y aura peut-être sept ou huit poules. Mais il y aura deux coqs. Alors, ce n'est aussi agréable.'

However, another development which emerged in the wake of the Nassau summit led to one of the most significant achievements of the decade in Anglo-American relations – a nuclear test ban treaty with the Russians. Having looked down the nuclear barrel in the Cuban missile crisis, Kennedy and Macmillan attached greater importance than ever before to making a start on disarmament. Macmillan's message to Khrushchev, which was overtaken by events when the Russian leader decided to withdraw his missiles from Cuba, had proposed discussions on disarmament. He nursed the idea in the months that followed, wondering how best to revive it, especially since the gloom from the 17-nation Disarmament Conference in Geneva indicated total deadlock.

The task appeared even more daunting when one of the most promising opportunities to have presented itself since the start of disarmament negotiations was let slip as a result of a miscalculation by the American experts advising Kennedy. The President had been eager for a breakthrough to a nuclear test agreement ever since his inaugural speech. His advisers were conscientious enough in probing for ways to come to terms with the Russians, but they remained extremely suspicious of them. The crux of all manoeuvres for an agreement on banning nuclear testing was how to work out a system of verification to discourage cheating. For years the stolid Soviet delegate at Geneva, Semyon Tsarapkin, said 'Nyet' to any inspection on Russian territory on the grounds that it would be a pretext for Western espionage. In an attempt to get the Russians into the numbers game, the Americans dropped their demand for a quota of on-site inspections from a total of 20 to seven. There was no immediate change from the usual Russian response until Khrushchev suddenly let it be known that Russia would be prepared under certain conditions to accept three on-site inspections. This was the sort of offer that should have been snapped up immediately. But the Americans refused to budge. They calculated that to make allowances for a margin of error the minimum number of inspections had to stay at seven. Yet they should have realized that the risk of being found out cheating was as effective a deterrent at a quota of three as at one of seven.

Undaunted, Macmillan set out the challenge and the options in trying to end the stalemate in a long letter to Kennedy running to some 3,500 words on 16 March. Discounting Macmillan's penchant for seeing every East–West problem in terms of an instant summit, Kennedy responded enthusiastically with ideas of his own about a fresh attempt to get an agreement. After hot-line telephone discussions there was some more influential brokerage in Washington by Ormsby-Gore. This proved to be a factor of more than momentary relevance. Kennedy's respect for the authority of Ormsby-Gore, a family friend for 25 years, on disarmament went back to 1959 before Kennedy became a candidate for the presidency. After a period of protracted wrangling with the Russians in Geneva, Ormsby-Gore, then Minister of State at the Foreign Office, sent Kennedy a long analysis of the problem of dealing with Russia on disarmament. Thereafter Kennedy took many opportunities to discuss the nuclear test ban negotiations with him.

The outcome of Ormsby-Gore's to-ings and fro-ings on the test ban in the spring of 1963 was a joint letter from Kennedy and Macmillan which was dispatched to Khrushchev on 15 April offering to send 'very senior representatives who would be empowered to speak for us and talk in Moscow directly to you'. The door was left open for a summit at the end of the negotiations with the suggestion that the emissaries might bring matters close enough to a final decision 'so that it might then be proper to think in terms of a meeting of the three of us at which a definite agreement on a test ban could be made final'. Khrushchev's reply railed at the West for continuing to 'harp on espionage – why? For purposes of espionage', but he agreed to receive the emissaries.

What really broke the stalemate was Kennedy's Commencement Address at Washington's American University on 10 June which Khrushchev described as 'the best speech by any President since Roosevelt'. This memorable address, carefully drafted by Ted Sorensen with suggestions from McGeorge Bundy, sent a message from the university campus to Moscow that a re-examination by both sides of their attitudes could be the first practical step to peace. Instead of a catalogue of complaints about the Soviet record, Kennedy appealed for genuine coexistence: 'If we cannot now end our differences at least we can help make the world safe for diversity.' Amid all the fine phrases, such as a promise to work for 'a world of peace where the weak are safe and the strong are just', he sent a clear signal to Khrushchev that the United States had decided to stop nuclear tests in the atmosphere. He soon knew that the message had been well received: for the first time since the beginning of the Cold War, the entire speech of a US President was printed in *Izvestia*, the Soviet Government newspaper.

The two emissaries for the talks starting in Moscow on 15 July were chosen with great care. Macmillan picked Lord Hailsham, Lord President of the Council and Minister of Science with a well-honed legal brain used to spotting traps in documents. Kennedy put his trust in Averell Harriman, former US Ambassador in Moscow with immense experience as a trouble-shooter and conciliator. If Macmillan nurtured any ambitions of using Hailsham as a mediator between the two superpowers, they were quashed at the outset when Kennedy insisted that Harriman would be the leader of the team, speaking for the United States and Britain. Knowing that it was futile to return to the numbers game, since the Russians were no longer prepared for on-site inspections, Kennedy and Macmillan worked out a new narrowly defined mandate for the emissaries.

This directive was given its detailed form during a two-day meeting with Kennedy at Macmillan's family home at Birch Grove in Sussex at the end of June. Before the final review, Macmillan recalled Ormsby-Gore from Washington for a series of conferences at Chequers with Home, Thorneycroft and two scientific experts, Sir William Penney and Sir Solly Zuckerman. They came to the conclusion that it was pointless trying to make progress on the 18-point draft for a comprehensive test ban which was deadlocked at Geneva. Instead they concentrated on a five-point draft for a partial test ban as the key for an agreement covering outer space, the atmosphere and underwater but excluding underground testing. It was a choice, in Macmillan's view, between aiming too high and achieving nothing or being realistic and accepting that underground tests were no longer a major source of concern. The Birch Grove communiqué stressed the urgent need for a nuclear test ban and held out further incentives for the Russians: 'The achievement of such a treaty would be a major advance in East–West relations and might lead on to progress in other directions.'

Khrushchev kept Kennedy and Macmillan guessing from the opening of the talks on 15 July until the end ten days later, with a series of gambits to test their nerves in between. First, the Russians tried to link the test ban treaty to an East–West non-aggression pact, but the Harriman–Hailsham team sidestepped that by stating that they had no mandate to commit their NATO partners. Next, they sought to have a moratorium on underground testing. But Harriman ruled that out knowing that his Joint Chiefs of Staff, who opposed any halt to underground testing, would marshall powerful support in Congress if a concession were made to the Russians on this issue. Then came a last-minute hitch over the proposals that other countries should be encouraged to adhere formally to the test ban treaty.

Macmillan was alarmed that stipulations requiring an instrument of adherence to be deposited in all three signatory countries might cause the negotiations to founder. The danger he foresaw was that the United States, which did not recognize East Germany, would refuse to accept its adherence and that Formosa's adherence would be rejected by the Russians. Lord Home, who had performed an important role in Downing Street speedily devising new drafts to overcome difficulties, telephoned a get-out clause to Ormsby-Gore who drove straight to the

White House to put it to Kennedy. Ormsby-Gore persuaded him to authorize a provision enabling adhering countries to register their assent only in countries with which they had diplomatic relations. That cleared the final obstacle to the initialling of an agreement in Moscow on 25 July.

For Macmillan, it was 'one of the great purposes' he had set himself for his premiership. For Kennedy it was 'a step towards peace, a step towards reason, a step away from war'. In the assessment of his biographer and close companion Ted Sorensen: 'No other single accomplishment in the White House ever gave him greater satisfaction.' Both Kennedy and Macmillan saw it as a peak in their partnership. They decided to send their foreign ministers for the signing ceremony in the Kremlin's Palace of St George on 5 August as an earnest of their willingness to keep the momentum of the newly agreed coexistence going. Even so, Lord Home advised Khrushchev not to expect rapid results since the pace of the disarmament negotiations which he and Rusk doggedly pursued in Geneva had been like that of the tortoise in the fable. With a sly allusion to the Russian manoeuvres to test the nerves of the Anglo-American partnership, he told Khrushchev: 'The tortoise won in the end because, although he was slow, he knew where he was going and did not allow himself to be distracted from his goal.' It was to prove extremely astute advice, since the next major step in superpower disarmament was not achieved for 25 years – and when the Intermediate Nuclear Forces Treaty was signed in Washington by President Reagan and President Gorbachev in December 1987, the British had been marginalized to a purely peripheral influence in nuclear negotiations.

Two months after the test ban treaty was signed, Macmillan resigned on 18 October following a prostate operation ten days earlier. Two months later Kennedy was shot dead in Dallas, Texas. A single sentence in Macmillan's memoirs on the last farewell to Kennedy at the end of their meeting at Birch Grove in June as he left for his helicopter encapsulated a partnership which bridged the generation gap: 'Hatless, with his brisk step, and combining that indescribable look of a boy on holiday with the dignity of a President and a Commander-in-Chief, he walked across the garden to the machine.'

Even without these two fateful events, circumstances were combining to threaten an end to this partnership. Just before the Birch Grove meeting the latest of the political troubles to cast an ominous shadow over Macmillan's premiership erupted – the Profumo scandal, followed by the Judicial Inquiry under Lord Denning into the security aspects of the situation, which caused the resignation of the Secretary of State for War over his association with a prostitute, Christine Keeler. Conservative Party morale was low and there was much whispering about the need for a change of leadership. Even Macmillan started canvassing his senior Cabinet colleagues about whether he should resign before the resumption of Parliament in October to give a new leader a year to chart a fresh direction for the country before the next election was due. In the event he decided to carry on at the helm, but even before he was struck down by ill-health Macmillan had begun to behave like a man whose zest for the challenges of Anglo-American relations had become jaded.

This decline in enthusiasm for the commanding role which Macmillan had earlier claimed for himself has prompted some critics to invest more credence in the notorious waspish observation of Dean Acheson than it received when he first made it in a speech at the Military Academy at West Point on 5 December 1962:

> Great Britain has lost an empire and has not yet found a role. The attempt to play a separate role – that is, a role apart from Europe, a role based on a 'special relationship' with the United States, a role based on being head of a 'Commonwealth' which has no political structure or unity or strength and enjoys a fragile and precarious relationship by means of the sterling area and preferences in the British market – this role is about played out. Great Britain, attempting to work alone or to be broker between the United States and Russia, has seemed to conduct policy as weak as its military power.

Macmillan gave his response in a letter to Viscount Chandos, President of the Institute of Directors, who demanded that the matter be taken up with the US Government as 'a calculated insult to the British nation'. In his usual Olympian style he replied:

> Mr Acheson has fallen into an error which has been made by quite a lot of people in the last 400 years including Philip of Spain, Louis XIV, Napoleon, the Kaiser and Hitler. He also seems wholly to misunderstand the role of the Commonwealth in world affairs. In so far as he referred to Britain's 'attempt to play a separate role ... is about to be played out' this would be acceptable if he had extended this concept to the United States and every other nation in the free world. This is the doctrine of interdependence which must be applied in the world today if peace and prosperity are to be assured.

Acheson's strictures failed to acknowledge how quickly Macmillan had eradicated the imperialist image of Britain in America resulting from Eden's Suez adventure. If Macmillan had not established the sort of new role Britain was capable of playing, he could not have persuaded Kennedy to make the Nassau deal on Polaris missiles. In fact, Macmillan established a new image of Britain in the United States with a global role as leader of a new Commonwealth with multiracial unity after the 'Wind of Change' speech in Cape Town in January 1960. With the subsequent enforced departure of South Africa from the Commonwealth and the acceleration of independence conferences by Colonial Secretary Iain Macleod, Britain was able to retain an influence in all continents which, the Kennedy Administration recognized, was not enjoyed by any other European nation. As a country with over half a million men in its armed forces – at the time more than double those of West Germany – Britain was seen as the one European country which could fulfil a firefighting role alongside the United States, as happened in 1958 when the Americans sent troops to the Lebanon and British paratroopers went to Jordan.

Other critics of Macmillan's attitude to transatlantic relations have tended to assume that it was guided, or rather misguided, by the aphorism attributed to him when he was working with the Americans as Minister in Algiers in 1942: 'These Americans represent the new Roman Empire and we Britons, like the Greeks of old, must teach them how to make it go.' His rescue operation on Anglo-American relations in the six years of his premiership after the depths to which they had sunk under Eden could not have been achieved if he had behaved as a sophisticated Greek to ignorant Romans. Macmillan was more subtle than many of his detractors would have subsequent generations believe. He had a sense of history, anchored in his own experiences of the carnage of World War I and the devastation of World War II, which gave him the aura of a wise elder statesman to Kennedy, a generation younger. As a politician's politician, Macmillan had a shrewd appreciation of the balance of power in Washington which made him a realistic partner to Kennedy. Equally important – and all too rare in international politicians – Macmillan had a sharp sense of humour and an amusing style as a raconteur which, Kennedy found, made him an attractive companion at the dinner table at the end of a day's discussion of serious political issues. The Kennedy–Macmillan days of the transatlantic partnership revived a relationship between the leaders of the two countries which was underpinned by a degree of personal friendship such as had not existed since Roosevelt and Churchill forged the original bond. Like the founders of the Special Relationship, they were men of stature whose vision engaged their interest beyond the daily agenda of problems to be tackled. Macmillan, as the junior partner, clearly had much greater reason than Kennedy to keep the friendship in good repair, but his judgement of where Britain's best interests lay, which made him attach so much importance to Anglo-American relations, was buttressed by the conviction that it was also a matter of kinship. In the lean years that followed it was the weakening of this sense of kinship which accounted for the reality of the Special Relationship falling so far behind the rhetoric.

VIII

The Lean Years of the Almost Forgotten Friendship

*'Britain has so far faced only half the truth about her position.
That she is no longer a great world power in the American–Russian
class is accepted. That there is no divine right whereby she will,
without exertion, automatically stay a leading second-class power
has not yet sunk in.'*

Leader in *The Times*: 30 January 1963

*'Of all the British political leaders Heath was the most indifferent
to the American connection and perhaps even to Americans
individually. ... Heath dealt with us with an unsentimentality
quite at variance with the special relationship.'*

Henry Kissinger: 1982

Even the most ardent Atlanticists were surprised at the sudden cooling
of the Special Relationship so soon after the end of the Kennedy–
Macmillan era. The sense of kinship, which was the glue keeping the
partnership together, did not disappear overnight as new leaders took
over in London and Washington. Lord Home, transformed from the
14th Earl into Sir Alec Douglas-Home so that he could lead the
Government in the House of Commons, still held to the view that
Britain's interests were best served by working in close co-operation
with the United States. He liked the Americans and had enjoyed
dealing with them as Macmillan's Foreign Secretary. Lyndon Baines
Johnson, pitchforked into the presidency after the assassination of John
F. Kennedy, boasted of his British ancestors and his preference for buy-
ing Hereford cattle from England for his Texas ranch. A tough political
operator who entered the House of Representatives in 1937 at the age
of 29, Johnson was basically a homespun politician but he had a
fondness for recalling the 'wartime buddies' – Roosevelt and Churchill.

For both Home and Johnson, however, the main priority in the months that followed their unexpected propulsion into high office was not to spend time nurturing transatlantic relations but to garner enough domestic political support to gain a personal mandate for continuing in that office.

Their first encounter after a perfunctory greeting at Kennedy's funeral was one which indicated much less tolerance of differing attitudes than had existed in the Camelot times at the White House. It came in an angry telephone call from Johnson to Home on Tuesday, 7 January 1964. Johnson was enraged at the announcement that day that Britain had agreed to a contract with Cuba on five-year credit terms to supply 400 Leyland buses worth $10 million with another $1 million for spare parts and an option for 1,000 more buses. This was not the way to help an ally isolate the Cuban regime and weaken its economy, the President fumed. Sir Alec was in no mood to be told what Britain should sell abroad, or that a double-decker bus was going to threaten the nuclear defences of the United States. He pointed out that Cuba was a traditional market for Leyland buses and 200 had been supplied in 1959.

The row cast a cloud over Home's visit to the White House on 12 February. While Home reaffirmed Britain's support for US policy in South Vietnam, there was no endorsement from him in the part of the communiqué which stressed the President's concern over the Caribbean situation and 'the subversive and disruptive influence of the present Cuban regime'. Johnson was still furious at Britain giving 'aid and comfort' to America's enemy, even though Home emphasized that the deal had no strategic significance and that Britain's total trade in 1963 with Cuba was only £1.9 million compared with £15 million in 1959. Nor was the President's temper calmed when Home told a BBC interviewer: 'Nobody of the nature of Castro is brought down by economic sanctions and boycotts.' It rankled long afterwards with Johnson, but it had no direct impact since Home failed to win a mandate to continue in office when the general election was held in October. In any case Johnson left transatlantic relations well down his agenda while he concentrated on securing a 'mandate for unity' in the United States after the upheavals following Kennedy's death. For him the priorities were a tax reduction bill and a civil rights bill.

By the time he faced Harold Wilson as the new Prime Minister Johnson had won a landslide victory in November 1964, trouncing Barry Goldwater by 15 million votes. He was in such a strong position that he could afford to lavish treacly rhetoric on Wilson, who was desperate for any support he could get at a time when his parliamentary majority was a wafer-thin four seats and the British economy was lurching from one crisis to another. Johnson ladled it on at one White House lunch when he compared Wilson to Churchill: 'You personally are asking of the British people the same fortitude, the same resolve, that turned the tide in those days. England is blessed now, as it was then, with gallant hardy leadership. In you, Sir, she has a man of mettle.'

Wilson was not averse to such a comparison and played along with the rhetoric by claiming that there was a kinship between the Texan and himself on the grounds that his county, Yorkshire, was 'the Texas of England'. America had held a special fascination for him, he maintained, ever since his first visit in October 1943 when he described Washington as 'a wonderful city, the loveliest I've seen'. But on his first visit as Prime Minister in December 1964 Wilson made a break with tradition by redefining Anglo-American relations. Intentionally or not, he did it in such a way that set the scene for a decline which continued for 15 years until Margaret Thatcher rekindled the special warmth of the partnership with Ronald Reagan. Wilson chose his words with care at a White House lunch: 'Some of those who talk about the Special Relationship, I think, are looking backwards and not forwards. They talk about the nostalgia of our imperial age. We regard our relationship with you not as a special relationship but as a close relationship governed by the only things that matter, unity of purpose and unity in our objectives.'

However, a commitment to that unity of objectives was the price Wilson was asked to pay for American help in keeping pressure off sterling to avoid devaluing from 2.80 dollars to the pound. By the following December, when Wilson was back at the White House, the dominant objective for Johnson was waging the campaign in Vietnam – one in which he expected the maximum amount of support from his friends. When he took over from Kennedy there were 18,000 American troops in various capacities in South Vietnam. In December 1965 there were almost 200,000 – a commitment which rose over the next three years to over half a million men. Johnson had taken a close interest in Vietnam ever since he visited Saigon in May 1961 as Vice-President with a message from Kennedy that the United States was ready to join President Ngo Dinh Diem 'in an intensified endeavour to win the struggle against Communism'. In that struggle he looked to Wilson to demonstrate his support with the dispatch of British troops, continually urging the Prime Minister to do so 'if only on a limited – even a token – basis'. At one stage Johnson became so irritated by the lack of response that he complained that 'a platoon of bagpipers would be sufficient' just for the sake of showing the Union Jack alongside the Stars and Stripes.

Johnson had enough experience of handling Congressional opposition over the years that he should have understood the domestic political difficulties for Wilson on this issue. Not only was there strong resistance from the left wing of the Labour Party to any commitment of British troops to Vietnam but there were persistent calls for the Americans to stop bombing towns in North Vietnam. What angered Johnson in these circumstances was that Wilson both denied him the commitment of troops which the Australians were prepared to make and insisted on intervening with proposals and peace initiatives which the Americans believed had no relevance to the situation. It soured the relationship, when Johnson was devoting five times the amount of money to the Vietnam War as Britain spent on her entire defence budget, that Wilson felt it his duty to tell the Americans what their policy should be and to seek a solution to their problem on his own.

Wilson was not easily discouraged even when he met with a blast from the President's earthy vocabulary. During the night of 11 February 1965, Wilson woke up worried about the prospect a heavy punitive air strike by the Americans in retaliation for a Vietcong attack on a club in Saigon used by US servicemen. At 3.30 in the morning he got on the hot line at Downing Street to the White House with the suggestion of flying at once to Washington to discuss the situation. Johnson did not take kindly to the call and, according to Wilson, 'let fly with an outburst of Texan temper'. Drawing a parallel with Wilson's problems in Malaysia, where there were over 50,000 British troops involved in the 'confrontation with Indonesia', Johnson retorted: 'If one of us jumps across the Atlantic every time there is a critical situation, next week I shall be flying over when Sukarno jumps on you and I will be giving you advice.' He dismissed Wilson's concern about escalating the crisis: 'I have met escalation in many places and I take it in my stride and I do not think our personal visits would do anything but dramatize and heat it up.' His final advice was blunt: 'I won't tell you how to run Malaysia and you don't tell us how to run Vietnam. If you want to help us some in Vietnam, send us some men and some folks to deal with these guerrillas.'

The one occasion when a British intervention won praise in Washington and removed some of the sourness from Anglo-American relations at this time was not the result of an initiative by Wilson. It was by his Foreign Secretary, Michael Stewart, who braved the wrath of the left wing of his party and the jeers of undergraduates to speak up for the United States at a teach-in on Vietnam being televised by the BBC from the Oxford Union on 16 June 1965. In the style of the former schoolmaster that he was, Stewart took on the rowdy students with all the assurance of a skilled debater from his days as President of the Union in 1929. Welcoming the chance of being present at the teach-in, he won a hearing by stating that he would rejoice 'when students in China, the Soviet Union and even in North Vietnam would have the same freedom to express their views'. Critics who scorned the Americans for supporting what they called a rotten democracy were met with the observation that one million people had fled to South Vietnam from the Communist regime. He emphasized that the barrier to a negotiated settlement was not the policy of the Americans: they had offered to talk; it was the governments of North Vietnam, China and Russia which refused to negotiate. His performance drew applause from his audience – a rare experience for the quiet-spoken Foreign Secretary – and from the Administration in Washington.

This credit was completely squandered on the following day when Wilson decided to use the Commonwealth Heads of Government conference at Marlborough House in London to launch another Vietnam peace initiative. Instead of trying to grapple with a far more urgent problem for Britain, such as Rhodesia, Wilson devised a plan for four Commonwealth leaders from Britain, Ghana, Nigeria and Trinidad to visit Washington, Moscow, Peking, Saigon and Hanoi to seek the basis of a Vietnam settlement. Not only did he keep this a secret from President Johnson, he did not even tell his own Foreign Secretary. More embarrassing still was the fact that the first the Commonwealth leaders knew about the plan was on their way into the afternoon session of the conference on 17 June when they read it in a front-page story leaked to the London *Evening Standard*. It did not endear Wilson to Johnson – nor to the Communist leaders since the Russians, Chinese and North Vietnamese refused to meet the mission.

An even more forlorn venture was undertaken in the following month with the dispatch of Harold Davies, the worthy, well-intentioned MP for Leek, who had paid a number of visits to the area. The 61-year-old junior minister, Joint Parliamentary Secretary at the Ministry of Pensions and National Insurance, made secret contacts with two North Vietnamese journalists in London, Cu Dinh Ba and Nguyen Van Sao, who organized his visit as a guest of North Vietnam's Fatherland Front. Again, Wilson did not tell Johnson what he was doing. He did inform Stewart who tried to talk him out of the project but failed. In the hope of easing the way for Davies he sent one of the Foreign Office experts, Donald Murray, on the trip. However, the North Vietnamese refused Murray a visa and Davies flew from Vientiane on his own to Hanoi. On the day he arrived, 8 July, the *Daily Mail* carried an exclusive front-page lead report under the headline: Wilson's Secret Peace Move. The Communist leaders were not impressed with Wilson's gimmick. Neither Ho Chi Minh nor any of his senior ministers met Davies, who had to be satisfied with a meeting with Tran Troy Quat, Head of the Western Department at the Foreign Ministry. Wilson was furious and claimed that the hopes of a breakthrough had been 'dashed by a serious, indeed disastrous, leak in London'. In fact, it was recognized as one of Wilson's Walter Mitty delusions that a little-known Welsh MP could suddenly become an international peace-broker. Even Wilson's Principal Private Secretary, Sir Derek Mitchell, wrote it off from the outset as 'bloody nonsense'.

Undeterred, Wilson persisted in his quest to be the statesman who brought an end to the war in Vietnam. Lord Chalfont, Minister of State at the Foreign Office, was dispatched during what Wilson proudly proclaimed was his 14th visit to Moscow on another peace probe in February 1966. While Wilson was having talks with Premier Alexei Kosygin he sent Chalfont secretly round to the North Vietnamese delegation in Moscow. Although Chalfont was a much more intelligent interlocutor than Davies, he was unable to produce any more hopeful signs of an imminent breakthrough. Wilson had to wait for another year, until February 1967, for a fresh chance to intervene with one more initiative. By then his own position had been greatly strengthened by the general election of 31 March 1966 which increased his majority from four to 97 seats. On the other hand the larger majority eased party discipline and increased the clamour of the left wing with their placards around him at every public meeting with the slogan 'No Support for Murder in Vietnam'.

Wilson's impatience was ended with the opportunity presented by an official visit of Premier Kosygin on 6 February 1967. Wilson saw his chance of reactivating the role of Britain and Russia as co-chairmen of the 1954 Indochina Conference – remembering the success of Eden in Geneva – to coincide with the ritual Tet truce at the time of the Vietnamese New Year. It also coincided with a letter from Johnson to Ho Chi Minh – which Wilson claimed he knew nothing about at the time although Johnson insisted that he had told Wilson about it. Wilson always believed he had a special status with the Russians and that through them there could be Anglo-Soviet mediation. This was not a view which filled Johnson with any enthusiasm. He was convinced that if the Russians thought they could devise a settlement acceptable to the North Vietnamese which might appeal to the Americans then they would negotiate directly as one superpower to another. Nonetheless, he was prepared to let Wilson have a go and sent the experienced CIA agent Chet Cooper back to his former base in London to advise the Prime Minister.

No one on either side of the Atlantic accepted responsibility for what happened, but whoever was to blame it was Wilson who was made to look exceedingly stupid. He presented one proposition to Kosygin for transmission to Hanoi: the famous 'Phase A – Phase B Plan' which set out first a stop to American bombing then a reduction of the fighting by restricting the movements of US and North Vietnamese forces. In fact, that had been overtaken by Johnson's letter to Ho Chi Minh which stated that the bombing would stop 'as soon as I am assured that infiltration into South Vietnam by land and sea has stopped'. Johnson was adamant that Wilson was informed of the prerequisite of 'an assured stoppage of infiltration'. After anguished exchanges on the hot line from Downing Street to the White House, Wilson had to revise the proposition for Kosygin to pass to Hanoi.

By the time the plan was cleared with Washington on Friday, 10 February, the Tet truce had 24 hours left to run and there was a problem over the time needed to get an answer back from Hanoi. Johnson therefore agreed to suspend the bombing for a further period. This resulted in a Mack Sennett chase across London late at night to catch up with Kosygin. Wilson sent his Private Secretary racing in a car in an attempt to catch the Premier's cortège on its way to King's Cross Station for the overnight train to Edinburgh. The Russians were in their compartments and the guard was about to wave his green flag for the train to depart when Wilson's envoy rushed onto the train with his message. Foreign Secretary George Brown, who had not been consulted by Wilson, was annoyed at the message being sent to the train since there was nothing the Russians could do with it until they reached a secure telephone or cipher machine in Edinburgh. He felt that the seven-hour train journey isolating Kosygin could have been used in Downing Street to try to get a different formula out of the Americans.

Johnson had little sympathy for Wilson in his embarrassment despite admitting afterwards that it was 'a diplomatic mix-up for which we shared a certain amount of responsibility'. He believed that Wilson should have understood the change involved in the letter to Ho Chi Minh. Brown always maintained that Wilson was overeager, trying to push the peace feelers beyond the limits. Ho Chi Minh slammed the door on the plan and the American planes resumed their bombing missions on North Vietnam a few hours after Kosygin landed back in Moscow. Johnson was confirmed in his view that it was easy to take initiatives when the lives of one's own soldiers were not at stake. His verdict on the episode was typically down-to-earth: 'The British Government's general approach to the war and to finding a peaceful solution would have been considerably different if a brigade of Her Majesty's forces had been stationed just south of the demilitarized zone.'

Whatever the criticism of Wilson – and his tactics were not well thought out at times – it was not an easy role for him to play. Wilson could never be sure whether Kosygin really had the power to deliver a deal on Vietnam, and after the last-minute revision of the 'Phase A – Phase B Plan' the Russians kept wondering how much Wilson was in the confidence of the Americans. George Brown was left with serious doubts about the strength of the Special Relationship: 'The Prime Minister's hot line to President Johnson was not as reliable as it ought to have been. I think the fact of the matter was that Mr Johnson didn't really like the Prime Minister much, and the hot line from Number 10 that allegedly went directly to the President was inclined to go instead to Mr Rostow [Johnson's National Security Adviser].'

Yet it was George Brown who retrieved British diplomacy in American eyes – at least for a time. This was all the more surprising to Washington's political pundits since Brown did not make a good impression on his first visit to the White House in 1964 when he was Shadow Foreign Secretary. Having been ingratiatingly over-familiar at his meeting with Johnson, Brown went out to tell White House correspondents afterwards how successful the talks had been with 'my old friend Lyndon' – which irritated his host since protocol required any reference in public to be made to 'the President'. Although his disregard for diplomatic etiquette made him many enemies throughout the capitals of the world, George Brown's energetic commitment to causes won him widespread respect. None more so than his diplomatic endeavours to find a framework for stability in the Middle East after the Six Day War between Israel and Egypt in June 1967.

There was no disguising the difficulty of framing a resolution which could command sufficient support at the United Nations Security Council as well as being saleable to the Arabs and the Israelis. The record of failures was daunting. For 20 days round the clock the ten non-Permanent Members of the Security Council tried to find a form of words which would be acceptable to every party to the dispute. Exhausted and dispirited, they admitted defeat on 3 November. Three other resolutions were in draft form – one from the United States, another from Russia and one jointly sponsored by India, Nigeria and Mali – but were failing to win any large measure of approval. For Brown to step forward at this stage was a bold move, especially since he had the complex credentials of a highly emotional and impulsive politician, known to be an anti-Zionist married to a Jewish woman.

His faith was in his formula – a carefully balanced set of principles as the basis for 'a just and lasting peace'. The British resolution he hammered out with his advisers was a judicious blend of precision and vagueness encapsulating the essence of Arab recognition of Israel in return for Israel giving up occupied land. No one could have worked harder for success than George Brown in arduous 18-hour days at the United Nations building. He had a team of secretaries working in relays taking notes and typing revised drafts as he negotiated with delegates.

In one day he had separate talks with 30 ministers, each having to be persuaded that the draft in Brown's hands was the best that could be achieved. The outcome was UN Security Council Resolution 242 which remained thereafter, with the subsequent Security Council Resolution 338, the foundation for all further peacemaking in the Middle East. Brown handed over to Britain's UN Ambassador, Lord Caradon, the final round of keeping everyone in line for the resolution to be passed unanimously on 22 November 1967. Throughout the Six Day War Johnson had virtually lived in the Situation Room at the White House with the hot line to the Kremlin – operating effectively for the first time – in constant use. For him the ceasefire was the end of the tension, but it was Brown's persistence in seeking something more stable than a temporary ceasefire agreement which made the

Americans for once genuinely appreciative of British skills in Middle East diplomacy.

Two months later that dividend from Brown's finesse at the United Nations was dissipated by a decision which for many of Britain's friends abroad marked a watershed in British history and for some of them the end of Britain as a global power. There had been hopes in Washington right until the last minute that the decision to withdraw from East of Suez might be postponed. It had been part of Labour policy for years. When the party came to power in October 1964 the Foreign Office mandarins, ever-ready for any eventuality, had prepared a detailed planning paper for politicians intent on carrying it out. Sir Michael Palliser, as Head of Planning, had set down all the consequences of withdrawal and how they could be handled in the most orderly fashion. However, very soon after Wilson settled into his office at 10 Downing Street, he was made to realize that Johnson would only provide the financial support the British economy needed if there was no devaluation of sterling and no withdrawal of British troops. While he struggled to defer the decision as long as possible, Wilson found that the economic and financial pressures for substantial cuts left him no alternative but to sound the retreat. This was announced in the Defence White Paper on 18 July 1967 which stated that there would be a total withdrawal of Britain's 51,800 forces from East of Suez 'in the middle of the 1970s'.

Before that announcement Johnson made one more appeal to Wilson to stay his hand. At a long discussion in the White House on 2 June, Johnson urged him repeatedly to reconsider the seriousness of the step he was proposing to take. One of the most revealing descriptions of this episode was given by Anthony Howard from Washington in the *Observer*: 'One presidential aide compared the Prime Minister's response to a "kind of Morris dance: every time the President asked him a question he'd simply take two steps backwards, two to the side and end up wagging a tassel". A more austere account of the same incident was offered by another official: "I'm afraid on this occasion the two of them didn't interrelate at all," he admits bleakly. "It wasn't a case of a special relationship, there just was no relationship at all."' Wilson found it increasingly difficult to pirouette and play for time in the autumn as sterling came under further threats and the authority of the government to defend it was undermined by a sea of industrial troubles. Despite their irritation over his performance at the White House in June, Wilson looked to the Americans for a lifeline. A message sent via Sir Patrick Dean at the Washington Embassy urged Johnson to give him a financial moratorium for a month. But Johnson was not in a mood for further philanthropy. The devaluation of sterling from 2.80 to 2.40 dollars to the pound was announced on 18 November. Wilson tried to make light of it with the phrase that came to haunt him for the rest of his time in Parliament: 'It does not mean that the pound in the pocket is worth 14 per cent less.'

What the devaluation did mean was an acceleration of the defence cuts. On 16 January 1968, Wilson announced that British troops would be withdrawn from East of Suez by the end of 1971, that bases in Singapore, Malaysia and the Persian Gulf would be closed, and that a $1 billion order for 50 swing-wing F-111 planes from the United States would be cancelled. Defence spending had to be cut by 1972–3 to £1.625 billion, a reduction of £415 million from the previous estimate. Not only Johnson was annoyed. Singapore's Prime Minister, Lee Kuan Yew, was bitter at being let down so quickly after having to make emergency plans for the vacuum in 1973 instead of the mid-decade deadline given in the original Defence White Paper. Even Wilson appeared to recognize how much it downgraded Britain in American eyes as he quoted lines from Kipling's 'Recessional' in the House of Commons: 'Far-called our navies melt away – On dune and headland sinks the fire – Lo, all our pomp of yesterday Is one with Nineveh and Tyre.'

Yet two years later, if Johnson's successor had had his way, all the old warmth would have been restored to Anglo-American relations. Richard Nixon, without even a tenuous link to the Pilgrim Fathers so many others claimed, had a fondness for old England. He liked to think that he could get on well with the British – although perhaps not all of them. On his first visit as President on 25 February 1969 he was invited to attend a Cabinet meeting at 10 Downing Street. But Wilson's gimmick was too theatrical even for Nixon and they did not hit it off. Nixon distrusted Wilson's smooth talk. When Wilson suggested after their first handshake that they should get on first-name terms, Henry Kissinger graphically described the reaction: 'A fishy-eyed stare from Nixon squelched this idea.'

However, the arrival of Edward Heath in Downing Street as victor in the general election of June 1970 could have changed the entire nature of the relationship. To Nixon he seemed the ideal transatlantic partner, and as Kissinger commented: 'There was no foreign leader for whom Nixon had a higher regard, especially in combination with Sir

Alec Douglas-Home, Heath's Foreign Secretary, whom Nixon posi-
tively revered.' That admiration for Home was greatly enhanced when
he ordered the expulsion of 105 Russians from Britain as spies on 24
September 1971. It was this inner core of toughness in Heath and
Home that attracted Nixon to them, but Heath kept his distance from
Nixon and made it clear that the overriding objective of his premiership
was the admission of Britain to the European Community. If co-
operation with the United States suffered in consequence, that was a
price he was perfectly prepared to pay.

Heath, with an impressive war record on the Normandy invasion
beaches working alongside the Americans, could not be fairly categorized as anti-American. It was just that he had little interest in, or
enthusiasm for, the Americans at that time. Heath made no effort even
to have a good day-to-day working relationship with Nixon. There was
clearly the opportunity of a close confidential link between the White
House and Downing Street, but Heath was not interested in taking
advantage of it. There was also the matter of temperament, making a
relaxed relationship more difficult between these two politicians. Heath,
as Lord Carrington emphasized in his memoirs, could be 'abrasive and
sometimes contrived to seem at the same time both touchy and
autocratic'. Nixon, though an experienced public speaker, had no small
talk. He often appeared nervous in company and had a tendency to
make cutting remarks. Neither Heath nor Nixon had the knack of
making friends easily, but on coming to office Heath seemed to go out
of his way to be cool and aloof to Nixon. The President normally
avoided taking telephone calls made on the spur of the moment by
other heads of government. For Heath there was no such barrier. The
White House telephone exchange had standing instructions to put
Heath through direct to Nixon at any time. But Heath did not pick
up the telephone.

On his first visit as Prime Minister to the White House in December
1970, one month after the death of de Gaulle, who had twice vetoed
Britain's entry into the European Community, Heath went into extraordinary verbal gymnastics to avoid using the phrase Special Relationship. It was important for the success of Britain's third bid for Common
Market membership that he said nothing which would encourage
France's Premier, Georges Pompidou, to believe that Britain would be
a Trojan Horse for the Americans in Europe. Nonetheless, Nixon made
no attempt to conceal his eagerness to revive the pattern of familiarity
achieved in the Kennedy–Macmillan era, and when he kept on referring

to the Special Relationship, using it seven times in public during the visit, Heath appeared to squirm with embarrassment. As if scared to use the phrase in case it had a hidden meaning, Heath resorted to talking about a 'natural' relationship between Britain and the United States, or alternatively a 'happy' relationship. Combining the two variants, he then referred to a 'happy and natural' relationship. He seemed almost to sigh with relief at escaping from a Press Conference without following Nixon's example and talking about the relationship as special.

Heath's persistence in putting Europe before the United States with even more vigour after Britain joined the European Community in 1972 should have alerted the White House to the need for careful preparation before any American initiative on Europe was launched. Yet without any notice to Heath or any other European leader the United States announced that 1973 was the Year of Europe. The first that Home knew of it was when a Private Secretary at the Foreign Office handed him a news agency report. It was to have been proclaimed by the President himself in unveiling the Nixon plan for a new Atlantic Charter – an over-ambitious attempt to modernize the concept set out by Roosevelt and Churchill in their eight-point code of principles 32 years previously. Instead it was set out by Dr Kissinger at the annual luncheon of the American news agency, Associated Press, in the Waldorf-Astoria Hotel in New York on 23 April 1973.

Heath and his partners in the European Community were surprised that four months into the year it had suddenly been decided in Washington to call 1973 the Year of Europe. If Kissinger was intending to enlist the sympathy and support of Europe's leaders in establishing closer transatlantic co-operation, he went about it in a very strange way. All the standard complaints about Europe ignoring 'its responsibilities in pursuing economic self-interest too one-sidedly' and 'not carrying its fair share of the burden of common defence' were recycled and trotted out at the luncheon address. Kissinger condemned the way that European nations, as recipients of aid under the Marshall Plan, had failed to work with the United States to 'ease many of our international burdens'.

However, the gravamen of his argument was the 'sometimes petty, sometimes major economic disputes' which he felt were isolating America from Europe: 'The prospect of a closed trading system embracing the European Community and a growing number of other nations in Europe, the Mediterranean and Africa appears to be at the expense of the United States and the other nations which are excluded. In agriculture, where the United States has a comparative advantage, we are particularly concerned that Community protective policies may restrict access to our products.' This was to become a familiar lamentation over the years, but the way it was so brusquely placed on the agenda without any prior consultation left a bitter taste.

If the Americans genuinely expected Edward Heath to respond to such a head-on challenge then they were mistaken. Heath was not the sort of politician who kept looking over his shoulder at the United States. His main interest was in Europe, and if the Americans wanted an answer to Kissinger's message it was not Heath's responsibility but that of the rotating president of the European Community, the Danish Prime Minister, who would speak on behalf of the Nine. Heath made it clear to Nixon that in matters concerning the United States and Europe there could be no separate consultations with Britain. Being a member of the European Community in Heath's view meant that a collective attitude had to be worked out towards problems with the United States. Ironically for Kissinger, whose views on Europe were seen as Gaullist, it was the French who reacted most strongly to his arguments. Led by Foreign Minister Michel Jobert, who had an American wife and an extensive knowledge of the United States, they deeply resented American interference in purely European affairs.

In the end, a detailed economic response was produced for the Danes to give to the Americans after a marathon meeting of EC Ambassadors in Luxembourg which began at nine o'clock in the morning and continued through the night until eight o'clock the next morning – a reply which caused irritation in Washington by the precision with which the American charges were countered. The political response teasingly reaffirmed the European contribution to the burden of Western defence which Heath had set out at the National Press Club in Washington during his visit for talks with Nixon on 1 February. Heath made the point that Europe's share was significant: the Europeans provided 90 per cent of NATO ground forces, 80 per cent of naval power and 75 per cent of air force strength. He had driven home his argument with the claim that ten West Europeans were under arms for every US serviceman in Europe.

The gulf between the United States and Britain widened drastically during the Arab–Israeli conflict, known as the Yom Kippur War, which broke out on 6 October 1973. Throughout the dramatic 16 days of the war, United States policy was largely in the hands of Kissinger since

Nixon was embroiled in the Watergate affair; Vice-President Spiro Agnew resigned on 10 October over a financial scandal, and his successor Gerald Ford, though nominated on 12 October, was not sworn into office until 12 December. It was a highly complex operation in which Kissinger kept his cards close to his chest and did not inform the British of his secret commitments to Israel's Premier Golda Meir, such as a promise to re-equip Israeli forces immediately for all weapons lost in battle so that they could fight flat-out in the war. He also made a secret pledge to the Israelis that the United States would outstrip Russian supplies to Egypt and Syria – and in one day had 1,000 tons of arms delivered to Israel.

Anglo-American differences began on 10 October when the United States became angry with Britain for refusing to supply spare parts for Centurion tanks to Israel. Apart from the standard British policy at that time of not supplying arms to 'battlefield countries in the Middle East', there was a very strong incentive for all European countries not to be seen favouring Israel: the risk of retaliation against oil supplies from the Arab countries. The United States could ignore that risk since it relied on the Middle East for only 6 per cent of its oil supplies, whereas the Europeans were dependent on the Middle East for 66 per cent of their oil needs. The row flared up again on 17 October when Heath banned American planes from using the Royal Air Force facilities on the British sovereign base in Cyprus for airlifting arms supplies to Israel.

The worst 24 hours in transatlantic relations for many years occurred during a tense period from the late evening of 24 October until well into 25 October when an American warning to Russia over the Middle East put US army, naval and air forces on a nuclear alert. What created alarm among America's allies was that only one was told officially – Britain, and that was a matter of being informed, not consulted. Other European partners, particularly Germany where the US forces were stationed, were incensed to learn initially from news agencies that these forces had been put on 'DefCon III' – the highest alert in peacetime below stations for an imminent attack.

The crisis began with a telephone call at 9.35 p.m. on 24 October to Kissinger from Russia's Washington Ambassador, Anatoly Dobrinin, stating that the Kremlin wanted joint action to halt Israeli violations of the ceasefire agreed under UN Security Council Resolution 338 passed on 22 October. With Israeli forces cutting access to Suez City, they had the Egyptian Third Army virtually encircled. The urgency of the situation was emphasized in one sentence of the message from President Brezhnev to President Nixon read at dictation speed over the telephone to enable Kissinger's secretary to take it down: 'If you find it impossible to act jointly in this matter, we should be faced with the necessity urgently to consider the question of taking steps unilaterally.' The last thing the Americans wanted was Russian military intervention in the Middle East. They knew that the Russians could make it legitimate, since the Egyptians would invite Russia into Egypt to enforce the ceasefire following America's refusal to answer President Anwar Sadat's call for intervention to ensure its implementation.

Kissinger did not disturb Nixon that night with crisis consultations, believing that he had enough to worry about facing the threat of impeachment after dismissing Watergate prosecutor Archibald Cox. Instead, he summoned an emergency meeting of senior Cabinet members of WSAG – Washington Special Actions Group – and with the endorsement of White House Chief of Staff Alexander Haig set in motion the nuclear alert at 12.20 a.m. Just over half an hour later, at 1.03 a.m. on 25 October, Kissinger awakened the British Ambassador, Lord Cromer, with a long telephone call to inform him of the alert and his message back to Brezhnev. Cromer was made aware that Britain was America's only ally to be informed at that stage and that the other NATO partners would not be told until noon in Brussels – that is, after the US message had been delivered in Moscow. As Kissinger explained in his memoirs: 'It was a classic example of the "Special Relationship" with Britain as well as the limits of allied consultation. We shared our information as a matter of course, despite the fact that the Heath Government was doing its utmost to distance itself from us in Europe and had rather conspicuously underlined its different perspective in the Middle East.'

In Downing Street, however, there was strong resentment at the way Kissinger had handled the crisis, especially since it was quickly shown that there was no real threat of Russian intervention and that the Americans had overplayed their hand. By the morning of 25 October Sadat indicated that following the US refusal to undertake peacekeeping he would not be inviting the Russians into Egypt and would approach the United Nations instead. Brezhnev made a low-key reply as well, acknowledging that UN observers might be the answer to the problem of monitoring the ceasefire. Afterwards Nixon claimed that he had been at the nerve centre all the time, describing it as 'the most difficult crisis we have had since the Cuban confrontation of

1962' and maintaining that it was his toughness which resolved it: 'That is what made Mr Brezhnev act as he did.'

Home, who had been at Macmillan's side during the Cuban missile crisis, was not convinced that there was any comparison. When the Americans claimed that the CIA had reported unusual Communist activity indicating preparations to airlift troops to Egypt, he called for a thorough check from all Foreign Office sources. After exhaustive enquiries Home was assured that there was no collateral Intelligence to confirm that the Russians had taken any steps to justify an American nuclear alert. This exacerbated the annoyance in Downing Street that the White House had denied them the degree of consultation which Macmillan got from the Americans during the Cuban crisis.

Whereas Kennedy had discussed the question of a blockade with Ormsby-Gore and Macmillan in 1962, there was no consultation over the ceasefire crisis in October 1973 – partly because Kissinger was willing to delay its implementation to enable the Israelis to seize more territory from the Arabs. There was anger in Downing Street that by the time Lord Cromer received Kissinger's call all the American decisions about the nuclear alert and the form of reply to Brezhnev had been taken. Being informed was no substitute for having a chance to discuss the implications that the decision might have for allies in Europe. The European allies were even more outraged when they heard Kissinger's comment: 'I don't care what happens to NATO. I'm so disgusted.'

Home was so angry at the way Kissinger escalated the confrontation with Russia that he decided to make a personal intervention to the Kremlin in order that the brinkmanship did not get out of control. He rushed back to the Foreign Office from the House of Commons and telephoned direct to Russia's English-speaking Foreign Minister, Andrei Gromyko, with whom he had dealt for over 12 years. Gromyko assured him that Russia had no intention of interfering in the Egypt–Israel crisis and agreed to make public gestures to help calm the situation. Home then telephoned Kissinger to tell him that Gromyko wanted to assist in stabilizing the crisis on the assumption that the United States would restrain Israel from further violations of the ceasefire. That conversation took some of the tension out of the situation but left two points requiring clarification. These were cleared up after further calls by Home to Britain's Ambassador, Sir John Killick, who went to the Soviet Foreign Ministry to obtain specific assurances on them. Even after the initial heat was taken out of the crisis, Home was busy mollifying his European partners in order to avoid a post-mortem showdown between them and Kissinger. Premier Pompidou wanted to convene an emergency summit of the nine-nation European Community in order to put the United States in the dock for introducing a nuclear alert on European soil without adequate consultation. The French broadcast their proposal on the radio and drew immediate support from Chancellor Willy Brandt who was aggrieved at the Americans taking action in West Germany directed at Russia without first discussing it with him. Home stepped in with the advice that a public showdown was not the way to settle differences with the United States – an intervention for which the Americans were very grateful.

It was not, however, an episode which ministers in London were content to let simmer down as a mere temporary aberration by the Americans. That was confirmed in an unusually sharp letter to Kissinger from Home, who was not a politician given to carping. It was a reflection on the state of the Special Relationship that the move expressing concern was made by Home and not by Heath, but as a statesman who gave top-priority to Anglo-American relations Home felt the drift had to be stopped. Knowing that Kissinger would not resent criticism from someone he regarded as 'the wisest and most decent man' he had met in politics, Home set down some lessons to be learned in Washington from what he believed had become lean years in Anglo-American relations.

There was no question, in Home's view, that the British Government was always ready to stand four-square behind the Americans and give them the benefit of the doubt if there was any uncertainty about the circumstances. 'But,' he insisted, 'you must from your side do every-thing possible to reduce the area of uncertainty – that is to take us more systematically into your confidence and consult with us during the period of the build-up towards crisis and confrontation. I think this applies to the Middle East also where, if I may say so, I think that over the years American administrations have not given enough weight to such policies as ourselves and others, which have a lot and, perhaps more than a lot, to be said for them.' He ended his homily on a gentle note of optimism: 'I am sure that our aim should be to restore the old intimacy and I can see no reason why this should not be possible.' Home's message struck a chord with Kissinger. Having reflected that American consultation had not been as readily offered as it might have been, Kissinger told Home that he was prepared to try harder in future. The problem about fulfilling that promise was that as Nixon's immersion in the Watergate scandal deepened transatlantic partners saw it as a political liability to have close links with him.

On the professional diplomatic level, however, Kissinger had more than compensated for the weakened political links between Heath and Nixon. He ensured easy access for Cromer far beyond anything available to any other envoy in Washington. The result was a good working relationship demonstrated by Cromer's response when Kissinger had called at one o'clock in the morning to tell him of the nuclear alert: 'Why tell us, Henry? Tell your friends, the Russians.' Kissinger made a habit of having a meeting every two months with Sir Burke Trend, the Cabinet Secretary, for a review of the global agenda. He attached a lot of weight to Trend's assessments of situations, especially on matters which had an Intelligence connection. On one particular occasion, when Kissinger asked for advice on how to handle a tricky drafting problem over proposals from the Russians on 21 July 1972, he was bowled over by the response.

It came from Sir Thomas Brimelow, at that time Deputy Under-Secretary of State at the Foreign Office, whose knowledge of the Russians – their language, mentality and diplomatic manoeuvring – made him the ideal adviser for Kissinger. For Kissinger to turn to an expert from London instead of an American one was a measure of the high reputation of the British Diplomatic Service in general and of one member of it in particular – the 'cherubic, unflappable' Brimelow who was 'not quite successful in obscuring his penetrating intelligence behind the bland exterior of the perfect civil servant'. The subtlety of the Brimelow operation was to transform a Soviet proposal seeking to trap the Americans into renouncing nuclear weapons without the Russians fully realizing that what finally emerged was an agreement renouncing brinkmanship by threatening force. No one imagined that Brezhnev and Nixon could be brought to sign a treaty virtually undermining the basic concept of the Cold War and that it would be enshrined in terms drafted by an English diplomat.

The assignment given to Brimelow was so secret that he was warned not to talk about it to anyone inside the Foreign Office. As this meant that Brimelow could not dictate his preliminary drafts to his secretary, he sat down at a typewriter and tapped out his counterproposals himself to the Russian draft on one side of a sheet of paper – never a man to waste time with two words when one will do. Aware that, while Soviet foreign policy was based on an ideological struggle which postulated the avoidance of major wars, the doctrine endorsed by the two recent Communist Party congresses did not exclude wars of national liberation, Brimelow had to devise a form of words which did not require Brezhnev to run the risk of being accused of heresy. At the same time he had to have enough precision for a code of conduct for the superpowers which Kissinger required to ensure that if crises arose they would be handled in such a way as not to lead to nuclear war. Once he had worked out a formula it was sent off under seal in the diplomatic bag for delivery to Kissinger. When Kissinger sought some clarifications Brimelow flew to Washington, worked out amendments over a working lunch with Kissinger's assistant Helmut 'Hal' Sonnenfeldt, and took a plane back home that evening. The Americans were amazed that he could work with such speed on an intricate subject full of pitfalls and talk with the precision of a speaking clock.

The eight-article treaty signed by Nixon and Brezhnev on 22 June 1973 had the essence of Brimelow's skill in Article One which stated: 'The Parties agree that they will act in such a manner as to prevent the development of situations capable of causing a dangerous exacerbation of their relations, as to avoid military confrontations, and as to exclude the outbreak of nuclear war between them and between either of the Parties and other countries.' It gave the Russians the impression of *détente* without actually providing any substance for it. At that stage the Russians were obsessed with the fear of war, so Western strategy was to devise a form of words diminishing those fears and therefore scaling down the threat of Soviet deterrence. Kissinger was delighted with the outcome, hailing Brimelow's role as 'an example of the Anglo-American Special Relationship at its best'. He admitted the unique trust that he had in the British: 'There was no other government with which we could have dealt so openly, exchanged ideas so freely, or in effect permitted to participate in our deliberations.'

Ironically, the American draft did not meet with the approval of the departments in the Foreign Office handling the subject who were unaware that the author was the person about to become Head of the Foreign Office five months later. They were worried that the Americans had been naive in doing a deal with the Russians which might weaken the resistance of other allies to Soviet propaganda on peaceful coexistence. It was thought in the Western Organizations Department that so much emphasis on *détente* would encourage some governments to cut their defence budgets and make it hard to sustain a strong defence posture in NATO. When the treaty was tabled at NATO

Britain's Ambassador, Sir Edward Peck, was highly critical of it and sent back a report of his warnings which caused a Cheshire cat smile to illumine Brimelow's face when it landed on his desk.

Kissinger's trust in the British had its limitations. He kept the Foreign Office in the dark about his plans for a secret visit to China in July 1971 and this secrecy made Britain's diplomatic manoeuvres at the time much more difficult than they need have been. It was accepted that Kissinger needed a smokescreen to keep the Press from tailing him. President Yahya Khan provided that when Kissinger arrived in Islamabad, letting it be known that he was 'slightly indisposed' and had gone to rest in the hills at Nathiagali. Then, after midnight, the President drove Kissinger to a remote part of the tarmac at Islamabad airport where he boarded a Pakistan International Airlines Boeing 707 for Peking, leaving his own Boeing 707 in full view of the terminal building to make it seem as if he was still in Nathiagali.

The ploy caught all the Press off-guard except for the local correspondent of the *Daily Telegraph*, Mohammad Beg. He was at the airport when he thought he caught sight of a familiar figure heading for a Pakistan International Airlines plane. When he asked one of his airport contacts if it was Kissinger his guess was confirmed. His next question was 'Where's he going?' Back came the answer: 'China'. For the industrious 'stringer' Beg this was the scoop he had waited years to file to London. Even with a five-hour time advantage on London he knew he could not wait for any more details. He raced back from the airport and filed his story – not at Urgent rates since the *Telegraph* did not approve of stringers running up big telex bills, but knowing the operator he got it punched out quickly. His scoop landed on the Foreign Desk where the assistant foreign editor could not believe what he was reading. Surely, the American Press Corps following Kissinger around the world could not have missed such a story, he thought. He re-read it and still could not believe it, so the scoop never reached the front page. It was spiked, according to Fleet Street legend, with the comment: 'That bloke must be drunk. Really, Kissinger going off to China – ridiculous.'

If Kissinger had not been so secretive, it would have been easier on the Foreign Office which was negotiating with the Chinese on the terms for upgrading Britain's diplomatic representation to ambassador level. Foreign Secretary Home insisted that the Americans not only be informed but consulted at every stage of the negotiations. However, when the Chinese realized that they had hooked Kissinger for talks which were to lead to President Nixon's visit their enthusiasm for upgrading British representation was greatly diminished and, in the words of one diplomat, 'it meant the price went up'. The result was that the appointment of Sir John Addis as Britain's first Ambassador to Communist China did not take place until 13 March 1972. Yet there are those in Downing Street who maintain that Number 10 was co-operating in the deception over Kissinger's visit. They claim that Kissinger's game plan was communicated privately to Number 10 from the Washington Embassy which had a direct link with the White House, where a young Lieutenant-Colonel Alexander Haig was in charge. In that case Number 10 kept the secret so well that not even the Foreign Office knew about it.

Whatever genuine trust existed on a political level had virtually petered out by the end of the Nixon–Heath era. Attention was focused almost entirely in Britain on the struggle for political survival – with the miners on strike, a three-day working week and steadily increasing economic chaos. It ended in Heath's defeat and the return of Wilson with a minority government in March 1974. This was not the dynamic Labour leader of the 1960s fired by the 'white heat' of the technological revolution. Wilson had lost most of his fire, certainly on the international front. He made it clear to James Callaghan as his Foreign Secretary that apart from EC summits he was interested in only two foreign affairs questions: Israel and South Africa. The rest he left to Callaghan to decide in terms of priorities for Britain's place in the world. Wilson had no marked enthusiasm for the United States, in contrast to Callaghan who was an unrepentant Atlanticist and made it his objective to end the aloofness of the Heath premiership. One of the first items on his agenda when he arrived at the Foreign Office was to tell his advisers that he regarded the Special Relationship as having supreme importance irrespective of the commitment to Europe which had been Heath's top priority.

Callaghan, however, was in a delicate situation. He had to tread warily in Europe since he relied upon the goodwill of his EC partners to ease his path in the complex process of renegotiating the terms of Britain's membership – or at least the interpretation of them – in order to keep a general election pledge. He knew that he could not tear up the Treaty of Accession, but he sought a tolerant acknowledgement that he required some cosmetic changes. At the same time he wanted closer co-operation with the United States and warned the Germans on his first visit as Foreign Secretary to Bonn on 22 March 1974: 'We cannot build a wall around Europe and leave the Americans outside.' One week later he persuaded Kissinger to stop off in London for talks on his way back from Moscow. With his Foreign Office advisers alongside him, Callaghan assured Kissinger that he was determined to end the 'mutual needling' that had been going on between London and Washington.

Despite these good intentions they got off to an ill-tempered start. Callaghan felt badly let down by Kissinger when the first major international crisis of his time at the Foreign Office erupted four months later with the coup in Cyprus deposing Archbishop Makarios and setting up a puppet presidency under Nicos Sampson. After rescuing Makarios by RAF helicopter, Callaghan then turned to Kissinger in the hope of co-ordinating the British and American response. He was convinced that the best chance of avoiding bloodshed on the island was for American leverage to be applied to the Greek junta so that its behaviour could not be used by Turkey as a pretext for sending in troops. Having intervened twice before – in 1964 and 1967 – to head off a Turkish invasion, the United States was best placed, in his view, to avert it again. For Callaghan the first step was to affirm that Makarios was the only legitimate authority and that he should be enabled to return to Cyprus. Kissinger stayed on the fence. He refused to support Makarios since the Americans regarded him as the 'Red Bishop' and the 'Castro of the Mediterranean'.

Facing increasing pressure from the Turks for joint police action by Britain and Turkey to prevent clashes between the two communities on the island, Callaghan appealed again to Kissinger to exercise America's influence on the Athens Government. He believed that tension would be greatly reduced if the Americans prevailed upon Prime Minister Adamantios Androutsopoulos to withdraw the 650 Greek officers from the Cyprus National Guard, which was involved in the conspiracy to oust Makarios. Once more Kissinger prevaricated. Even when Callaghan looked to Kissinger for help in urging Turkey's Prime Minister Bülent Ecevit in late-night talks in London to stay his hand, he refused to become involved directly. Instead he sent his deputy Joseph Sisco to London but with no new proposals to persuade Turkey's National Defence Minister Hasan Isik that the United States was prepared to help restore stability to Cyprus. When Sisco pleaded for more time to enable him to fly to Athens for further talks with the junta, Callaghan realized that it was merely a gesture. He knew that the Greeks, who had refused to come to London for talks, would not be argued out of supporting the illegal Sampson regime by Sisco.

The day after Ecevit left London empty-handed the Turkish invasion of Cyprus began – and once more Callaghan was frustrated at the Americans. For the entire first day of the invasion – Saturday, 20 July – Callaghan could not get in touch with Kissinger because he had been summoned from Washington to San Clemente in California to hold Nixon's hands as the Watergate noose tightened round the President's neck. Callaghan would have welcomed some assistance on the diplomatic front while he was coping with the problems of ensuring the safety of British holidaymakers and those in the British sovereign bases. It took ten long telephone calls from Callaghan to Kissinger on Sunday to make up for lost time in the manoeuvres for an agreement on a ceasefire on 22 July.

Callaghan was left on his own to wrestle with Foreign Ministers George Mavros of Greece and Turan Gunes of Turkey on the terms for a settlement at the Palais des Nations in Geneva – not easy, since the Turks with 15,000 troops now held a large sector of the north of the island. Even though he secured a standfast agreement on 30 July, it was just a breathing space for further parleying at Geneva and a final military thrust by the Turks to give them one-third of the island. With Kissinger seeing out the last phase of the Watergate drama – Nixon resigned on 9 August, the day the Geneva talks resumed – Callaghan's frustration got the better of him again. He dropped a heavy hint that British troops would be authorized to fire on Turks to stop any breach of the ceasefire – and that produced a bitter backlash from Washington.

Throughout the crisis Callaghan had been diplomatically correct in keeping the Americans informed about every move he was making in Geneva. He felt that Gunes was under instructions to walk out of the conference unless there was acceptance of Turkish proposals for the creation of six separate cantons with complete autonomy for Turkish-Cypriots – and therefore some deterrent was necessary to warn the Turks against breaking the ceasefire to achieve what they had failed to get at the conference table. This was explained to Arthur Hartman, an American career diplomat sent by Kissinger to hover around the Inter-Continental Hotel and keep an eye on the proceedings. When Hartman delivered a stiff response from Washington stating that any more warnings of British military action would be unhelpful, Callaghan snapped back that it was the United States that was being not only unhelpful but ineffective in its dealings with the Turkish Government.

Callaghan reinforced his outburst with an angry telegram to Kissinger pointing out that there was more at stake than American concern for Turkey's place in NATO's south-east flank and that America's attitude was damaging the basic trust between Britain and the United States.

Even allowing for the political upheavals in Washington as Nixon resigned, which made it difficult for Kissinger to concentrate, Callaghan resented what he regarded as America's off-hand attitude in treating Cyprus as a little local problem. For Callaghan it was an issue requiring military as well as diplomatic pressure. There was much at stake for Britain in Cyprus in Callaghan's view: the plight of a fellow Commonwealth country under military threat, the safety of thousands of British tourists, the security of British sovereign bases surrounded by refugees, the responsibilities of British soldiers with the United Nations force sent there in 1964, and Britain's obligations as a Guarantor Power under the Lancaster House agreement of 1959 for the independence of Cyprus.

Callaghan ignored American strictures over threatening force against the Turks when the UN commander, General Prem Chand, cast a ring of troops round Nicosia airport and declared it a UN protected area as Turkish troops moved towards it with heavy tanks and artillery. When the General said that he needed reinforcements, Callaghan did not hesitate. He did not wait for any more UN Security Council resolutions. He warned the Turks that Britain would not stand by and see Turkish troops attack the airport in violation of the ceasefire. To show that it was not an idle threat, Callaghan authorized two companies of the Coldstream Guards and two armoured reconnaissance squadrons to be moved up from the British sovereign bases. When they reported to Brigadier Francis Henn, Chief of Staff of the UN force, they were issued with blue berets and deployed round the airport perimeter with anti-tank guns.

Brigadier Henn then went to Sir Stephen Olver, British High Commissioner, with a request for stand-by air power. Again, Callaghan responded at once regardless of any American reservations. To leave no doubt about British resolve, 12 RAF Phantom jets flew from England to Akrotiri to be on call. Until then the Turks had been dismissive of the UN with a mere 120 men guarding the airport. But this quick response to General Prem Chand's request for reinforcements deterred the Turks and kept the airport as a UN enclave, a success which gave Callaghan immense satisfaction even though the Americans disapproved of it for having run a serious risk of clash between Britain and Turkey as NATO allies.

During this tense period Callaghan felt that Kissinger was being devious with him when he had been completely open to Hartman about British moves. Although a stand had been made over Nicosia airport, Callaghan realized that despite assurances of Washington's support for maintaining the ceasefire, the Americans were not serious about applying strong pressure on the Turks to observe a standstill all along the line. After his worst fears materialized with the breakdown of the Geneva conference at 2.30 a.m. on 14 August as the prelude to further territory being seized by the Turks, Callaghan wrote Kissinger an angry letter accusing the Americans of disgraceful and duplicitous behaviour.

After his experience of the Americans playing both ends against the middle over Cyprus, Callaghan should have been more alert to the risks of a repeat performance when Kissinger decided to devote his attention to solving Britain's problems over Rhodesia. Veteran Rhodesia hands in Whitehall advised extra caution over the American intervention. Having seen three major British attempts at a solution founder – Wilson's negotiations with Premier Ian Smith on HMS *Tiger* in 1966 and HMS *Fearless* in 1968, and Home's 'agreement' with Smith in Salisbury in 1971 – they were highly doubtful that America could succeed where the British had failed. There was the added irony of an American intervention being made at a time when the United States Government was in breach of the UN mandatory sanctions through its import of Rhodesian chrome from the rebel regime.

This did not inhibit Kissinger from adopting a high moral stance in supporting racial justice in southern Africa as 'not simply a matter of foreign policy but an imperative of our moral heritage'. However, there were some critics who believed that the main reason for Kissinger involving himself in African politics was to block further Communist infiltration after the Russians outmanoeuvred the Americans by securing a dominant influence in Angola. These suspicions were heightened by the alarm in Washington at reports in February 1976 that the Russians had offered Rhodesia's nationalist leader Joshua Nkomo military advisers and vast arms supplies during a secret meeting in Budapest.

By that time Callaghan had inherited the premiership from Wilson and handed over foreign affairs to Anthony Crosland, but as an old Africa hand he still kept a watchful eye on issues such as Rhodesia.

By then Kissinger's authority had increased too, since Gerald Ford had taken over as President all too aware of his inadequate credentials in foreign affairs and very much dependent upon the experience of his much travelled adviser. In fact, Kissinger was not informed in any depth on Africa until he decided to turn his mind to Rhodesia and set out to acquire his expertise on a 13-day trip to Zambia, Tanzania, Kenya, Liberia, Senegal and Zaire in April 1976. After six months of shuttle diplomacy, he appeared to have pulled off an impossible feat of persuasion in securing the agreement of the African nationalists, the Smith regime and its South African backers for a constitutional conference.

Echoes of Wilson's boast at the Commonwealth conference at Lagos in 1966 that the Smith rebellion would be over in weeks rather than months should have warned the optimists forecasting that the Kissinger deal would settle the problem by the end of the year. What they overlooked was that each delegation read a different meaning into the terms, a miscalculation magnified by the error of not publishing the proposals in London or Washington beforehand. Instead, Premier Ian Smith was allowed the first opportunity to announce them in a broadcast to Rhodesia on 24 September, and he promptly put his own gloss on them. Crosland was clever enough not to become personally involved in trying to get an agreed common framework for a settlement. He passed that bed of nails to Britain's Ambassador to the United Nations, Ivor Richard, who was assigned to Geneva to chair the conference.

It was a frustrating task for Richard, a man of immense patience and legal expertise, to drive from the lakeside Beau Rivage Hotel to the Palais des Nations for a daily review of the deadlock with the delegations – sometimes as short as 15 minutes. When Smith complained that he had been brought to Geneva under false pretences, Kissinger met Crosland in London to review the impasse. But he left the British to handle the problem and refused to have a further meeting with Smith in an effort to get genuine negotiations going. After seven weeks the conference collapsed amid sour observations that whatever else Kissinger had achieved by his Middle East shuttle, he had not brought the Rhodesian problem an inch nearer a solution – nor had he done much to improve Anglo-American relations.

The end of the Kissinger era six months later aroused hopes of a fresh start towards better Anglo-American relations with the arrival of Jimmy Carter at the White House and the appointment of Cyrus Vance as his Secretary of State. Initially the omens looked very promising. Carter was impressed with the way the British Embassy in Washington had alerted Downing Street well in advance of everyone else that he would be the next President. All the missions in Washington – except three – had come to the conclusion that Carter had no chance: the British, the Russian and the Israeli. Carter's campaign advisers discovered that long before the votes were counted the British were first with the right answer. That was due to the inside knowledge of the British Consul-General in Atlanta, Frank Kennedy, a diplomat whose experience of tribal politics in Nigeria for 11 years enabled him to evaluate candidates whose potential was ignored by others.

Having come to know Carter and his campaign team well, Kennedy advised the Ambassador, Sir Peter Ramsbotham, to take Carter seriously as the next occupant of the White House. That was precisely what Ramsbotham did and he earned Carter's gratitude. Unfortunately for Ramsbotham, however, the new Foreign Secretary, David Owen, who was appointed on 22 February 1977 after Crosland's death, did not share Washington's high opinions. Three months later Owen banished him to Bermuda to make way for Callaghan's son-in-law, Peter Jay. The shock at the surprise appointment was almost as widespread in Washington as in London where it was strongly criticized as nepotism at its most blatant. While Ramsbotham was being denigrated as an old fuddy-duddy under newspaper headlines such as 'Snob Envoy Had To Go', his departure was a matter of great regret in Washington since he was a man whose influence on Capitol Hill was envied by other ambassadors who admired the way he overcame Congressional resistance to British Airways landing Concorde in the United States.

Owen and Callaghan made their mark quickly with Carter and Vance. In his first public speech as Foreign Secretary, Owen paved the way for a warm reception at the White House for Callaghan the following week by giving human rights the top priority accorded to them by Carter as an integral part of foreign policy. He pledged to take a stand on human rights issues in every corner of the globe with the promise: 'We will not discriminate; we will apply the same standards and judgements to Communist countries as we do to Chile, Uganda and South Africa.' Progress on human rights in his view, however, was not just the result of making speeches about injustices; they had to be combined with pressures in private. To hammer home his point he had the Russian Ambassador, Nikolai Lunkov, carpeted at the Foreign Office and given a list of 44 cases of 'great personal tragedies' – families kept divided by the Russians either denying travel permits or refusing emigration applications.

Callaghan's first visit to Carter in March 1977 – flying by Concorde, the first Prime Minister to fly to America in the plane – established an ease of communication and a surface cordiality which he hoped to develop into a deeper relationship. To symbolize the start of the new partnership Callaghan took a present for Carter: dark-blue cloth for a suit with the initials 'J.C.' woven into it. He had purchased it from Moxon's of Huddersfield when they made him a gift of a suit-length for himself – Callaghan was still wearing his 'J.C.' suit on his 80th birthday but Carter's was returned to the US Government on ceasing to be President under regulations governing gifts. Callaghan rolled out a special red carpet for him two months later when Carter flew to London for an economic summit and took him to Washington Old Hall, the ancestral home in north-east England of the first American President. There was an even greater salute for Carter at Newcastle Town Hall when he responded to the mayor's welcome with the local rallying call 'Hawaay the lads' which Callaghan had rehearsed him to pronounce with an almost authentic Geordie accent.

Owen's main concern in his first year as Foreign Secretary was to find a solution to the problem of Rhodesia and he turned to the Americans to make it a joint venture. He won the co-operation of Carter and Vance but he was saddled with the impulsive, outspoken upholder of black civil rights, Andrew Young, the American UN Ambassador, as a travelling companion. Young's off-the-cuff remarks often made Owen wince, as when he asked publicly whether the British 'were going to run out and leave us with 30 years of trouble as they did [in Palestine] in 1948'. It required all of Owen's diplomatic patience to limit himself to the observation: 'He does sometimes shoot from the hip a bit.' Owen could not be criticized for lack of effort or commitment: he was prepared to travel anywhere, even to Salisbury for talks with Smith and to Malta for meetings with African nationalist leaders Robert Mugabe and Joshua Nkomo. The obstacles were not just in Africa itself – the duplicity of Smith, the suspicions of Tanzania's President Julius Nyerere, and the resistance of Nkomo and Mugabe to a transitional period in which control of security was not in the hands of the Patriotic Front.

Owen was handicapped by the basic policy differences on both sides of the transatlantic partnership. The Americans saw the Rhodesia problem largely in terms of an extension of black civil rights: they approached it as a question of ensuring racial equality with a settlement to end the injustice of white minority rule. Because there was initially strong African nationalist reluctance to have any American involvement, Carter went out of his way to meet their demands for amendments to Owen's seven-point plan for a settlement which was presented as the Anglo-American proposals on 1 September 1977. Behind him on his own side of the Atlantic, Owen had to accept strong reservations not only from the Labour back benches but in the Cabinet to British troops being committed as peacekeepers during any transitional period to independence. Former Defence Minister Denis Healey, sitting alongside Callaghan as his influential Chancellor of the Exchequer, was adamant that a Commonwealth force was not feasible since its main element would be British and a Labour Government could not send British troops into such a volatile situation.

Although Owen won over the Americans to the choice of Field Marshal Lord Carver as Resident Commissioner to govern Rhodesia during the transition to black majority rule, Carter scuppered the chances of the transition arrangements being acceptable to the whites. Smith agreed to the framework of a settlement on the understanding that his security forces would be in charge during the transition period and supervise the elections. Owen produced a formula which sought to fudge the issue for both sides by stipulating that there would be a combination of all the forces to ensure security. But after Julius Nyerere, Mugabe's backer, put pressure on Carter the Americans agreed that the new national army would be 'based on the liberation forces', which meant that the Patriotic Front would be in charge. That put paid to the seven-point plan since neither Smith nor his South African supporter, Prime Minister John Vorster, was prepared to have the Rhodesian army 'integrated with terrorists and made subordinate to them'.

While Owen insisted that he was still committed to the role of peacemaker, any further Anglo-American efforts had to take account of the 'internal settlement' organized by Smith under the so-called Salisbury Agreement of 3 March 1978. Officially, white minority rule ended as Smith stepped down as Prime Minister, but the change won no recognition or respect outside the country as the whites retained the reins of power with Bishop Abel Muzorewa a mere puppet Prime Minister. Differences between the Americans and the British surfaced again as Carter came under pressure from the right wing in Congress to take some initiative, such as sponsoring a conference which Muzorewa wanted to legitimize his regime. Callaghan came to the rescue by sending the former Commonwealth Secretary, Cledwyn Hughes, on a mission to Africa which bought time, Hughes returning with the predictable report that the circumstances were not appropriate for a fresh attempt at a settlement.

Owen's efforts at solving the Rhodesia problem did not demonstrate the Anglo-American partnership in its best light, even though Owen claimed that he paved the way for his successor, Lord Carrington, to achieve the long-sought prize of an agreement after 14 weeks at the Lancaster House negotiations on 21 December 1979. One significant dividend, however, emerged 15 years later when the partnership was resumed between Owen and his 'wonderful friend, a Mr Valiant-for-Truth', as he described Cyrus Vance, in their joint venture to seek a peace agreement in the former Yugoslavia. Although it was not strictly an Anglo-American operation, since Vance was the appointee of the United Nations and Owen of the European Community, those who worked with them attributed the success of the partnership – despite the failure of the Vance–Owen plan to win approval from the Serbs – to their previous transatlantic co-operation.

American co-operation over Rhodesia did not extend to Middle East peacemaking. An Egypt–Israel settlement was a question of fundamental importance to the United States, and since Carter held all the cards which mattered he was determined to play them on his own. At one stage Callaghan felt that Carter was concentrating too much on the Middle East and not paying enough attention to global economic and financial problems that he bludgeoned him into hosting a one-day summit. Backed by Chancellor Schmidt of Germany and President Giscard d'Estaing of France, Callaghan cornered Carter into reviewing with them world trade, effective use for capital surpluses and currency stability on 23 March 1978. But it did not divert Carter for long from trying to halt the steady deterioration of relations between Egypt and Israel as each month passed.

While Callaghan tried to keep a dialogue going with Israel's Prime Minister Menachem Begin, it was more a matter of courtesy than serious consultation for the Israelis to discuss with the British their plans for Palestinian autonomy. Egypt's Anwar Sadat also recognized that while Britain had a long-standing interest in the Middle East it was the United States which had the leverage through its funding of Israel. Britain's main role was to provide a neutral venue for talks on 18 July 1978 when Vance arrived at Leeds Castle in Kent for two days of negotiations with Foreign Ministers Moshe Dayan of Israel and Mohammed Kamel of Egypt. Although the meeting failed to break the deadlock, it produced the first hint of flexibility in a personal memorandum from Dayan to Vance about the possibility of discussing sovereignty over the West Bank and Gaza. Carter was so encouraged by that hint and the consequences which flowed from it that he decided to convene a summit at Camp David with Begin and Sadat on 5 September.

It was an interesting reflection on the decline of Britain's status on Middle East matters in American eyes that during all the intensive preparations for the summit the British were kept as much apart from them as the Japanese. In view of Britain's role in securing the linchpin of a peace agreement in UN Security Council Resolution 242 and of her long-standing close relations with Jordan, Callaghan could have legitimately expected some consultation on the general strategy for the negotiations. Carter was meticulous in his own homework for the summit, reading accounts of previous negotiations, studying maps, analysing profiles of the participants, and even taking along a copiously annotated Bible to enable him to counter quotations by Begin. But he did not think it necessary to check notes with Callaghan or Owen. While Carter was naturally cautious about revealing details of his negotiating strategy in advance, it surprised the British that he did not sound them out about the prospects of having British co-operation in the monitoring of an agreement between Egypt and Israel – an issue which was to become a matter of contention subsequently between Alexander Haig and Lord Carrington.

For the entire 13 days of the Camp David summit the British had no inkling as to the outcome. When Carter produced two framework agreements on 17 September – one for an Egypt–Israel peace treaty and a second on achieving Palestinian 'full autonomy' – the diplomatic congratulations from Downing Street were tinged privately with relief that there was no British responsibility for the deal. While the Arabists in Whitehall joined in the welcome for the Israeli evacuation of Sinai with its oilfields and settlements, they pointed to the basic flaw in the deal that Begin had avoided any direct link between the peace treaty and fulfilling the commitments to the Palestinians. Those who argued that the British were fortunate after all not to have been involved in the negotiations claimed that they were justified by the outrage in the Arab world against the Camp David accords. Sadat was bitterly denounced for selling out the Palestinians and taking back territory as a prize while other Arab lands remained under Israeli occupation. The British were able to stay on the sidelines, excluded from blame, when an Arab summit in Baghdad unanimously condemned Sadat for falling into the 'trap of Camp David' and Saddam Hussein branded him as a traitor 'mentally and psychologically unfit to lead his country'.

There was a strong temptation for the British to say 'I told you so' when it took the Americans six months, not the expected three, to transform the framework agreement into a signed peace treaty. It was pointed out that the treaty signed on 26 March 1979 on the White House lawn not only paved the way for Israel to open an embassy in Cairo but required Egypt to stay neutral if Syria or Iraq attacked her. That temptation was even greater when the last Israel soldier left Egyptian soil on 25 April 1982 with the Arabs not one step nearer the achievement of Begin's Camp David pledge for negotiations to 'recognize the legitimate rights of the Palestinian people and their just requirements'.

The British Government's determination to keep its distance from the consequences of Camp David led to a sharp disagreement between Callaghan and Carter. With the Abu Rodeis oilfields in Sinai being handed over by Israel to Egypt, Carter asked Callaghan for a secret assurance that in an emergency Britain would sell North Sea crude oil to the Israelis. His request coincided with a warning from Syria's Deputy Foreign Minister, Abdel Khaddam, in London that any government supporting the Camp David accords would face economic reprisals for endorsing 'the sell-out of Palestinian rights'. Although Callaghan was in no mood to be told what to do by the Syrians, he was equally anxious not to be part of a secret codicil to Camp David. His hand was strengthened by his Energy Minister, Anthony Wedgewood Benn, who was a stickler for maintaining the government's integrity on oil policy. He had written six weeks previously to 13 oil-exporting companies laying down precise guidelines that they should sell North Sea crude oil only to traditional buyers in the markets of the International Energy Agency and the European Community. Since Israel was not among these traditional customers he insisted that the ruling could not be changed for political reasons. Callaghan decided to face the wrath of Carter rather than have Britain's reputation for fair trading jeopardized in the oil world.

After the Camp David summit Carter sent his National Security Adviser, Zbigniew Brzezinski, to London, Bonn and Paris to organize a Big-Four Western summit which by a quirk of circumstances played a part ultimately in eliminating Callaghan from the transatlantic partnership. In September it seemed a very agreeable arrangement to avoid the harsh winter weather in Washington by having a summit in January hosted by Carter on the French island of Guadeloupe in the West Indies. There were serious transatlantic matters to discuss. Brzezinski had switched Carter from his pursuit of *détente* to a firm stand against the threat of Russia's intermediate-range SS-20 missiles. Carter was looking for strong support from Callaghan as his most reliable partner in Europe, but Callaghan thought that Carter was being precipitate in trying to rush the Europeans into a decision on counter-measures.

France's Giscard d'Estaing was enthusiastic about the West meeting the Russian threat but did not wish to be beholden to the Americans for the weapons with which to do so. Germany's Chancellor Schmidt seemed 'very contentious' to Carter. Schmidt was the one who wanted American Cruise and Pershing II missiles, but he would only accept deployment of missiles on German soil when other Europeans had agreed to have them. Carter argued that Germany must accept the deployment in order to strengthen the Americans in negotiating with the Russians for a scaling down of arms. Callaghan was disappointed by Carter's approach to the Russians since he believed that the Americans had made modernization of their missile programme their first objective and relegated negotiations on arms control to a much lower place on the agenda. As a result Callaghan aimed to get the best of both worlds by having the Americans go ahead with the construction of the required number of missiles while negotiations with the Russians took place but leaving the decision on deployment until the missiles were all ready. Callaghan justified his tactics by quoting a well-known aphorism of the Clydeside Socialist Jimmy Maxton: 'If you cannot ride two horses at the same time you shouldn't be in the bloody circus.'

Defence was always a delicate issue for Labour Prime Ministers in Anglo-American relations. Callaghan found himself in an embarrassing position when Carter told him that he was under strong pressure in February and March of 1978 to give the go-ahead for the production of ER – enhanced radiation – weapons, popularly known as the neutron bomb. Germany's Foreign Minister, Hans-Dietrich Genscher, was eager for the United States to announce a start to production. Germany wanted it deployed but insisted on other countries having it as well. However, in Britain the left wing of the Labour Party and their allies in the Campaign for Nuclear Disarmament aroused a tide of public opposition against a bomb which could kill a large number of people by intense radiation yet leave buildings relatively lightly damaged. Callaghan was able to calm some fears by stating that neutron bombs would not be launched from Britain. His problem was how to respond to any request for the bombs to be stored in Britain for use in Continental Europe. Callaghan admitted to Carter that it would be a very difficult issue for him and was greatly relieved when the Americans decided to defer production.

The impact of the protracted American negotiations with the Russians on strategic arms, SALT II, which were initiated by Nixon and not concluded until the agreement signed in Vienna on 15 June 1979, frequently produced diplomatic tremors in transatlantic relations. Schmidt found a very sympathetic audience in London when he warned the International Institute for Strategic Studies in October 1977 that an American agreement on SALT II would create tensions in Europe by magnifying 'the disparities between East and West in nuclear, tactical and conventional weapons'. Callaghan acknowledged that there had to be a compensating parallel agreement if Europe were not to be under greater threat by Russia being left with its superiority in medium-range nuclear weapons and its vast strength in conventional forces. Consequently, British concern for the dangers of an imbalance in Europe was used by the Americans to justify their tendency to treat Britain's views as part of the overall European defence problem.

One particular embarrassment for Callaghan at Gaudeloupe was the dilemma over making tentative confidential enquiries to Carter about the prospect of Britain replacing its ageing Polaris missiles with Trident. In one respect he did not want to give the impression that he was wondering whether there would be problems over making Trident and its technology available. Even once over that hurdle he had to move gingerly around the question of the price since the rumoured estimate of the programme's cost, $10 billion, put it beyond his calculations for the British Defence budget. In another respect Callaghan felt that his hands were tied because of the political circumstances. With an election in sight he had to tread with extreme delicacy: his deputy Prime Minister Michael Foot, a long-standing member of CND, was inflexible about adhering to the Labour Party's 1974 general election manifesto pledge not to buy a new generation of missiles for Britain's nuclear deterrent. At the same time a special report on nuclear options had been commissioned from two senior civil servants – Sir Antony Duff, Deputy Under-Secretary of State at the Foreign Office, and Sir Ronald

Mason, Chief Scientist at the Ministry of Defence – to be available for the government to be formed after the forthcoming election. Its verdict, which was delivered to Callaghan just before he went to Guadeloupe, was an unqualified recommendation for Trident.

Despite the contradictions in his position as a Labour Prime Minister, Callaghan decided that it was in the national interest for him to test Carter's reactions to what he confided was a purely hypothetical case of the next British government choosing to modernize its Polaris missiles with C4 Tridents. Carter helped him over the first hurdle by assuring him that under the terms of the Anglo-American nuclear programme there would be no difficulty over technology transfer. He was even more helpful – somewhat to Callaghan's surprise – in recognizing that the costs might appear prohibitive to the British Treasury and therefore there would have to be some flexibility in reaching satisfactory terms. To demonstrate his readiness to help the British in a way that was offered to no other American ally, Carter proposed that technical and financial details should be worked out in Washington without any final commitment from Britain at that stage.

Callaghan took up the offer at once and nominated Sir Ronald Mason and Sir Clive Rose, Deputy Secretary in the Cabinet Office, as his team for talks in Washington with Defence Secretary Harold Brown. It was one of Callaghan's most successful ventures in personal diplomacy, since Carter's response left him totally uncompromised so far as the Labour Party was concerned, regardless of his personal conviction that Trident had to be bought, and yet left the door open for Margaret Thatcher as his successor to take up the option. As Callaghan had shrewdly decided to set down in writing his understanding with Carter – and have it corroborated by him – the correspondence was on her desk when Mrs Thatcher moved into 10 Downing Street.

On the main Four-Power discussions the Guadeloupe summit ended inconclusively, but in public relations terms in Britain it turned out to be a disaster for Callaghan. It was not his fault if pictures in the newspapers showed him sitting in the sunshine under a straw umbrella assessing international issues while Britons shivered in the grip of the winter of discontent with strikes curtailing hospital services, uncollected garbage piled in streets, cemeteries unable to bury the dead and two million workers threatened with being laid off. His mistake was to treat the problems too dismissively on his return with the comment: 'I don't think other people in the world would share the view that there is mounting chaos.' The damage was done by a newspaper headline in the *Sun* which stuck with him, although the words were never his: 'Crisis? What Crisis?' These three words echoed round the country when voters went to the general election in May; they helped to turn the country against him and usher in the Thatcher era.

For Carter there was a further period of 18 months at the White House, but for over a year he had no interest in improving Anglo-American relations. His attention was focused almost exclusively on one problem: the detention of 52 members of the American Embassy in Teheran taken hostage when an Iranian mob seized the building on 4 November 1979 in retaliation for the Americans allowing the Shah of Iran into America for cancer treatment. When Carter sent Vance to Europe for support in his confrontation with Ayatollah Khomeini there were assurances of solidarity in Downing Street, but the government was careful not to invite a backlash from Iran by signing up for an overt economic blockade. The British Embassy had been invaded two days after the American Embassy was seized, but the cool-headed acting ambassador Arthur Wyatt talked his way into reasserting control. After the mob withdrew great care was taken in Teheran and London not to give the Iranians any excuse for a second invasion. Carter's anguish was aggravated by the disastrous failure of an American rescue mission sent to bring out the hostages from the embassy in April 1980, and for the rest of his presidency the issue dominated most of his waking hours. Forty minutes after his successor Ronald Reagan was inaugurated the hostages were freed from their 444-day ordeal.

During the two decades after the golden days of Kennedy and Macmillan whatever remained of the Special Relationship was so occasionally in evidence that it had become for most of the time largely a matter of nostalgia. If it was not dead, as most political pundits asserted, then there were long periods when it seemed so dormant as to be almost comatose. Anglophiles in the United States who looked for better days after the rhetoric of the Johnson–Wilson era failed to mask the lack of warmth in their relationship had their hopes dashed by Edward Heath. His main interest was the French connection to achieve his European designs for Britain which left Nixon and Kissinger with the frustration of a series of rebuffs. For a long time afterwards Kissinger kept asking the question: 'Did he really have to pay the price in intimacy with Washington to establish his European credentials, especially at a time when Brandt and Pompidou were heading in the opposite direction of strengthening their countries' ties with us?'

Callaghan tried hard to get the transatlantic partnership back on course in a pragmatic way. His was a step-by-step approach, in contrast to the Kissinger method of devising one great concept to deal with global problems whereby all difficult issues were put together to be resolved as a single challenge. Callaghan wanted to know what lessons were to be learned from Kissinger's débâcle over the Year of Europe and make a fresh start. Sir Derek Thomas, as Head of the North American Department at the Foreign Office, was commissioned to analyse what went wrong and what were the best steps to take to refurbish whatever was valuable in the Special Relationship. It resulted in a more realistic attitude to Anglo-American relations with the recognition that while Britain's importance to the United States was decreasing there remained certain areas where Britain's experience was of greater value to the Americans than that of any other ally.

This conclusion encouraged Callaghan to believe that he could re-establish close Anglo-American co-operation, but although he succeeded in forming a warm friendship with Carter their personal relationship was never enough in itself to enable Callaghan to have a substantial influence on policy-making in Washington. Carter appreciated it when Callaghan smoothed over differences between Schmidt and the Americans as he did at the London Economic Summit in May 1977. However, when there was a major issue to be faced, such as Middle East peacemaking at Camp David, Carter took sole charge and had no time for any advice from Britain. The British were eager to know what was going on at Camp David and did not disguise their irritation at not being taken into Carter's confidence. Carter worked with a small team – Vance, Brzezinski, Brown, Assistant Secretary of State Harold Saunders and his own Middle East expert William Quandt. There were no nightly calls to Downing Street as in Kennedy's time during the Cuban missile crisis; no private briefings given to Ambassador Peter Jay in the way that Ormsby-Gore was informed and consulted by Kennedy and his brother.

Initially, Carter gave every indication of wanting a good transatlantic relationship, but as he came to rely more and more on the hardline advice of Brzezinski and became engrossed in serious challenges such as Middle East peacemaking and later the Iran hostage crisis, many of his good intentions evaporated. Callaghan had some success at the outset of his premiership in getting the political barometer of trans-atlantic relations away from the 'Stormy' or 'Changeable' sector where it was stuck during the Heath era. But at best it never went beyond

'Fair'. When Callaghan left Downing Street and, after a further agonizing 18 months, Carter left the White House, there were more gloomy predictions that even though the pessimists had been wrong in the past this time the Special Relationship was beyond reviving. Historians were poised once more to bury it as a relic of the days when kinship still counted for something. They reckoned without the seductive charms of Margaret Thatcher giving it a kiss of life when Ronald Reagan came under her spell.

IX

'Soul Mates': The Reagan–
Thatcher Years

*'Their chemistry is right. They've stared down the same gun barrel.
They hit it off.'*

James Brady, White House spokesman: 1 March 1981

*'I liked her immediately – she was warm, feminine, gracious and
intelligent – and it was evident from our first words that we were
soul mates when it came to reducing government and expanding
economic freedom.'*

Ronald Reagan, *An American Life:* 1990

*'We sometimes seem to be a partnership as indissolubly linked as
Astaire and Rogers.'*

Margaret Thatcher on Ronald Reagan's 82nd birthday

Few would have forecast that the election of an actor with 53 films to
his credit as President of the United States and the people's choice of
a Grantham grocer's daughter untutored in the arcane skills of international diplomacy as Britain's first woman Prime Minister would have
restored the Special Relationship to the splendid partnership its wartime
creators had hoped to preserve for all time. Neither appeared to have
had the appropriate experience nor acquired the necessary perspective
for such a task. The new American President had no Congressional
apprenticeship in foreign affairs: his political training was in domestic
politics as Governor of California. Unlike the three previous Conservative Prime Ministers – Macmillan, Home and Heath – Mrs
Thatcher had not graduated to 10 Downing Street via the Foreign
Office. Until he went to the White House Reagan was not a travelling
man with much acquaintance of the outside world. When Mrs Thatcher
became Prime Minister her knowledge of 'abroad' was so limited –

despite a few brief visits overseas – that one minister observed after her first Cabinet meeting: 'She doesn't seem too sure where Calais is.'

Neither showed a great interest in foreign policy on coming into office. Initially, they decided to delegate the main burdens of global affairs to their specialists. Thatcher gave Lord Carrington a free rein as Foreign Secretary. The arrangement had two major advantages for her: it enabled Thatcher to concentrate in her first year on the country's economic problems knowing that Carrington would never be a challenge to her leadership since he had no desire to emulate Lord Home and leave the Upper House for the power house at Number 10. Even more important for her, Carrington was a former Defence Secretary who had served in four Conservative Governments and been High Commissioner of Australia; he knew more about foreign affairs than anyone else in the upper echelons of the Conservative Party – and he was actually very interested in foreign affairs.

It suited Thatcher to leave most things to Carrington so that she could devote herself to the 'Battle of the Budget' at European Community summits to get a rebate of 'my £1,000 million'. He was the only one of her foreign secretaries she really trusted. She hated his successor Francis Pym – despite having to lean on his parliamentary expertise during the tense days following the Falklands invasion. She despised Sir Geoffrey Howe, although she relied on his patient diplomatic skill to rescue her from troublesome confrontations in the Commonwealth, the European Community and Hong Kong. After Carrington resigned she left her foreign secretaries behind when she travelled except when they were required alongside her at European, Economic or Commonwealth summits.

Reagan chose a man of considerable experience, too, as his Secretary of State: the former Supreme Allied Commander in Europe, Alexander Haig, whose military career had given him a deep insight into international problems. In theory, it was an ideal delegation of authority on both sides of the Atlantic. In practice it did not work out well since Carrington and Haig did not get on with each other. Carrington had admired Haig as NATO commander, but he found Haig's impulsiveness and his tendency to assume that different views were tantamount to a vote of no confidence an increasingly awkward barrier to close co-operation. While Carrington was careful never to upstage Thatcher even on his own patch – such as when he patiently steered the 14-week Lancaster House negotiations to an agreement on

Rhodesia – he felt that on several occasions Haig was acting with an ambitious eye on the American presidency.

These difficulties were kept under control in the first year, since Thatcher was determined to transform Anglo-American relations on a personal basis from the very beginning. She had two factors of signal importance in her favour. First, she had made time to make an impact on Reagan long before he was even a candidate for the presidency. When Reagan was visiting London in April 1975 a chance meeting with Justin Dart, one of his kitchen Cabinet as Governor of California, led to an introduction to Thatcher as the new leader of the Conservative Party. None of the Wilson Cabinet found time to meet Reagan – the nearest he got to 10 Downing Street was 15 minutes with Roy Hattersley, then Minister of State at the Foreign Office. Reagan only expected a brief courtesy call on Thatcher but they continued talking – with his hostess, as was her way, doing most of it – for almost two hours and she had made a friend for the future. The other factor which paved the way for a new transatlantic partnership was the angry Russian denunciation of Thatcher after she warned the West in January 1976 not to drop their guard because the Kremlin was bent on world domination and intent on consigning the democracies to 'the scrap heap of history'. She was lambasted in the Soviet Press and given the nickname 'Iron Lady' by the army newspaper *Red Star* – a sobriquet which ensured that she was the first foreign leader invited to the White House after Reagan's inauguration.

This was the occasion which Thatcher used brilliantly to lay the foundations for the ideological bonding from which the Special Relationship blossomed as it had not done since the Kennedy–Macmillan era and which was to last until Reagan left the White House. Her arrival in Washington – accompanied by her husband Denis as well as Lord Carrington – for three days of talks from 25 to 28 February 1981 could not have been better timed. Two days beforehand President Leonid Brezhnev had unleashed a blast against the West in his address to the 26th Congress of the Soviet Communist Party. That gave her the text for her discussions at the White House and for her keynote speech in New York to veterans of the Office of Strategic Services under the title 'The Defence of Freedom'. She proclaimed the objective of the new transatlantic partnership as being 'to promote stability, to prevent aggression and to oppose tyranny' and issued an invitation: 'I call on the free peoples everywhere to join us.'

The rhetoric at the White House was deliberately hyped to match that of Thatcher. At the State Banquet Reagan turned to her and brought her almost – but not quite – to blushing with the disclosure: 'Our relationship goes beyond cordiality and shared ideals.' It was followed by a rare tribute to a visiting head of government when the President went to the residence of Sir Nicholas Henderson, the British Ambassador, for the return banquet given by Thatcher which normally would have been an occasion attended by Vice-President George Bush. After her speech Reagan paid her a heartfelt compliment with the observation: 'You are a hard act to follow, Prime Minister.' Her unqualified commitment to the causes he was eager to espouse had won him over from her first pledge on arrival on the White House lawn: 'The message I have brought across the Atlantic is that we in Britain stand with you. ... Your problems will be our problems and when you look for friends we will be there.'

From the very beginning, however, Thatcher had no illusions about the President's intellectual capacity. Sitting with him in the Oval Office she quickly became aware that after two minutes of any detailed discussion he had lost the thread of the argument. But she knew that they had the same gut instincts; there was no overstretch involved for her political credo. She had become a crusader against Communism long before Reagan talked about 'the aggressive impulses of an Evil Empire' in an address to the National Association of Evangelicals in March 1983. Until she met President Mikhail Gorbachev, Thatcher was tougher about the Russians than Reagan. She tried to stop Carrington going to Moscow, telling him that there was no point in talking to the Russians. When he insisted on going as the President of the European Community she made it clear that it was against her wishes.

In a sense it was also an attraction of opposites. Reagan was content with signposts giving the general direction of where the country should be heading; Thatcher wanted to know every twist and turn on the road and the pace at which they should be going. He was easily bored by briefing papers and preferred a broad-brush picture of objectives; she had a voracious appetite for documents and would have speaking notes revised and rewritten many times. He preferred his working day to end if possible by six o'clock; she was a workaholic able to operate with only four hours' sleep a night, prepared to come back from an official dinner at midnight, work until two in the morning, and then on rising spend an hour reading telegrams and policy notes before having a working breakfast with another head of government. Yet there was no denying that they were drawn to each other as no two other politicians of their time were. It was more than just seeing eye to eye with each other on most issues: Reagan gave her extra status on the international stage. Thatcher needed him so that she could stay in the Nuclear Club, even though it was just as a junior member. There was, clearly, an element of political seduction undertaken with a great deal of sophistication on Thatcher's part, but there is equally no doubt that, in private, she regarded him as an extremely nice man.

Her preparations for their first discussion at the White House were undertaken with immense care. Knowing that her views would be fully recorded by the White House notetaker even if they were not fully absorbed by her host, Thatcher set out her position on a number of key issues – a practice which she followed with considerable success for the next eight years. She subtly registered credit for Britain in the speed with which she responded to the outbreak of the Iran–Iraq war in September 1980 by stationing naval units in the Gulf. She made approving comments about a rapid deployment force and Britain's readiness to make a spearhead battalion available at 72 hours' notice. She pledged that Britain would continue to stand firm against further Russian encroachment following the Soviet invasion of Afghanistan.

There were also appropriate expressions of concern, for the Americans' benefit, about Cuban interference in El Salvador – combined with thinly disguised misgivings at the prospect of American advisers being sent to help the Government of El Salvador crush the left-wing uprising. Because Thatcher was accorded such a good hearing she was able to insist on the full commitment to the twin-track system of deploying Cruise and Pershing II missiles in Europe in parallel with a genuine attempt at negotiations. Pentagon pressures to drop the negotiating aspect had appeared to be gaining the upper hand in Washington and it was Thatcher's backing for the negotiating case being advocated by Lawrence Eagleburger, Assistant Secretary at the State Department, that restored the duality to the policy.

On her return Thatcher triumphantly reported to the House of Commons that her reception at the White House had been 'warm and generous', testimony to the glowing state of Anglo-American relations and the 'excellent understanding' which she and Reagan had established 'even before either of us had assumed our present responsibilities'. Apart from the mood music, however, the greatest dividend was to accrue in the 12 months following the visit when the nuclear relationship was renegotiated. Thatcher had taken advantage of Callaghan leaving the door open on Trident C4 missiles and signed an agreement on 14 July 1980 which enabled Britain to update from Polaris on cut-price terms by having to pay only 5 per cent of the research and development costs. But no sooner had Reagan taken over the presidency than it was decided to upgrade Trident C4 to the more accurate – and much more expensive – Trident D5. For Britain's already overburdened economy the new costs could have been exceedingly onerous. Again the Americans came to Britain's rescue.

The Anglophile Defence Secretary, Caspar Weinberger, arranged that the British would get the modernized system on easy terms with the US Government agreeing to waive research and development costs in excess of $116 million falling to Britain's account. It was not just a bargain offer; it was a pledge ensuring Britain a unique nuclear partnership indefinitely which the United States would not have contemplated making to any other ally. In a letter to Thatcher on 11 March 1982 formalizing the agreement, Reagan set out in remarkable terms the nuclear value of the Special Relationship: 'The United States' readiness to provide these systems is a demonstration of the great importance which the United States Government attach to the maintenance by the United Kingdom of an independent nuclear deterrent capability. I can assure you of the United States' willingness to co-operate closely with the United Kingdom Government in maintaining and modernizing that capability.'

Not every aspect of the relationship, however, was given a boost by that momentous first meeting of the Reagan–Thatcher era. The harmonious personal relations the two leaders enjoyed did not spread through their entire entourage, and certainly not to Haig and Carrington. Differences between them over the Middle East were aggravated at the meeting and became more sharply focused in the months that followed. The Americans had been needled by the way Carrington sought to encourage the Arab 'moderates' with incentives to show their followers that moderation paid off. Carrington's role in getting the European Community to make its Venice Declaration in June 1980 advocating self-determination for the Palestinians rankled with Haig. The Jewish lobby built up pressure on the Reagan Administration to secure a more helpful European attitude towards Israel instead of being supportive of those whom the Israelis branded as terrorists. It developed into a bitter clash over Carrington's unwillingness to involve Britain in the process of implementing the Camp David agreement –

a treaty worked out by Carter without any detailed consultation with the British.

Haig asked for British participation in the peacekeeping force being recruited to monitor the withdrawal of Israeli troops from Egyptian territory. Carrington thought it was one of Haig's more impulsive propositions and indicated his reservations as diplomatically as he could. What angered Haig was the contrast between that coolness and the warm welcome given by Carrington to Saudi Arabia's eight-point plan as a framework for Middle East peacemaking. Since the new Saudi Arabian plan acknowledged the basic problem for Arabs and Israelis and even nodded in the direction of recognizing Israel Carrington saw it as another example of moderation to be encouraged. Not so the Israelis, who condemned it as a betrayal of Camp David and criticized Britain for welcoming it. In turn Haig was furious that Britain was seen to be rocking the boat and blamed Carrington for using the occasion to arouse hostility in Israel towards any British participation in Camp David monitoring so that he would have an excuse for British troops not taking part. Haig's wrath was stoked by the fact that Carrington made his comments not just on behalf of Britain but for the entire European Community since he was the current President.

Haig was unwise enough to give vent to that wrath on 15 October 1981 at a staff meeting in the State Department which led to a leak of the famous phrase that Carrington was 'a duplicitous bastard'. Carrington was incensed at the report since he did not believe that the denigration was justified even to appease the Jewish lobby. He believed that he could not be silent as President of the European Community when Saudi Arabia made a serious proposal about Middle East peace. In the end Carrington received an apology, but he had to wait a long time before he was forgiven. A residue of resentment against him remained after Haig left the State Department.

His reputation in Washington as a 'difficult European' persisted after he resigned as Foreign Secretary and blocked his nomination as NATO Secretary-General for a time. Doubts about Carrington being tough enough were reinforced by the hawks in the United States who were critical of his attacks on those who indulged in 'megaphone diplomacy' in the belief that shouting abuse shamed opponents into coming to the negotiating table. It took a call on the hot line to the White House from Thatcher to have the obstacles to Carrington's appointment removed. Such was the opposition at the State Department and the

Pentagon – including Weinberger – that if Thatcher had not pushed very hard and secured Reagan's support Carrington would probably have withdrawn his candidacy.

In view of the lack of empathy between Haig and Carrington it was fortunate for transatlantic relations that they were not juxtaposed with each other during the intensive diplomacy following the Argentine invasion of the Falklands on 2 April 1982. Their differences on the eve of the attack drove Carrington into a fury. When he alerted Haig by telegram on 28 March to the prospect of imminent Argentine intervention in South Georgia, asking him to use America's influence with the Galtieri regime to head them off, he counted on Haig taking action quickly. Instead he received a bland reply from Walter Stoessel, Haig's Deputy Secretary of State, stating that this was a time for restraint and that the United States intended to stay neutral. Carrington was livid. He carpeted the American Chargé d'Affaires, Edward Streator, deputizing for Ambassador John Louis who remained on holiday in Florida until after the invasion. He also instructed Sir Nicholas Henderson in Washington to convey his strong feelings to Reagan's old friend, National Security Adviser William Clark.

Had this ill-tempered coexistence gone on much longer it could have had serious consequences for Anglo-American relations. In the event Carrington resigned on 5 April and it was only later that day that Haig seized what he believed might be his moment of glory and volunteered to mediate between Argentina and Britain. In contrast to the immediate response from Weinberger whose clandestine organization of vital war supplies for the British, as disclosed in Chapter I, was a classic demonstration of the value of the Special Relationship, the American diplomatic reaction was initially hesitant and confusing. Although Reagan responded promptly to Thatcher's plea on 31 March to intercede with Argentina's President Leopoldo Galtieri, his hour-long telephone call was far too late to halt the invasion fleet. Once the landings had taken place Reagan's attitude was 'flaky' in the Washington sense of being somewhat eccentric and ambivalent. While giving his approval for Haig to mediate, Reagan seemed uncertain not just about how far mediation should go but whether in fact the United States Government should have become involved in such a complex diplomatic operation.

At the outset Thatcher and her advisers were anxious that Haig's mediation might undermine Britain's hopes for unstinted co-operation from the United States. They wondered how Britain's best friend and most powerful partner could support her when America was publicly committed to mediation and therefore could not take sides. Memories of Suez, when America used all its diplomatic, economic and financial leverage to halt the military intervention in Egypt, also cast a cloud over British expectations. Ambassador Henderson and his Political Counsellor Robin Renwick spent a large part of the first 48 hours after the invasion getting one simple message across to the White House and the State Department: This is no Suez. They stressed that it was a case of unprovoked aggression against a British territory and this time, unlike in 1956, the entire country was united behind the Prime Minister with a loyalty such as had not been seen since the war. Because of fears that the United States might sit on the fence when the situation came to a crunch, Henderson laid it on the line: If the United States failed to back Britain, that could bring down the government and would have a devastating effect on transatlantic relations.

When Haig met Thatcher on 8 April at the start of his exhausting shuttle diplomacy between London, Buenos Aires and Washington – he logged 32,965 miles in the next 12 days – no one denied his sincerity in wanting to avert a conflict. The task, however, was quickly shown to be impossible: Thatcher insisted that until Argentina observed UN Security Council Resolution 502 requiring the withdrawal of troops from the Falklands there could be no talks; the Argentine junta wanted guarantees that talks would lead to their sovereignty over the islands before agreeing to withdraw. Neither was in a mood to compromise. Haig found Thatcher determined not to have the aggressor put on even terms with the victim of aggression, however neutral he aimed to be. The junta had no room to manoeuvre either: if Haig imagined that he could persuade Galtieri or his Foreign Minister, Nicanor Costa Mendez, to make concessions, he got his answer from the 300,000-strong crowd chanting 'Ar-gen-tina' like World Cup football supporters as he went into talks at the Casa Rosada, the presidential palace.

All that Haig had in his favour at the beginning was that neither side wished to reject outright any proposals and be blamed for the bloodshed that followed. His only hope was to devise an ambiguous formula which Downing Street could interpret as allowing the islanders the right to stay British while enabling the Argentinians to believe that by some foreseeable date the sovereignty of the islands would be theirs. But any slippery system of interim administration with two flags flying was anathema to Thatcher. The more she listened to Haig the less she liked his way of addressing the problem. She did not think that he had done enough homework on it and suspected that he was spelling out one set of terms in London and another lot in Buenos Aires. By the time of the second round of the shuttle, when there were some tense exchanges between them, Thatcher had come to mistrust him. In diplomatic parlance he was in her view 'unhelpful'.

There was a great sense of relief in Downing Street when Haig admitted defeat. His final proposals, presented on 27 April, were eventually rejected by Argentina – without any formal decision on them having to be taken by the British Government. Haig's abandonment of his mission opened the door for the US Government to give full backing for Britain as 'our closest ally' and to impose economic sanctions against Argentina as 'aggressors'. It meant open provision of military supplies instead of the clandestine operations organized by Weinberger, but Reagan drew the line at 'direct US military involvement'. Thatcher did not disguise her satisfaction that the period of diplomatic manoeuvring was over and that she could openly call upon the Special Relationship to ensure that Britain would have total victory in the war.

However, Anglo–American relations were not entirely smooth in the weeks that followed, as documents recently made available in Washington reveal. There were two acrimonious telephone calls between Thatcher and Reagan when the Americans were worried that the sweeping success of the British task force might make it look as if they were supporting 'colonial aggression'. This anxiety reached a point when Reagan actually appealed to Thatcher to agree to a ceasefire before the liberation of Port Stanley. A detailed account, disclosed in the National Security Council archives, of a telephone conversation on 31 May 1982 – when British troops were poised to storm into Port Stanley – suggests a President thoroughly 'handbagged' by Thatcher's response.

'Ron, I'm not handing over ... I'm not handing over the island now,' she snapped. 'I didn't lose some of my best ships and some of my finest lives to leave quietly under a ceasefire without the Argentines withdrawing.' When Reagan tried to plead for the Brazilian proposal, which sought to stop the fighting and install a neutral peace-keeping force on the islands, he was cut short. As he stammered 'Oh, Oh, Margaret, that is part of this, as I understand it', Thatcher interjected heatedly to ask how the Americans would react to a ceasefire if Alaska had been invaded and the US forces had sustained casualties in driving out the invaders. 'Now you've put all your people there to retake it and someone suggested that a contact could come in ... you wouldn't do it.' Reagan tried to parry her verbal assault: 'No, no, although, Margaret, I have to say I don't quite think Alaska is a similar situation.' Thatcher was not impressed: 'More or less,' she insisted.

Then Reagan changed tack to what he thought would be a more subtle way of persuading Thatcher to have second thoughts about total victory: 'Your impressive military advance could maybe change the diplomatic options. ... Incidentally, I want to congratulate you on what you and your young men are doing down there. You've taken major risks and you've demonstrated to the whole world that unprovoked aggression does not pay.' Thatcher appeared to calm down and said 'Well, not yet but we're half-way to that', then she paused to be more exact: 'We're not yet half-way but a third of the way.' Reagan pursued his point: 'I think an effort to show we're all still willing to seek a settlement ... would undercut the effort of the leftists in South America who are actively seeking to exploit the crisis. Now, I'm thinking about this plan....'

Before he could elaborate his thoughts, Thatcher chopped him off: 'This is a democracy and our island – and the worst thing for democracy would be if we failed now.' Each time Reagan tried to argue his case she intervened to prevent him finishing a sentence. After two more failures he conceded defeat: 'Well, Margaret, I know that I've intruded and I know how ....' All charm again, Thatcher replied: 'You've not intruded at all, and I'm glad you telephoned.' After putting down the telephone, Reagan is believed to have slumped back into his chair with his favourite comment on Thatcher: 'That's one hell of a tough lady.'

Reagan's appeal was not the only attempt to secure a gesture of magnanimity from the British. Haig tried it on the diplomatic level, since there was a growing concern in some quarters that America would suffer a backlash in South America from helping Britain to gain an overwhelming victory. In a long review of the situation with Ambassador Henderson and Counsellor Renwick at the State Department, Haig argued that there was a political case for avoiding a total humiliation of the Argentinians by halting the fighting on the wrong side of Tumbledown. The Ambassador put on his most incredulous look and dismissed it with thinly concealed contempt: 'How could you expect British troops to fight their way ashore and yomp through the mud all over the island just to stop 500 yards from Port Stanley?'

One final attempt at a diplomatic face-saver for Argentina was made at the UN Security Council on 4 June with a resolution tabled by

Spain and Panama for an immediate ceasefire. As Argentina had mustered nine of the 15 Security Council members to support it, Britain's UN Ambassador, Sir Anthony Parsons, left no one in any doubt that he would use the veto to defeat the resolution. That left the United States with a delicate decision in terms of America's relations with Britain and with Argentina: to register a No vote alongside its 'closest ally' or to avoid a further deterioration with the Argentinians by abstaining. The voting had been postponed to allow Reagan to review the situation after meeting Thatcher in Versailles where they were attending the Economic Summit. Before he left Washington, Jeane Kirkpatrick, who had received a delegation from Buenos Aires, had talks with Reagan urging him not to let the United States take a stand alongside Britain in casting a No vote.

America's diplomatic problem was complicated by communications difficulties. Haig had left instructions before flying to France that the United States should register a No vote, but he agreed to discuss the situation with Foreign Secretary Francis Pym. After an hour with Haig in Paris, Pym made it clear that he expected American support at the UN, stating: 'We are not out to humiliate Argentina. We are out to repossess the islands.' Shortly afterwards Haig received a message sent from Washington by his deputy Stoessel urging that America's best interests would be served by abstaining. Haig eventually agreed but felt he should inform Pym of the change. But by the time he managed to get through by telephone to Washington and had Stoessel contact Kirkpatrick, the vote had been taken.

There was, however, one more twist to America's diplomatic embarrassment. Kirkpatrick made an explanation of vote to the Security Council, stating: 'I have been told that it is impossible for a country to change its vote once it has been made known, but my Government has asked me to put on record that if it were possible to change votes I would change it from a No to an Abstention.' This left the United States in the worst of all possible positions: Britain was disgruntled at the apparent backsliding; Argentina was dismayed that America had not calculated earlier that a veto would damage Latin American relations. Reagan appeared bewildered by it all as he stood beside Thatcher in Versailles on the following day – perhaps partly because he had broken his reading spectacles and had to borrow a pair from Haig. Thatcher herself made light of America's UN débâcle, saying: 'If that's the only thing I have to worry about then I should be a very lucky woman.'

In fact, there was one very big thing to worry her apart from the final push to victory in the Falklands: the row over the Soviet gas pipeline. It had been sidestepped by Reagan at the Versailles summit, although it proved to be the cause of one of the roughest patches in Anglo-American relations during the Reagan–Thatcher years. Political differences are accepted as part of any relationship but when politics and business, especially big business with contracts worth hundreds of millions of pounds, become intermingled the dispute quickly rises to the top of the agenda. The row over the Urengoi Pipeline – a 2,790-mile steel conduit with high technology turbines being constructed by Western companies to bring Soviet gas to Western Europe – began as a political dispute.

The United States Government decided to take action against the pipeline on political grounds. It was described as 'Pentagon punishment' devised by Assistant Secretary of Defence Richard Perle – nicknamed in Britain the 'Prince of Darkness' – in retaliation for the imposition of martial law in Poland on 13 December 1981. Although martial law was declared by General Wojciech Jaruzelski, the Pentagon saw the hand of Soviet President Brezhnev behind it and announced sanctions against Russia on 29 December. Nothing was done to stop the sale of one million tons of American grain to Russia going ahead in February 1982, which brought the total US grain exports to Russia in 1981–2 to 12 million tons. Instead, Perle banned American companies from exporting gas and oil technology to the Russians. Among the list of items was pipe-laying equipment, which the Americans believed would halt or severely delay the Urengoi pipeline. Britain and other participating countries – Germany, France, Italy and Japan – criticized the ban as an ineffective political gesture since they believed that it would have no impact on the Polish crisis.

What turned it into a major row was the decision taken on 18 June to extend the ban to foreign subsidiaries and other companies making American-designed components under licence. The Americans calculated that this would prevent countries like West Germany becoming dangerously dependent on Russian energy supplies and would curb the capacity of the Russians to earn hard currency which they could use for military purposes. They assumed that Britain, with her North Sea oil supplies, would not be affected. However, if Perle, a fervent admirer of Thatcher for her crusade against Communism, imagined that he would have her fulsome support, he miscalculated. The ban had serious implications for four companies in Britain: John Brown Engineering of

Clydebank with a £104 million contract for 21 gas turbines; and three American subsidiaries: Baker Oil Tools of Aberdeen with a £14 million contract for oil and gas equipment; Smith International of Stroud with a £12.4 million contract for well-head equipment; and American Air Filters of Cramlington, Northumberland, with a £3.6 million contract for air filters.

Thatcher was very angry and made no attempt to disguise it. Reagan had given her only a few hours' notice and the ban was retroactive, applying not just to orders being fulfilled but to contracts made but not yet carried out. When she went to the White House on 22 June – her first visit since her Falklands victory and only four days after the new ban was announced – she thumped the table, insisting that a deal was a deal. The British could not renege on contracts, she warned her Oval Office audience of Reagan, Vice-President George Bush and Secretary of State Haig, who was to resign two days later partly because he disapproved of the way the pipeline issue had been handled. She pointed out that the Americans were not hurting the Russians half as much as their own transatlantic partners and that the damage done to American-Soviet relations was nothing compared to that done to Anglo-American relations. Thatcher made it clear that Britain would defy the attempt to impose American legislation on her and would honour the contracts with the Russians. Apart from the principle at stake she was well aware of the industrial repercussions with 2,000 jobs involved.

On her return to England she instructed Trade Secretary Lord Cockfield to invoke the Protection of Trading Interests Act empowering the Government to prohibit British companies from complying with legislation by other countries which would damage the United Kingdom's trading interests – a green light for companies in Britain to go ahead with production whatever the consequences. On the basic issue of extraterritoriality, Thatcher was adamant in the House of Commons: 'The question is whether one very powerful nation can prevent existing contracts being fulfilled. I think it is wrong to do so.' Other European countries followed her example. Trade Minister Peter Rees warned Americans during a visit to Washington for talks with Commerce Secretary Malcolm Baldridge that if the United States persisted with this policy there could be hostility on a large scale towards American investment. This produced counter-threats from some quarters in the United States that if the Europeans did not fall in line on exports to Russia then America would not feel obliged to maintain troop levels in Europe.

When Reagan's new Secretary of State, George Shultz, assessed his inheritance he was convinced that there had to be a quick rescue operation to extract his President from this transatlantic disarray. While he was astonished at the bureaucratic ineptitude of the Pentagon, he was even more appalled at measures that resulted in a confrontation with America's friends instead of her enemies. But Shultz's main argument in persuading Reagan to retreat was the damage done to the credibility of American business abroad when the sanctity of contract was overruled by government. In a series of discussions with his European partners, Shultz worked out a face-saving formula which enabled Reagan to lift the sanctions on 13 November 1982. In his usual bland style Reagan presented it as 'a victory for all the allies', demonstrating their determination to strengthen their cohesion. In fact it was a transatlantic battle that need never have been fought, and no sooner had Reagan congratulated himself on putting relations back on an even keel than another big squall left the Special Relationship looking somewhat tattered, especially to Sir Geoffrey Howe, who was new to the role of Foreign Secretary and unprepared for Washington's occasional economies with the truth.

The event that brought the Special Relationship to its lowest ebb during the Reagan–Thatcher era was in essence the tale of the two Howes: in Washington there was Admiral Jonathan Howe, Director of the Political-Military Bureau at the State Department; in London there was Sir Geoffrey Howe. For ten days there had been growing anxiety over what the United States would do following a coup in Grenada on 14 October 1983 which ousted one brutal Cuban-backed Marxist regime and installed an even more bloodthirsty Marxist one. Two additional ingredients in the situation indicated that the United States would be unlikely to stand idly by: the presence of 603 American students who could become hostages and the American claim that there were 1,500 Cubans on the island – although the true number subsequently turned out to be half that figure. As speculation intensified on Saturday, 22 October, the Foreign Office asked the British Embassy in Washington to find out urgently what the Americans were intending to do. The Head of Chancery, Robin Renwick, who was to become Ambassador in Washington eight years later, went for a long discussion with Admiral Howe and got what is known diplomatically as a bum steer: everyone was proceeding very cautiously and nothing would happen without consultation with Britain.

Since the Foreign Office wanted to be doubly sure, there were two further checks: one by the Minister at the Embassy, Derek Thomas, and another by the Ambassador, Sir Oliver Wright. On Sunday, 23 October, Thomas contacted Lawrence Eagleburger, Assistant Secretary at the State Department, who purveyed the same line of caution. The next enquiry by the Ambassador would normally have been direct to the Secretary of State, but George Shultz was not a man of many words and not given to confidences. He had kept relations with Wright to a chilly formality as a result of observations which the Foreign Office instructed the Ambassador to convey about American behaviour over United Nations resolutions on Argentina after the Falklands War. In any case Shultz had gone to Augusta, Georgia, for a golfing weekend with Reagan. Wright went instead to see Eagleburger who told him that the President had not made up his mind – which was true as of that moment.

Sir Geoffrey Howe accepted the assurance of his namesake Admiral in Washington and told the House of Commons on Monday, 24 October, that he was 'in the closest possible touch' with the US Government and knew of no intention of military intervention. At dawn the following morning Operation Urgent Fury began with 1,500 troops of the 82nd Airborne Division and 400 Marines landing on Grenada led by the operation's deputy commander, Major-General Norman Schwarzkopf – subsequently to acquire greater fame as commander of Operation Desert Storm to liberate Kuwait. Both Thatcher and Howe had assumed that they were each well-placed to be told of any last-minute decision by Reagan to order military action. On the Monday evening Thatcher was at a dinner given by Princess Alexandra for the departing American Ambassador John Louis. Howe was at a dinner of the American Banks Association alongside the American Minister Edward Streater. They both returned to 10 Downing Street at 10.30 p.m. having been alerted by the Foreign Office about telegrams from the Caribbean reporting rumours of imminent American military intervention. Enquiries were urgently undertaken seeking confirmation from Grenada and its neighbours. When Thatcher was convinced that the rumours were true she became incandescent with rage.

It was almost 2 a.m. when she got through to Reagan and unleashed her fury upon him. He was in the middle of a briefing for senior members of Congress who had also been kept in the dark. Thatcher left Reagan in no doubt that she felt badly let down and betrayed. If the Special Relationship which she had so carefully cultivated meant anything it should have entitled her to be consulted in advance about America's intentions over a crisis such as this. Grenada, she reminded him, had a long British connection and was a member of the Commonwealth with a Governor-General, Sir Paul Scoon, as the Queen's representative. Thatcher insisted that the United States had no business to get involved there and she urged him to call off the operation. It was too late because the troops were on their way but even then Reagan declined to tell her that. She was angered by the embarrassing comparison with the Russian invasion of Afghanistan and asked Reagan how the West could claim the high moral ground when the world saw the American intervention in Grenada in the same light. At one stage her invective became so strident that Reagan took the telephone away from his ear and exclaimed in admiration to those around him: 'She's great.'

At first it was thought that Reagan had been distracted from consulting Thatcher by the Lebanon crisis which forced him to fly back on Sunday from Augusta to deal with the aftermath of the bomb attack on the US marine barracks which killed 421 servicemen. But the Grenada secrecy was the outcome of a deliberate policy decision. Reagan had worried about leaks on two counts: that if Thatcher had heard early enough she would have made such a fuss that the operation might have had to be called off, and secondly that if Congress had discovered sooner there might have been strong opposition on Capitol Hill to the use of American troops, perhaps even attempts to restrict his powers as commander-in-chief. Thatcher's outrage was shrugged off as unjustified by Jeane Kirkpatrick who argued that the Prime Minister had misunderstood the whole basis of the US action and failed to appreciate one basic point: 'We cannot give our allies veto power over our national security.'

Thatcher's embarrassment was mercilessly exposed in the House of Commons when she was accused by the Labour Opposition of 'fecklessness' and of behaving like a poodle to Reagan. It took her longer than usual to recover her composure and resume the rhetoric about Anglo-American relations with her customary vigour. When she went on a BBC World Service phone-in six days later, she made no attempt to hide her anguish over America's behaviour. She was emphatic that the West could not assume the right to walk into other people's countries. Although she hated Communism and realized that many people living under it would like to be free of it, she insisted: 'That does not mean we can just walk into them and say "Now you are free." ' With an estimated global audience of 25 million people listening to her, she disclosed that on the Grenada operation the United States had not given Britain 'an opportunity of consultation in those last critical stages of the kind we would have wished.' Her warning against a repetition was a clear signal to the White House: 'If you are going to pronounce a new law that wherever Communism reigns against the will of the people ... the United States shall enter, then we are going to have really terrible wars in the world.'

At least Howe received an apology. When he took a telephone call from Shultz two days after the invasion he made the point that in view of the sort of relationship between the two countries it should have been possible for him to have been trusted with a clear indication of American intentions on the Sunday. The point was taken and an apology offered. Once the necessary amends were made there was a fresh start which led to one of the closest relationships between foreign ministers of the United States and Britain. Shultz and Howe were two men of similar characteristics and cast of mind. They were slow and deliberate in making assessments, never wanting to rush into commitments without carefully looking at all the options, including the choice of doing nothing. They both had a sense of history but no great gifts as phrasemakers in expressing it. Although often criticized as dull, they each had an engaging, quiet sense of humour.

With similar backgrounds in industrial relations and finance before coming to international affairs, they developed an affinity of thought on East–West relations. On three occasions Shultz stayed with Howe at the Foreign Secretary's residence at Chevening in Kent and had long discussions on ways of moving from East–West confrontation to a more stable relationship. Howe had a great admiration for the manner in which Shultz set out his views in speeches about relations with Russia and used them in talks with Soviet leaders. On one occasion, when he quoted two extracts of a Shultz speech to Gorbachev on his first meeting, the Russian leader quoted back a different part of the same speech.

This close relationship did not always make it easy to agree with emergency decisions of the Reagan Administration. The crisis over Libya's sponsorship of international terrorism provided a difficult test case. Reagan's patience was near exhaustion when an incident occurred to provide an opportunity for a punitive strike against Colonel Muammar Gaddafi. A bomb planted on 5 April 1986 at a West Berlin discotheque popular with US servicemen killed an American soldier and a Turkish woman, leaving 200 others injured, including 60 Americans. Four days later General Bernard Rogers, America's Supreme Allied Commander Europe at NATO, claimed 'indisputable evidence' that Libya was behind the blast, and on the same day, 9 April, Reagan in a televised Press conference branded Gaddafi a 'mad dog' – one of the worst insults in the Arab vocabulary. On the previous day, however, he had already given orders for an air strike to be prepared against Libya and made a secret request for Britain's co-operation. It was not a question of consultation with his 'closest ally'. There was nothing to consult about. The decision had been taken. It was just a matter of modalities.

The request from the White House reached 10 Downing Street in the middle of a banquet for South Korea's President Chun Doo Hwan. It was passed discreetly to Thatcher by her Private Secretary, Charles Powell. At the end of the dinner she signalled for Howe and Defence Secretary George Younger to stay behind and asked Powell to call in her foreign affairs adviser, Sir Percy Cradock. Reagan's message asked for the use of bases in Britain at Upper Heyford and Lakenheath for the American F-111s which he said were necessary for low-level precision bombing. Implicit in seeking the use of British bases, however, was the desire to have the British Government associated with the American policy of retaliation against Libya. Thatcher had strong views about combating terrorism. She had no time for the Libyans. She detested them on two counts: their supplies of funds and weapons to IRA terrorists, and their shooting of Woman Police Constable Yvonne Fletcher from a window of their embassy in St James's Square which led to the severance of diplomatic relations on 22 April 1984. Her main concern at the outset was whether Reagan's air strike could be justified under international law. Three months before Reagan's request Thatcher had reaffirmed her opposition to the use of force against Libya, telling the American Correspondents' Association in London: 'I do not believe in retaliatory strikes that are against the law. Once you start going across borders, I do not see an end to it.'

Howe and Younger were both worried about Britain being associated with any punitive action which could be condemned as a violation of international law. But Howe had other reservations. He was concerned about the dangers of a backlash against Britain in the Arab world and the consequences that an air strike might have against British subjects, especially those held hostage by Arab extremists. Discussions went on long after midnight and they decided that it was too important an issue for an instant answer to be given to meet Reagan's deadline of noon on 9 April. Younger was eager not to let the Americans down, especially when they had planes for the defence of the West on British soil. He was worried, however, about the risk of massive civilian casualties in Libya.

Younger suggested, with backing from Cradock, that a cautious message should be sent back to the White House, indicating a desire to be supportive but remaining non-committal until a list of supplementary questions was addressed. Top of the list was how the Americans would justify the action as consistent with Article 51 of the UN Charter providing for 'the inherent right of individual or collective self-defence if an armed attack takes place against a member'. Other questions sought answers on what the targets were, how the Americans would ensure that civilian casualties were kept to a minimum, whether it would be possible to make the strike from an aircraft carrier instead of land bases, and whether the action was to be confined to a single one-off strike.

The issue proved to a complex challenge to Thatcher's loyalty to Reagan. Further meetings on 10 April of ministers concerned – not the entire Cabinet – and officials such as Powell, Cradock, Cabinet Secretary Sir Robert Armstrong and Deputy Secretary Christopher Mallaby ended without conclusions being reached despite a flow of messages to and from the White House. The Attorney-General, Sir Michael Havers, advised Thatcher to suggest to Reagan that it would be better for the Americans to soft-pedal on the theme of retaliation and emphasize the self-defence aspect of the operation if they wished to carry any conviction in asserting that it was within the terms of Article 51. Outside the group of six Cabinet members in the Overseas Policy and Defence Committee there were a number of ministers hesitant about giving Reagan *carte blanche*. Lord Whitelaw as President of the Council had reservations, so did Norman Tebbit, himself a former pilot. Leader of the House John Biffen and Home Secretary Douglas Hurd were not against co-operating with the Americans, but they had certain forebodings about the operation unless it were very sharply defined. One rock-solid supporter of Thatcher in her eagerness to find a way to help the Americans regardless of the obstacles was Lord Hailsham. But when Howe reminded her of these obstacles Thatcher lambasted him as a fair-weather friend.

What helped to turn the tide was the visit of General Vernon 'Dick' Walters, America's UN Ambassador, at the start of a tour to win support from Britain, France, Germany and Italy. His exposition of the operation with fresh emphasis on the self-defence aspect to Thatcher and Howe at Chequers on the evening of Saturday, 12 April, and further meetings of ministers on the Sunday cleared most of the reservations. Younger did not attend the decisive meeting of the Overseas Policy and Defence Committee on Monday, but had let it be known that he was by then convinced it was right to give the go-ahead. Howe, who went off to a meeting of European Community Foreign Ministers in The Hague, claimed that he was not aware of final decisions either in Washington or London until he returned to London. Thatcher's firm support was important to Reagan, especially since all other European governments refused co-operation. The denial of the use of French and Spanish airspace meant that the 18 F-111 bombers and the four EF-111 electronic jamming aircraft from Lakenheath and Upper Heyford had to take a circuitous route over the Atlantic Ocean and the Strait of Gibraltar to strike at three targets in Tripoli early in the morning of 15 April.

Announcing the raid as 'a single operation in a long battle against terrorism', Reagan told the American people on television: 'Today we have done what we had to do; if necessary we shall do it again.' Thatcher began to have doubts as reports of the raids revealed that Gaddafi's adopted baby daughter had been killed, his wife and two sons injured at El Azziziya Barracks, and the French Embassy, though not on the target list, had been partly destroyed. Initially, she resolutely defended her co-operation with Reagan, insisting that it would have been 'inconceivable' to have refused the use of British bases. 'If you fail to take action because there might be some risks incurred, you are saying that you should never tackle or take action against State-sponsored terrorism – you would have to cringe before Colonel Gaddafi,' she warned. Even so, Thatcher acknowledged that there had been risks and she had 'pondered them deeply'. She carefully avoided any pledge to do what she did again. Thatcher assured her critics in Parliament that she had 'reserved the position of the United Kingdom Government on any question of further action' and made it clear that any future request would be very carefully examined on its merits.

Subsequent events soon made her aware of the heavy price paid in the backlash against Britain. Two days after the air strike two British teachers, Philip Padfield and Leigh Douglas, seized as hostages in Beirut on 28 March, were discovered shot dead in Lebanon with a note stating that it was in revenge for the raid. On that same day the

British television journalist John McCarthy was kidnapped in Beirut and held hostage in appalling conditions for over five years until his release on 8 August 1991. While opinion polls in America recorded 77 per cent in favour of the raid, in Britain Thatcher's popularity plummeted with 70 per cent of the people polled disapproving of her co-operation. Nonetheless, she did not waver over her tough policy on terrorism and won tremendous acclaim in America as the one ally who had stood side by side with them in defiance of the consequences. It demonstrated the value of the Special Relationship to the United States, that it was not one-way traffic. It reasserted Thatcher's place in the international league table, a position where she had the ear of the President and the chance to influence him, to some extent at least, by what she imparted into it.

That place owed a lot to the fact that Thatcher was the first leader in the West to make her mark with Gorbachev – even before he reached the top in the Kremlin. Through the ingenuity of the Foreign Office's Russian expert, Nigel Broomfield, who picked out Gorbachev early on as the rising star, an invitation attracted him to London in December 1984. After six hours with Gorbachev at Chequers, Thatcher had established an extraordinary rapport with the politician who was to transform Communism. In view of her reputation as the Iron Lady, Thatcher's verdict that Gorbachev was a 'man I could do business with' made a deep impression on a President determined not to drop his guard against a regime he described as an 'evil empire'.

Thatcher, however, was shrewd enough to realize that the Americans did not need an intermediary to do business with the Russians. Both Macmillan and Wilson had delusions about being able to mediate between the superpowers. Thatcher did not fall into the trap of trying to perpetuate that myth. There was no question of her presenting herself as a broker between Moscow and Washington. She saw herself as a trusted friend of Ronald Reagan and as such she could sound out Gorbachev, who respected her, and convey a measured assessment of the Soviet position to Reagan. It was, she recognized, up to the Americans to decide on any negotiations and what to negotiate about. As one of her advisers put it: Reagan and Gorbachev had the power; Thatcher had the influence of a well-informed bystander.

That particular influence was first put to significant use at the height of the controversy over Reagan's Strategic Defence Initiative, or Star Wars project as it was popularly known until it was abandoned ten years and £20 billion worth of research later by Defence Secretary Les

Aspin on 13 May 1993. When Thatcher went to see Reagan at Camp David in December 1984 after meeting Gorbachev, she had a number of concerns about SDI which needed to be pursued with finesse if she were to persuade Reagan to accept her advice. She was worried that it would be such a provocation to the Russians that they would try to match it. The outcome, in her view, might undermine the concept of nuclear deterrence which she believed would cause perturbation throughout the NATO alliance. She knew that it would be pointless to argue for the entire programme to be halted, but she realized that unless it were circumscribed with some restraints America's SDI activity could jeopardize the 1972 Anti-Ballistic Missile Treaty. Undaunted, Thatcher set out single-handed – without her Foreign Secretary or Defence Minister – to take on Reagan's team of Vice-President Bush, Secretary of State George Shultz and National Security Adviser Robert McFarlane. In an hour-long address that was a combination of a tutorial 'as a chemist', political analysis with direct knowledge of Kremlin thinking, and the summing-up of a barrister she proved her power to influence.

When they adjourned for lunch Thatcher's aides, her 'golden pens' Charles Powell and John Kerr, went to work drafting a concise formula to cover the requirements of the ABM Treaty and the preservation of deterrence. Their 61-word text enabled Thatcher to perform her 'handbag' trick and produce what she happened to have handy on a piece of paper as the solution to everyone's concerns. The famous four points, she suggested, would be a suitable substitute for a communiqué to give to the Press. In principle there was British support for the United States to continue with its dream of a protective shield of laser guns positioned in space which would make Russia's nuclear arsenal of intercontinental ballistic missiles 'impotent and obsolete'. That support kept the door open for British high technology to get contracts with the programme. But the essence of Thatcher's Camp David diplomacy restricted SDI to research and testing, deferring deployment to negotiations beyond the foreseeable future. To some extent this calmed the fears of Thatcher's European partners as well as some of Reagan's critics in the United States. Even so, the Camp David formula was not to everyone's liking – certainly not to the Pentagon which felt outmanoeuvred since Weinberger had not been invited to the talks because defence was not on the official agenda.

Three months later, when the Pentagon thought the worst of the insidious attempts to undermine Star Wars was over, there came a body blow which even caught Thatcher herself by surprise. It was subtly delivered by her Foreign Secretary in an address to the Royal United Services Institute in London when Howe asked a few basic questions in the style of a plain man's guide to Outer Space. These might just have been accepted as valid in October 1984 when the speech was originally due to have been made, but as it was delayed until 15 March 1985 the questions appeared to call into question the Camp David accord itself. Thatcher had been given Howe's text in advance on her way to Moscow for the funeral of President Konstantin Chernenko, but either the somnolent style of the opening sentences or her travel fatigue resulted in the key passages being left unread.

Howe's speech caused a furore in Washington by questioning the whole concept of Star Wars in the context of a new Maginot Line. American experts appeared to be held up to ridicule at the prospect of SDI being outflanked by simple counter-measures: 'Are there more cost-effective and affordable ways of enhancing deterrence?' Howe asked with a clear implication that there well might be. Research, like the concept of SDI itself, could prove elusive, he warned. 'As a research programme, it is also full of questions. The answers may be clear or obscure. They may not even emerge at all.' What if they provided only partial answers, he wondered. 'If it initially proved feasible to construct only limited defences, these would be bound to be more vulnerable to counter-measures than comprehensive systems. Would these holes in the dyke produce and even encourage a nuclear flood?'

In these circumstances, Howe asked: 'Might it be better to use the available funds to improve our capability to oppose a potential aggressor at a time of crisis with a credible, sustainable and controllable mix of conventional and nuclear forces?' The Pentagon was so angry that Assistant Defence Secretary Richard Perle, who was in London at the time, issued a bitter riposte: 'It was a speech that proved again an old axiom of geometry that length is no substitute for depth.' Confirming how much it hurt, Perle accused Howe of 'rewriting the recent history of the Soviet-American strategic relationship, rendering it unrecognizable to anyone who has charted its course'.

That stern rebuke was intended to head off any further attempts at outside intervention in Soviet-American nuclear relations. It was successful for the next 18 months, but it did not deter Thatcher from plunging into another lecture session at Camp David after a near-disaster at the Reagan–Gorbachev summit in Reykjavik on 12 October

1986. America's allies were aghast – none more so than Thatcher – at how close Reagan had come to being trapped into a nuclear disarmament deal which would have left Europe at the mercy of Russia's vastly superior conventional forces. Ironically, even with all his disarmament experts around him – Paul Nitze, Max Kampelman, Richard Perle and Kenneth Adelman – it was only Reagan's attachment to SDI which caused the negotiations at Hovde House in Reykjavik to founder. The steps to the brink were vividly recalled by Chief of Staff Donald Regan: 'What, Reagan asked Gorbachev, had he meant by the reference in his letter to "the elimination of all strategic forces"? " I meant I would favour eliminating all nuclear weapons," Gorbachev replied. "All nuclear weapons?" Reagan said. "Well, Mikhail, that's exactly what I've been talking about all along. That's what we have long wanted to do – get rid of all nuclear weapons. That's always been my goal." "Then why don't we agree on it?" Gorbachev asked. "We should," Reagan said. "That's what I've been trying to tell you." It was a historic moment. The two leaders had brought the world to one of its great turning points. Both understood this very clearly. Then came the impasse. Mikhail Gorbachev said: "I agree. But this must be done in conjunction with a ten-year extension of the ABM Treaty and a ban on the development and testing of SDI outside the laboratory." Outside the laboratory. Those words negated all that had been agreed upon,' Donald Regan revealed.

To avert any further confusion over nuclear disarmament being negotiated behind the backs of America's NATO partners, someone had to intervene with Reagan to establish unambiguous guidelines for Western security. There was no question of a mission by Chancellor Helmut Kohl or President François Mitterrand. There was only one voice in such a situation to which Reagan would listen: Thatcher's. She went to Camp David again on 14 November to prove once more that her Special Relationship enabled her to exert influence on Reagan in a crisis. Although Thatcher knew she would be facing the full American team with Shultz and Weinberger alongside Reagan, she left Howe and Younger at home once again. But she took her 'golden pens' – Charles Powell and John Kerr – knowing that it was a question of precise drafting to ensure the preservation of Britain's nuclear deterrent.

Reagan and his team acknowledged the need for clarification and accepted with only minor amendments the terms which the British draft proposed. They even allowed Thatcher to publish the new guidelines as part of her final Press Conference in Washington. While emphasizing the need for an East–West agreement abolishing intermediate nuclear weapons and the target of a 50 per cent reduction in strategic nuclear weapons, the statement reaffirmed the West's commitment to 'effective nuclear deterrence based upon a mix of systems'. It was also reaffirmed that Reagan would honour commitments to 'modernize Britain's independent nuclear deterrent with Trident'. The statement soothed anxieties in France and Germany that, given a chance, the Americans might try to resurrect the proposals for a denuclearized Europe. Although there was often resentment among other European Community members that Thatcher set such store on Anglo-American relations, this was one occasion when – at least privately – they were grateful for it. For Thatcher it was a source of considerable personal satisfaction that Britain's influence, which was so often derided by political and academic pundits, was demonstrated to have produced results at Camp David.

That influence enabled British Ambassadors to have an ease of access to the Administration which other envoys envied. The three ambassadors during the Reagan–Thatcher era – Sir Nicholas Henderson, Sir Oliver Wright and Sir Antony Acland – enjoyed an inside track which was of great benefit to government departments in Whitehall. It also enabled the envoys to convey Downing Street's views direct to those involved in decision-making. Americans often complained about how difficult it was for them to deal with the European Community because there were so many different competing national groups as well as Community agencies. But it was equally challenging for British Ambassadors even with all their advantages of access. With Washington full of competing authorities – White House, State Department, Pentagon, National Security Council, Central Intelligence Agency, Commerce and many others – outsiders are sometimes bewildered by policy clashes between them as they vie for presidential approval. Often the skill of the ambassador is in knowing which agency will have the final say in the decision-making process and homing in on it. On top of that he has to know where the power lies on Capitol Hill to enable him to lobby the influential members of Congress.

Senators can be very resentful of any manoeuvre which they regard as an attempt by a foreigner to challenge their authority. On one occasion it took all the suave diplomatic skill of Sir Antony Acland to prevent the wrath of the Democratic Senator from Ohio, John Glenn, being directed at the British. The Senator was trying to have a Defence

Procurement Bill amended to stipulate that no contract under the SDI programme should be awarded to a foreign company unless it could not be undertaken by an American company. When Ambassador Acland was instructed by the Foreign Office to take the matter up he emphasized to Senator Glenn that it was discriminatory and unfair. He also pointed out that the British Government had a memorandum of understanding signed by Defence Secretary Caspar Weinberger according British companies the right to compete for tenders on an equal basis with American companies. Senator Glenn was not impressed. He argued that there were two poles of authority at either end of Washington's Independence Avenue – one the Administration, the other Congress. It was all very well for someone to claim that a Government memorandum carried greater weight than anything else but on Capitol Hill there was a different view, Senator Glenn insisted.

Often it was the 'Advise and Consent' part of the lobbying that was the most complex. After three months of hard-pounding negotiations in 1985 led by Sir David Hannay, then Minister at the Embassy in Washington, all the hurdles in the way of the Supplementary Extradition Treaty drafted to ease the procedures for Irish terrorists to be brought back to Britain had been cleared with the Administration. The treaty signed on 25 June 1985 ensured that persons accused of a crime of violence could no longer escape extradition on the grounds that the alleged offences were of a political nature. However, it took a year to lobby for a majority in the Senate Foreign Affairs Committee which was heavily weighted on the Democratic side by senators from states with a large number of constituents with Irish connections such as Massachusetts, Connecticut and Rhode Island. It meant that Ambassador Wright not only had to keep making the British Government's case to Senator Richard Lugar, the Chairman of the Committee, but he had also to find a Democratic senator open to arguments to become a swing vote. After a considerable amount of shrewd reconnaissance on Capitol Hill he discovered that Senator Thomas Eagleton of Missouri, a lawyer not standing for re-election, was a candidate for conversion. Wright went about the task with the fire of an evangelist and when the treaty went to the full Senate had the satisfaction of seeing it passed on 17 July 1986 by 87 votes to 10. Reagan was so pleased that he telephoned Thatcher to inform her.

Reagan was prepared to be helpful over the British Government's problems in Northern Ireland despite the strong Irish lobby which claimed to represent over 25 million Americans with Irish ancestors.

Americans were impressed by the way Thatcher turned over a new leaf after her distaste for dealing with Ireland's Taoiseach Charles Haughey. It paid dividends when she reached a friendlier understanding with the new Taoiseach, Dr Garret Fitzgerald, and signed the Anglo-Irish Agreement on 15 November 1985 providing for some measure of co-operation between London and Dublin. Reagan promised that the United States would be more active in helping to stop the smuggling of guns and funds to the IRA and gave the signal to the FBI to be tougher in securing arrests. It also led to Congress setting up the International Fund for Ireland which allocated about $30 million a year promoting job-creation programmes and human rights projects.

Thatcher's recognition of the importance of the Irish factor in Anglo-American relations was emphasized in her address to a joint session of Congress on 20 February 1985 when she devoted a large part of her speech to the Irish question. Tip O'Neill, the Speaker of the House of Representatives who carried great weight in the formation of American policy on Ireland, had let it be known that he looked forward to a major statement of policy. Thatcher used the occasion to appeal for greater appreciation of the problems facing the British Government and stressed her readiness to work with anyone acknowledging the democratic rights of the majority to choose staying in the United Kingdom or being united with the Republic. Since the State Department had earlier in the month refused a visa to Gerry Adams, the Sinn Fein leader, because of his 'advocacy of violence', Thatcher thought it timely to urge Americans not to stoke violence with funds for Noraid. With memories still fresh of her narrow escape in the IRA bombing of her hotel in Brighton at the Conservative Party Conference the previous October, she warned against making contributions to seemingly innocuous groups: 'That money is used to buy the deaths of Irishmen north and south of the border – and 70 per cent of those killed by the IRA are Irishmen – and even the killing and wounding of American citizens visiting our country.'

Reagan helpfully echoed her plea the following month in his St Patrick's Day statement – which the White House always cleared in advance with the British Ambassador to check that it would not create difficulties for any current discussions on the Irish problem. He was emphatic: 'We in America must make every effort to ensure that, whether knowingly or unknowingly, no material, financial or psychological help originates from this side of the Atlantic for those who advocate and practice violence.' In a warning that men of violence would face the full rigour of the law, he disclosed: 'We have intensified our efforts to ensure that the United States is not the source of guns and money for such activities.'

Where influence deriving from the Special Relationship was less effective was in matters of trade, especially in disputes over trade with the Communist bloc. That was governed by the COCOM, the Co-ordinating Committee for export controls, which the Americans originally slipped into the small print alongside the Marshall Plan in 1947, and eventually grew to 17 members – the NATO nations less Iceland plus Australia and Japan. With a secretariat in Paris, COCOM issued lists of high-technology products embargoed for export to Communist countries in three categories: military, atomic energy and dual use – that is, products with a civil as well as a military application. Initially, there were about 260 items in the first list, 90 in the second and 100 in the third with an annual review to reduce the numbers or update definitions. Although COCOM had no legal standing in the form of a treaty and in theory no enforcement authority, it operated on the basis of allies of the United States being too scared to risk the wrath of the Pentagon. As an added incentive to observing the rules, the Americans had the Mutual Defence Assistance Control Act. That Act, which had been law since 1952, barred American financial, economic or military aid to any nation not complying with the embargo regulations.

In the first half of the 1980s, until East–West confrontation eased when Gorbachev came to power, the rigours of COCOM often strained day-to-day transatlantic dealings. For Commercial Ministers at the British Embassy such as Sir Rodric Braithwaite and Sir Derek Thomas the 'dual use' list was a challenge to their patience and ingenuity as they took up complaints of British companies whose orders for Eastern Europe were being blocked. They had to face a stern examination of all borderline cases since the CIA claimed that 70 per cent of Soviet high technology was achieved from clandestine imports of items on the COCOM lists.

Three senior men at the Pentagon took a lot of persuading: Richard Perle, Frederick Clay and Steve Bryant. There was always a suspicion in their minds that while American companies might back off from a borderline contract for fear of losing a Government order there was a European firm ready to cheat. Thomas and his successor, Braithwaite, sometimes had the impression that the Pentagon would be best pleased if all exports to Russia – except American grain – stopped. They would become locked in long arguments about computers which a British company wanted to export to Russia. The Pentagon team would insist that a laptop computer could be used for fighting a tank battle, to which the British would reply that any Russian tank commander who thought his replacement computer had to come from Washington would be in a desperate situation. Another American argument that Thomas and Braithwaite faced was that what seemed innocent little gadgets to a British company could be used in subaqua sonar devices which could create a serious threat to the United States and require them to spend millions of dollars to devise counter measures. In the COCOM challenges all the negotiations were so tough that the British side thought they were doing well if their success rate in borderline cases was better than 50 per cent.

Trade disputes over big issues such as specialized steel and the Airbus were pursued on the American side with little regard for any sentimental attachment to the Special Relationship. 'It did not really count when dollars and cents were at stake,' one veteran negotiator admitted. A basic problem encountered repeatedly by British negotiators was the American belief that they were the only people playing by the rules and that everyone else was cheating. If there was a clash with the European Community – such as happened when Howe flew to Bermuda in January 1987 for talks with Shultz after threats of an extra American levy of 200 per cent on gin which would cost British companies £50 million in lost exports – the Americans would complain that they had to take on 12 different governments plus the European Commission. The British would retort that in Washington they had to deal with numerous departments and agencies then ultimately Congress on a single issue. British ministers were often tempted to call a halt to all the preliminary scene-setting and say in effect: you have interests; we have interests; so let us admit that and get down to business. The Foreign Office came to the conclusion that there were so many special features about trade talks with the Americans that a policy paper was commissioned as a child's guide for diplomats going to the United States who were unfamiliar with American negotiating techniques.

One aspect of British expertise which came to be highly regarded in the last two years of the Reagan–Thatcher era was Tea Party Diplomacy at the United Nations. It enabled the Americans to get action taken at the Security Council which otherwise might have been blocked as a superpower's bid to bulldoze the rest of the Council. Britain's status as being friendly with, but being seen as not unwilling to disagree with, the United States provided the Americans with a means of securing results without appearing to be directly involved. This new British diplomatic gambit was initiated by Britain's UN Ambassador Sir John Thomson in November 1986 and continued by his successor, Sir Crispin Tickell, and was responsible for devising the formula for a ceasefire to end the eight-year Iran–Iraq war. After there had been six years of savage fighting in the Gulf at a horrendous cost in lives, Thomson decided that the five Permanent Members of the Security Council had an obligation to do something about it. The Big Five envoys knew each other well but did not normally meet as five. Thomson thought that it was high time they did and came up with the suggestion of regular meetings away from the Security Council chamber. It was not something he discussed with the Foreign Office – he did not even secure their approval for the initiative in advance. He went ahead on his own and never put anything down in writing.

His first move was a telephone call to sound out the French Ambassador, Claude de Kemoularia, a close friend, who gave his instant support. Vernon Walters, the American Ambassador who was frequently sent on missions, was not available so Thomson telephoned his deputy, Herbert Okun, who ran the delegation most of the time. He was keen but insisted on getting approval from Washington. The State Department was enthusiastic. Russia's Ambassador, Aleksandr Belonogov, agreed without asking Moscow's permission. China's Ambassador, Ling Qing, did not commit himself or his government but he turned up because he did not want to be thought impolite. The inaugural tea party at Thomson's elegant New York apartment looking down over the East River was typically English with waiters serving Earl Grey tea and cucumber sandwiches from 4.30 p.m. until 6 p.m. Thomson made it clear that it was not to be just a talking shop but a meeting which would in the current diplomatic jargon be 'action-oriented', producing positive steps towards ending the Gulf War.

The enterprise took off with éclat from the first meeting. Thomson had a follow-up meeting two days later and kept up the momentum with six further meetings in the first three weeks. There was no atmosphere of a cabal by the Big Five: the UN Secretary-General, Javier Perez de Cuellar, was kept informed of the ideas circulating at the meetings and approved the scheme as an example of the practical application of the UN Charter. It was the foreign ministries of the Big Five which became alarmed because the pace of diplomacy was going much faster than that to which they were accustomed. When their ambassadors began producing a sheaf of resolutions with a variety of options for implementation and enforcement the desk-bound mandarins in the five capitals had to apply the brakes to give them time to assess the implications. Walters sought an ultimatum against the Iranians which threatened trouble with the Russians and Chinese. The Americans, not disguising their pro-Iraq stand, wanted a warning inserted that if the Iranians did not accept the procedures following a ceasefire there would be an economic embargo imposed, but Thomson smoothed over the others' objections by indicating that no one would take that seriously.

When Tickell took over from Thomson at the Security Council on 29 May 1987 he remained chairman of the Big Five tea party meetings for two years as the pace of activity accelerated with a flurry of telegrams on draft amendments back and forth from the five capitals. Two months later on 20 July they recorded their first success in Security Council Resolution 598 which set out the terms for a ceasefire as the first step to a peace settlement. But it took another year until Iran, which was wanting Iraq condemned as the aggressor, notified Perez de Cuellar on 18 July 1988 that it was willing to implement it and return to the pre-war borders. The intervening period was full of alarms over incidents threatening to jeopardize the whole enterprise. The worst of these was the bitterness aroused by an Iranian Airbus being shot down on 3 July 1988 off the island of Henghan by a missile fired by the USS *Vincennes* with the loss of 290 lives. It resulted in Iranian threats of retaliation which Reagan went out of his way to avert by describing the shooting as a 'terrible tragedy' and offering compensatory payments to Iranian families of the bereaved. As a test of Western solidarity, only the British gained credit in Washington from the episode. While other NATO allies sat on the fence, refusing to give any public support to the Americans, Thatcher issued a statement combining an expression of regret for the loss of life with an acknowledgement of 'the right of forces engaged in such hostilities (such as the *Vincennes*) to defend themselves.'

Seeing Security Council Resolution 598 through to its conclusion and keeping the tea party diplomacy going in the years that followed was proof of how effective Anglo-American co-operation could be. As the Five extended their collaboration to a wider range of issues the system required more structured organization. Each ambassador brought an assistant as a notetaker, but the intimacy of the gathering was never sacrificed. Tickell made it work smoothly because he had a close personal relationship with Walters and his successor, Thomas Pickering, and because the Foreign Office communications system was the best in the Security Council. It was difficult for the American delegation at times to get a quick answer because there were often arguments between the various government agencies in Washington. The French were not very fast because the Quai d'Orsay did not always attach great importance to Security Council action. Russia's Belonogov often had problems locating his Foreign Minister, Eduard Shevardnadze, to get approval for a draft. China's Qing was always last since the committee system in Peking took a long time to deliberate and produce an answer. But when Tickell needed to move quickly in a crisis he could rely on the Americans to help mobilize support from the ten non-permanent members of the Security Council.

The great advantage for the British in having Walters alongside them as an experienced political operator at the UN was that he was prepared on occasion to take decisions and tell Washington afterwards. It was not the Americans who brought the permanent British chairmanship of the tea party diplomats to an end. France's Foreign Minister, Roland Dumas, did not like President Mitterrand's envoy having an inferior status to the British Ambassador and insisted on a rotating chairmanship. Even then, with Tickell out of the chair, the close collaboration between the Americans and the British was maintained at the UN in private meetings between sessions. While Pickering lacked the charisma of Walters he had a highly trained professional mind which quickly identified areas of sloppy drafting that could cause trouble for the Anglo-American partnership when a resolution was tabled.

Anglo-American harmony at the United Nations was neither automatic nor constant. The extent to which it existed varied according to the issues and the importance each side attached to them. Sometimes, over resolutions on questions such as negotiations with Argentina over the Falklands, there was a wide gulf between the United States and Britain, but the closeness of co-operation which generally prevailed was often a surprise to Thatcher herself since she had no great regard for what happened at the United Nations. She much preferred direct partnership instead of operating in a multilateral forum where consensus – a word she detested – was the objective. When Thatcher wanted something done she went straight to the source of power – the White House, not the United Nations which she rarely recognized as being more than a debating society.

Throughout Reagan's eight years at the White House, Thatcher made it clear that she regarded her own relationship with him as the linchpin of the Special Relationship and the thought of the Anglo-American partnership weakening at the end of his second term weighed heavily with her. In recognition of that anxiety Reagan made a significant gesture, demonstrating how much he appreciated her contribution to the partnership: he invited Thatcher to be his last guest at a State banquet on 16 November 1988 with his successor, George Bush, alongside him. The spectacular White House tribute to her was so lavish that those who witnessed it realized that for Thatcher it could never be the same again.

It was an event full of pomp and ceremony. There was a 19-gun salute, the highest accorded to any visitor who is not royal, a fanfare of trumpets and a guard of honour to welcome her. There was a special ceremony with a presentation by Secretary of State Shultz. He explained that Americans wished to pay tribute to her ability, at the end of sometimes difficult negotiations, to bring tedious discussions to an end by producing the right words on a piece of paper she just happened to have in her handbag. 'I have been watching that handbag for a number of years – it's time you had a new one,' said Shultz. Handing over a capacious model for more communiqués, he told Thatcher: 'You are the first and only recipient of the Grand Order of the Handbag.'

The banquet was an occasion for the 'soul mates' to salute each other with rhetoric so rich in affection and admiration that no one could recall anything like it since the days of Roosevelt and Churchill. Saluting Reagan's presidency as 'one of the greatest in America's history', Thatcher had a tremor in her voice when she said: 'We had the same political dreams and the same way of achieving them.' Reagan responded with a tribute to her part in achieving an 'extraordinary change' in international relations: 'Yours was the part of courage and resolve and vision. Something sure has happened. We have transformed this decade into a turning point of our age – and for all time.'

This was the moment when he sought to pass the baton of the partnership, which Thatcher cherished, on to his successor in the White House. The parting message to Thatcher which he left for George Bush to contemplate was: 'Continuing in this work it is profoundly reassuring to me and to all those who care about freedom that you will continue to share with America your vision and steady hand – and this is especially critical to us at this moment of transition in our government.' How the baton would be picked up by the new

President she had to wait and see. But there was a lump in Thatcher's throat as she left the Oval Office and observed to those around her: 'I'm sad I will not see him sitting in that chair again.'

X

How Thatcher Missed the Bus –
and Caught It Again

'There will always be difficulties in the transatlantic relationship.'

Lord Carrington, *Reflect on Things Past:* 1988

'It's only with friends that you can take the gloves off and talk from the heart.'

President Bush: London, 1 June 1989

'You will always be able to count on Britain – when there is danger, when you need us. That is why the relationship is special.'

Margaret Thatcher to President Bush, two months before Iraq invaded Kuwait

Gunter Schabowski was not accustomed to announcing good news. His job was to make statements of the Communist party line and these were not regarded as good news even by the party faithful. No one in the West was prepared, therefore, for the announcement he made at six o'clock on the evening of Thursday, 9 November 1989. It was expected to be just another propaganda exercise. Instead it was the most momentous declaration Schabowski ever made in his entire career in the politburo of the East German regime. His 22-word announcement stunned his audience: 'Today the decision was taken that makes it possible for all citizens to leave the country through East German border crossing points.' A Reuter bulletin at 18.03 hours broke the news to the world that the Berlin Wall was being abolished after 28 years as the most infamous barrier erected by a government to keep its people inside its borders. Even Chancellor Kohl was taken by surprise. He was on an official visit to Poland and abandoned it to rush back to Bonn in time to receive a call from a worried President Gorbachev seeking assurances that any threat of violence would be

207

checked and that the Red Army in East Germany would not be in any danger.

As jubilant Germans celebrated with champagne that Checkpoint Charlie had suddenly become no more than a tourist's turnstile the implications of the symbol of a divided Europe being demolished became clear. It meant that the doors were open for people to choose where they should live. Once they tasted the freedom of that choice it was only a matter of time before it opened the next door for the two Germanys to be united. For years the Western leaders had ritually looked forward in their communiqués to the day when the two Germanys would be one again. It was an easy pledge to make when it seemed that there was no risk of having to do anything about it. The actual possibility of unification being just around the corner forced them to address a prospect none was ready to face. The end of the division of Europe was immediately acknowledged as an historic turning point affecting relations between countries from the Atlantic to the Urals. What was not so quickly realized was that it opened up a serious gulf between the governments of the United States and Britain.

While the Americans jumped in at once to make the most of the opportunities of the Berlin Wall coming down, the British were left totally outstripped by events. One person alone was responsible for Britain being marginalized in the midst of what historians have come to regard as the most astounding sequence of events since the Cold War began: Prime Minister Thatcher. Her attempt to put the brakes on German unification as something not be rushed but to be carefully evolved over a period of ten to 15 years was the most serious misjudgement of her career in international politics. Time and again President Bush tried to make her face the reality that unification was inevitable and coming fast: that Kohl had no choice but to take over East Germany speedily as people were streaming into West Germany in their hundreds of thousands, public services were crumbling, hospitals were being left unstaffed and the economy bankrupted. Despite the assessments from her experts – Sir Christopher Mallaby in Bonn, Sir Antony Acland in Washington and Sir Rodric Braithwaite in Moscow all sent similar warnings – Thatcher got it wrong. No one could shift her from her rigid views – neither her Cabinet colleagues, the ambassadors in the capitals concerned, nor her own advisers.

In the end Bush shrugged off Thatcher as irrelevant and went his own way to get the divisions of Europe healed as fast as possible and have a united Germany solidly in the Western camp without the

Russian troops stationed there being able to do anything about it. As one of the White House team explained: 'Bush is not the sort of man to go on arguing when he meets a stone wall.' What amazed the Americans was that while they had learned the lessons of history in Europe someone like Thatcher, who had grown up with that history, had failed to learn them. The idea of trying to slow down unification and keep Germany short of full sovereignty was, in America's view, a dangerous misreading of the history of Europe in the twentieth century.

Thatcher was shunted into the sidelines because of a combination of factors. She was worried about the emergence of a greater Germany of 81 million people with the economic and political strength to be a dominant force in Europe, inside the European Community and in world trade. That was an understandable concern but, as the Americans pointed out, it was a fact of life since nothing could stop the Germans coming together once the East Germans started chanting 'Ein Volk' in the streets of Leipzig. President Mitterrand was concerned about it, too, but he was more subtle than to shout about it as Thatcher did. Thatcher was anxious about the impact of moves towards unification upon the security of Europe. She was worried that Chancellor Kohl might be so eager to achieve unification that he would pay too high a price to the Russians and undermine the West's defences.

Thatcher was obsessed with preserving Gorbachev's position. She regarded Gorbachev as essential for a balanced East–West relationship and looked upon him with what some of her entourage felt was close to hero-worship. She was against any rapid change which might destabilize Gorbachev in the Kremlin and give the diehard Red Army chiefs the chance to topple him. Bush had a more realistic view of Gorbachev's fragile position. He took the view that the sooner an agreement was reached on an orderly process for unification and the withdrawal of Russian troops the better, because the longer it was left the more difficult it might be for Gorbachev to deliver Russia's part of the deal.

Two months after the winds of change blew through Eastern Europe, Thatcher claimed that she had been 'way ahead' in foreseeing the disintegration of Communism. This claim was substantiated by a passage in her famous Bruges speech on 20 September 1988 at the College of Europe which was overlooked at the time when the focus was on her attack on the concept of a 'European super-state'. Then, she held forth a vision of a Europe open to the world, making the point: 'We must never forget that east of the Iron Curtain peoples who once enjoyed a full share of European culture, freedom and identity have been cut off from their roots. We shall always look on Warsaw, Prague and Budapest as great European cities.' But while her heart was for democracy rolling across the plains of Europe to the Urals there was in her mind a basic deep distrust of the Germans. Those around her thought it derived from the fact that many of her generation never put the memories of the war against the Nazis behind them. Some of her Cabinet colleagues believed that it was a gut reaction which they suspect may have been absorbed from the attitudes of her husband Denis who served as a major in the Royal Artillery during the war.

The challenge of German unification came at an awkward time for Thatcher since it became entwined with two other complex issues which launched her on a collision course with the Americans. It coincided with a NATO review of the problem of scaling down conventional and short-range nuclear weapons in Europe in view of the diminishing threat of East–West military confrontation as Communism collapsed in Eastern Europe. Here, again, Thatcher was on NATO's highly conservative wing, urging caution about the West dropping its guard. The Americans, faced with serious budget difficulties, were much more disposed to consider arms reductions at a faster pace. The other major challenge, which was posed simultaneously, was the drive towards greater economic and political union inside the European Community. Germany and France were eager to accelerate the process, but Thatcher strongly resisted any moves towards centralizing power in Brussels at the expense of British sovereignty. Bush was not content to stay on the sidelines. He let it be known that the interests of America would be best served by having a cohesive Europe so that the United States could have a closer structural relationship with the Community. The idea that Britain had a role as a bridge between America and the Community was an outdated concept in Bush's political thinking. In seeking to distance herself from a strong, united Europe, Thatcher was at the same time undermining her status with the Americans who wanted to see Britain at the heart of Europe.

Another unfortunate coincidence with the emergence of these problems for Thatcher was the changing of the guard in Washington. Naturally, she was reconciled to the warmth of the Reagan years not surviving into the Bush era, but she was not braced for the sharper terms of doing business. The new atmosphere of Anglo-American relations was more than a difference in tone. It was clear from the start that Bush was not a man to be lectured to as Reagan had been; he left visitors in no doubt that he was in charge as the man in the driving seat. Conversational in his approach, which Thatcher was not, Bush was a good listener to what she had to say – provided she did not take too much time to say it. Although he was no intellectual, Bush had a deep knowledge of international affairs which enabled him to counter Thatcher's arguments based on her own extensive experience. Having served as United States Ambassador at the UN, as America's envoy in China and as Director of the CIA, he came to the White House better equipped than most incoming presidents and was not a sitting target for Thatcher's handbag diplomacy.

These differences were accentuated by the changes at the State Department under James Baker. It did not take long for Downing Street to get the impression that there were people in the State Department determined to redress the balance after what they regarded as the far too cosy relations with Britain during the Reagan presidency. They thought that Thatcher had been allowed too much latitude by Reagan in helping to shape American policy; they resented seeing State Department recommendations being turned on their head as a result of a Thatcher telephone call to the White House. It was this attitude that contributed to a swing in Washington policy-making away from Britain and towards the burgeoning influence of the Germans.

Thatcher put herself at a disadvantage by having three different foreign secretaries in the first nine months of the Bush Administration as a result of Cabinet reshuffles. Her relations with Howe had deteriorated in progressive frigidity until he was frozen out completely in July 1989. His successor, John Major, had barely time to read all the background briefing telegrams during his summer vacation before he was switched to the Treasury after three months. Douglas Hurd, a former diplomat and Minister of State at the Foreign Office, knew the map of the world well enough and the problems erupting in various parts of it but he was thrust quickly into the deep end with the Berlin Wall coming down only a fortnight after he became Foreign Secretary. It took him a considerable amount of time to get on close terms with Baker, a secretive person who was slow to give his trust to others.

As a man skilled in doing deals, Baker negotiated with his cards close to his chest. By the time Hurd was settled into his job Baker had come to grips with the complexities of the European problem and the ramifications of the unification process. He called for a solution at top speed from his skilled Washington team – Robert Zoellick, State

Department Counsellor, Dennis Ross, Planning Director, and Raymond Seitz, Assistant Secretary for European Affairs who was such a brilliant diplomat that he was subsequently promoted by Bush to be America's first career officer appointed Ambassador in London and kept there by Clinton. They produced the game plan which the other three guarantor powers initially opposed but were eventually persuaded by Baker to accept as the only practical way to deal with the tide of events threatening to sweep aside all political procrastination.

At the head of the procrastinators was Margaret Thatcher. The resistance which resulted in her being sidetracked began nine months before Schabowski's startling announcement on 9 November 1989. If a precise date had to be fixed for the start of her troubles it would be 12 February 1989 when Baker began a six-day tour of NATO capitals to discuss the question of modernizing the alliance's tactical nuclear missiles, in particular the Lance based in Germany. On his first day he realized after talks in London with Thatcher and in Bonn with Kohl that there was a cloud building up ominously for the NATO summit in May. Thatcher was adamant that modernized nuclear weapons had to be sited on German soil. Kohl, who had argued that the option of the 'Third Zero' – elimination of short-range nuclear weapons as well as intermediate and long-range ones – should be kept open in Europe, was equally emphatic in opposing Lance modernization. One good reason for Kohl taking that attitude was that he had to face elections in 1990. While Thatcher stressed the need for 'prudence and realism', Kohl asked what was realistic about updating Lance with its range of 70 miles by a weapon with four times the range if the targets were to be Prague and Budapest where the winds of change were already beginning to blow.

Baker's discussions in the next three months pushed Thatcher further into isolation as the rest of NATO lined up with Germany, except for the Dutch who backed the British stand on keeping nuclear weapons up-to-date on German soil. The Americans took note of a public opinion poll showing that 80 per cent of the German population were in favour of a non-nuclear Europe. Thatcher remained defiant. In talks with Kohl at Deidesheim on 30 April, she insisted that short-range nuclear weapons were 'absolutely vital' for Europe's defence and even threatened to withdraw Britain's Rhine Army troops if they were not properly protected by tactical nuclear weapons. Kohl responded by calling on the Americans to open negotiations with the Russians on abolishing all theatre nuclear weapons in Europe. When the Mayor of

Deidesheim, Stefan Giullich, sought to lighten the gloom by naming a vine in her honour, Thatcher Kabinett, she responded after sampling a glass of a similar quality: 'It is very suitable for me – very dry with a touch of sweetness.' And, ever so softly, someone behind Kohl whispered in flawless English: 'If only it were the other way round: very sweet with just a touch of dryness.'

Faced with this split in the alliance Baker chose to do a deal with the Germans but advised Bush to fudge it at the NATO summit in Brussels on 28 May to ease the blow for Thatcher. Bush took the spotlight off the nuclear quarrel by announcing a proposal for the superpowers to cut their troops in Europe by 20 per cent. He presented the offer as an attempt to scale down the military map of Europe and open up 'Eastern Europe to Western values and freedoms', but he could not disguise the gulf opening up with Britain as he accepted eventual negotiations on short-range nuclear weapons with the Russians. After a conventional forces agreement on reducing arms, Bush agreed that the United States, 'in consultation with the Allies concerned, is prepared to achieve a partial reduction of American and Soviet land-based missile forces of shorter range to equal and verifiable levels'. Thatcher's discomfiture was humiliatingly revealed by the pathetic way her aides disclosed that she had secured the underlining of the word 'partial' in the communiqué.

The extent to which Thatcher was being left behind by the Americans was highlighted by Bush in the next 48 hours, first in Germany and then in England. The focus of the President was not on nuclear weapons but on concepts of change: 'The division of Europe is under siege not by armies but by ideas,' he proclaimed. At the Rheingoldhalle in Mainz on 31 May Bush coined a phrase that was to haunt the British throughout the next 12 months in the twists and turns over German unification: 'The United States and the Federal Republic have always been firm friends and allies but today we share an added role – partners in leadership.' He set out a goal with an immediacy that underlined how much Thatcher was out of step: 'We seek self-determination for all of Germany and all of Eastern Europe; and we will not relax, and we must not waver. Again, the world has waited long enough.' But it was the three words 'partners in leadership' which, her advisers realized even if Thatcher did not understand, indicated that she was in danger of becoming a back number in the Washington index.

When Air Force One, the presidential plane, brought Bush on to

London – cynically described by one of his entourage as 'just a little pit-stop' – the situation deteriorated still further. On the steps of 10 Downing Street alongside Bush his hostess was asked in the light of the Mainz speech: 'Is Britain America's most important ally in Europe?' There was a steely look in her eye when Thatcher answered: 'I think you might put it more tactfully.' But she made the best of an awkward situation: 'We pride ourselves in being among the foremost of United States friends and we always will be. I think it is quite wrong that because you have one friend you should exclude the possibility of other friendships as well.' She used the talks to emphasize the need to 'avoid euphoria' over the changes taking place in Eastern Europe and the prospects of substantial arms reductions. Forecasts of completing an agreement on conventional forces in Europe in six to 12 months she dismissed as 'over-optimistic' – to which Baker retorted 'optimistic but not unrealistic'.

The banquet at Downing Street was to have been the occasion when the rhetoric saved the day with extravagant praise from both sides. There was the ritual salute to the Special Relationship, Bush declaring that it was continuing and 'will continue on an even keel'. But when he responded to Thatcher's congratulations on his success at the NATO summit in Brussels, he gave her a left-handed compliment by saying that he could not have done it 'without an anchor to windward'. Thatcher took it as a tribute to her steadfastness in preventing a drift into dangerous waters. Others regarded it as a shrewd observation that faster progress would have been made but for Thatcher trying to hold everyone back until it was known precisely where the summit ship was going.

Thatcher's dead-weight role was to come under increasing criticism as events gathered pace across Eastern Europe, but she seemed impervious to the fact that everyone else was prepared to go with the tide. As one who abhorred consensus politics, Thatcher took pride in being one against 15 in NATO. Even when her advisers warned her that the Americans were going ahead behind her back, she took it as a sign of virtue that she was the odd one out. It would have been easier for her if she had behaved like François Mitterrand, who did not like what was happening but confined his objections to discreet mutterings. She often boasted of not being diplomatic and in consequence her strident tones irritated the Americans as much as the objections.

Thatcher's first reaction to the Berlin Wall coming down was to stress the need for order to be maintained. She was against any discussion of German unification or of border issues when Mitterrand convened a one-day emergency summit of the European Community in Paris on 18 November. Her priorities were on security: 'All military matters should continue to be conducted through NATO and the Warsaw Pact. This arrangement has suited us all very well and at a time of great change it is necessary to keep this background of security and stability.' Ten days later when she was angered by Kohl announcing a ten-point plan for a German confederation – without any consultation, not even with his own Foreign Minister Hans-Dietrich Genscher – Thatcher formed the view that this was an issue first and foremost for the Big Four Powers responsible for Berlin.

This view was being strongly advanced by the Russians whose Ambassador to East Germany, Vyacheslav Kochemasov, convened a meeting of the four ambassadors at the Allied Control Council headquarters in West Berlin on 11 December – the first such session since the Four-Power agreement was signed in 1971 – to emphasize 'the importance of stability in and around Berlin'. Mitterrand modified his earlier reservations after talks with the new East German Government of Hans Modrow. He told people in Leipzig on 22 December: 'German unity is first and foremost for the Germans. France will not stand in the way.' But he added the rider: 'The German people must take the European balance into account.' At that stage no one envisaged change occurring quickly. Even Kohl was contemplating a process taking three or four years.

One person saw it more clearly: the trouble-shooter from the days of Haig's Falklands shuttle, the Libyan air strike and the Gulf ceasefire talks at the UN – Vernon Walters, who was now American Ambassador in Bonn. He was convinced that German unification was on its way – faster than most politicians dared to think. Once he set out his analysis to Baker, the Secretary of State took a firm grip on the diplomatic machine and crashed it into top gear. After a visit to East Germany in December – the first American minister to do so for over 40 years – Baker saw that a united Germany could emerge immensely more powerful, with all that implied for Europe and the European Community. In Berlin he launched proposals for 'a new Europe on the basis of a new Atlanticism'. This concept of a new architecture for Europe came as a shock to Thatcher since Baker had discussed the problems of Germany with her on his way to Berlin without disclosing anything of his grand design, a fact which set off more alarm bells for those trying to warn her that she was being increasingly sidetracked in the dialogue on the future of Europe.

The details were even more disturbing to Downing Street. Baker stressed that the United States wanted transatlantic co-operation 'to keep pace with European integration and institutional reform' in striking contrast to Thatcher's attempts to slow down that pace. The biggest surprise to her was the suggestion of a formal American presence in EC institutions: 'We propose that the United States and the European Community work together to achieve – whether in its treaty or some other form – a significantly strengthened set of institutional and consultative links.' This proposal was partly designed to offset the risk of tariff barriers against the Americans with the inauguration of the Community's Single Market, but its emphasis on political consultation carried a warning for Thatcher's advisers that it could mean a watering down of Anglo-American consultation.

Baker's review of German developments with Walters convinced him that it was in America's interest to be the main driving force helping Germany. He realized that it was essential to have a united Germany totally in NATO. For the United States the main dividend was to get the Russians out of East Germany and have the Red Army of 380,000 men pushed back behind the Russian border. With Kohl facing elections in 12 months' time, Baker calculated that America would benefit from having him installed as Chancellor carrying forward the unification process instead of the uncertainty of the Socialists in office with the risk of Germany being lured into neutrality. Another major factor in Baker's calculations was the danger that the backlash from Eastern Europe's gropings towards democracy could force changes in the Kremlin. That made Baker conclude that any deal with Gorbachev had to be done in a matter of months.

Thatcher still saw no need to rush into big decisions and deliberately chose to send warnings to Washington in a carefully phrased presentation of her case published in the *Wall Street Journal* on 25 January 1990. Knowing that every word would be studied carefully in Bonn and Washington, she argued in an hour-long interview for a measured pace in the steps towards change. She insisted that unification 'must come at a rate which takes account of other obligations and which gives us time to work things out – otherwise, that could destabilize everything. And if I may say so, the person to whom that would be most bitterly unfair is Mr Gorbachev, without whom it could never come about.' For her, the future of Gorbachev appeared to be every bit as important as that of Germany, if not more so. Paying tribute to his vision in taking what she called the right turning, she asserted: 'If we cannot visibly support him, then we shall be cheating future generations.' The risk of trying to push him too far too fast and thereby causing him to be replaced by a repressive government that would undo what had been achieved was a danger she signalled to the Americans: 'It is in the interest of everyone who believes in democracy, everyone who believes in human rights, that Mr Gorbachev stays in power.'

For Thatcher the way ahead was for the Big Four to agree among themselves on the international aspects, and once the external issues were settled then have the two Germanys tackle the problems of integration. It was a question of dealing with the situation in what she termed the 'wider context' – a sideswipe at Kohl and his Foreign Minister Genscher for not putting the encouragement of Europe's progress to democracy and a market economy before narrow, nationalist objectives. This stance was taken as a result of a major policy review held at Chequers on 27 January – two months before the notorious seminar which caused a furore when a report of it was leaked. Thatcher listened to assessments from Hurd, Major as Chancellor of the Exchequer, Alan Clark, Defence Minister of State, and a number of senior officials such as Sir Percy Cradock from the Cabinet Office, Sir John Weston, the Political Director, Sir Charles Powell, her Private Secretary handling foreign affairs, and Sir Rodric Braithwaite, Ambassador in Moscow – and still went her own way.

Anglo-American differences on Germany were compounded by Thatcher's strong reservations on what she believed were precipitate moves by the Americans on conventional force reductions in Europe. She was critical not only in private but publicly of the proposal by Bush in his State of the Union message suggesting that the United States and Russia should both scale down their troop levels in Central Europe to 195,000 men each. Thatcher warned that what she called piecemeal reductions could prove highly damaging to Western security. She insisted that the proper way to get troop reductions was at the Vienna conference so that there could be effective cuts negotiated in Warsaw Pact forces with the necessary verification procedures. For once she was not alone on this aspect of disarmament; others accepted that she had a point in warning the Americans because some members of NATO might take it as a signal to make reductions in their force levels without consultation.

Her views on focusing first on the quadripartite aspect of the German question were supported in Moscow where she was applauded for her determined stand against what the Russians suspected would be a renewal of German revanchism. But being praised by Moscow's old guard did not do Thatcher any good in Washington. Her arguments for starting with 'Four plus Zero' were swept aside by Baker who was adamant that Germany's future was a question for Germans as well as the Big Four. Kohl turned the tables on Thatcher at a meeting with Gorbachev on 10 February when he won over the Soviet leader, who agreed not to oppose unification and to negotiate it in the context of 'Two plus Four'.

Hurd had flown to Washington on 29 January for talks with Baker with a firm mandate laid down by Thatcher at the Chequers seminar two days previously for a resolute stand on 'Four plus Zero'. But he realized that Baker was in the driving seat and would not be diverted from bringing in the two Germanys at the beginning, so he gave his consent. The French were won over from 'Four plus Zero' on 6 February when Foreign Minister Roland Dumas met Baker during a 5 a.m. refuelling stop by the American Secretary of State at Shannon Airport in Ireland on his way to Moscow. The deal was struck when the quadripartite ministers met secretly at the 'Open Skies' conference in Ottawa on 13 February behind the backs of the other NATO foreign ministers and agreed to start formal negotiations in Bonn on 5 May.

Nonetheless, Thatcher sustained a vigorous rearguard action in the months following the Ottawa agreement. She had a habit of inveighing against the Germans on every occasion that a willing listener crossed her path. Even unwilling listeners became her victims so frequently that she was given the nickname of the Ancient Mariner of Downing Street for a time. Her entourage were often taken aback at the way she buttonholed a distinguished visitor who had come to the Prime Minister with high hopes of gaining her support for some worthy initiative. Instead, in Coleridge's Ancient Mariner style, Thatcher would divert the conversation, taking her guest by the arm and exclaiming: Do you know what these Germans are up to now? For the next ten minutes the visitor would be transfixed by her sharp blue eyes as she recited her list of calamities in store for Europe if German aggrandisement went unchecked.

The Americans were bewildered by the contrast between her public pronouncements and those of Hurd at the Anglo-German Konigswinter conference in Cambridge. Her address on 29 March highlighted the international aspect of German unification: 'Just as the conditions for German unification were created by the efforts and resolve of many different countries, so the consequences of that unification affect us all. We are all entitled to express our view on the implications for NATO, for the European Community, for Four-Power rights and responsibilities and for Germany's neighbours and their borders.' She recycled her warnings about the need for force reductions to be carried out 'in a co-ordinated and disciplined way by NATO, not in some wild scramble'. She renewed her demand for nuclear forces to be 'based forward on the Continent of Europe' and for nuclear weapons to be kept ready on German soil.

Yet 24 hours later the Americans heard totally different tones from the British Government in the Eton-honed diplomatic accent of the Foreign Secretary. Here was Hurd admitting to the Germans that there had been 'not a disastrous but a difficult phase' in relations during the last few months. He even confessed to British shortcomings which inevitably caused smiles not just to his audience at St Catherine's College but to those in Washington: 'I would admit in retrospect there was a certain lack of imagination on our part.' Who was to blame for that? He was too diplomatic to mention his Prime Minister but he went on to explain how it happened: 'I think we were perhaps slow to understand the emotions which were driving this process, the feeling that there was an opportunity for divisions which had been so destructive and so damaging, to bring those to an end.' Again, without naming any individual, Hurd warned: 'There will be continued argument and there will be tension – but it is creative tension.'

It was that tension – creative or otherwise – which seemed to surface at Chequers on 24 March when Thatcher assembled experts to advise her on how to live with a greater Germany, what were the characteristics of the Germans and what was likely to happen after unification. One of the most surprising features of the seminar was the absence of the one person employed to know best what was going on in Germany: Her Majesty's Ambassador Extraordinary and Plenipotentiary in Bonn – Sir Christopher Mallaby. He was not invited despite the fact – perhaps because of it – that he had sent several telegrams about the dangers of trying to slow down the inexorable tide towards German unification. Thatcher's foreign affairs adviser, Sir Percy Cradock, was not present because he was on leave. Instead, around the table at Chequers alongside Thatcher, Hurd and Powell were two English historians, Lord Dacre and Norman Stone, two American historians, Fritz Stern of Columbia University and Gordon Craig from Harvard University, George Urban, former research director of Radio Free Europe, and journalist Timothy Garton Ash.

The tremors from the leak of the seminar report written by Powell registered almost as high levels on the political Richter scale in Washington as in Bonn because Baker was still in the midst of difficult manoeuvres between the Germans and the Russians at the 'Two plus Four' talks. Although Thatcher did not have the report circulated to her Cabinet, a copy was leaked to a newspaper, the *Independent on Sunday*, which published it on 15 July. That was just a few weeks after a tense meeting in Berlin when Soviet Foreign Minister Eduard Shevardnadze stalled the 'Two plus Four' talks over Russia's concerns at East Germany suddenly switching from the Warsaw Pact to NATO. In a bid for more time he proposed an extension of Four-Power rights for five years following unification and only after that would a united Germany have full sovereignty to conclude treaties. Baker rejected it and the meeting adjourned in deadlock.

What Thatcher absorbed from the Chequers teach-in alarmed the Germans and the Americans since it appeared to justify the reservations the Russians had. It warned of certain attributes which were abiding features of the German character: '*angst*, aggressiveness, assertiveness, bullying, egotism, inferiority complex, sentimentality. Two further aspects of the German character were cited as reasons for concern about the future. First, a capacity for excess, to overdo things, to kick over the traces. Second, a tendency to over-estimate their own strengths and capabilities.' There was agreement at the seminar on one pointer to the future: 'a kind of triumphalism in German thinking and attitudes which would be uncomfortable for the rest of us.' One consolation was noted: 'There was no evidence that Germany was likely to make further territorial claims, at least for the foreseeable future.' However, there was a rider: 'It was likely that Germany would indeed dominate Eastern and Central Europe economically. But that did not necessarily equate to subjugation.' No formal conclusions were presented to Thatcher but an overall message was left with her by the experts: 'We should be nice to the Germans. But even the optimists had some unease, not for the present and the immediate future, but for what might lie further down the road than we can see.'

There was no immediate indication of Thatcher turning nice to the Germans and bridging the gulf between the Americans and herself.

Americans were as dismayed as the Germans by a further eruption of anti-German sentiment in an article in the *Spectator* magazine on 14 July based on an interview with Nicholas Ridley, the Trade and Industry Secretary and a former Foreign Office Minister. Although the article was geared to a visit to London by Klaus-Otto Pohl, President of the Bundesbank, the main diatribe was against the dominance of a greater Germany, Ridley citing the plans for EC economic and monetary union as 'a German racket designed to take over the whole of Europe'. The offence was compounded by a cartoon on the magazine's cover showing Chancellor Kohl with a Hitler-style moustache. That was a reflection of Ridley's comment: 'I'm not against giving up sovereignty in principle but not to this lot. You might as well give it to Adolf Hitler, frankly.' Since he was Thatcher's closest political partner, the views he expressed were assumed to be ones that she was privately inclined to share. Although the outburst led to his resignation from the Cabinet, Thatcher's comments on Independent Television News revealed her sympathies: 'Naturally, some people, particularly those who lived through the last war, feel a number of apprehensions and there's nothing unusual about that.'

In the end the bridge-builder turned out to be Gorbachev, who had a change of heart – at a price. On the day after the leak of the Chequers seminar on Germany, on 16 July, Gorbachev made a deal with Kohl at Stavropol, in the northern Caucasus, allowing a united Germany to be 'sovereign in every way' and free to choose to belong to NATO. That enabled the 'Two plus Four' meeting in Paris on the next day to agree on all the external aspects of unification. There was a bill to be paid by the West Germans. What Genscher called 'the price of German unity' was doled out to the Russians in dollars – $7.6 billion over four years to cover the cost of withdrawing the Soviet troops and rehousing them in Russia, plus an interest-free loan of $1.8 billion to help Russia pay maintenance costs of the troops until their withdrawal.

With the signing of the Final Settlement treaty in Moscow on 12 September Thatcher stifled her reservations and kept her fingers crossed for Gorbachev. The main prize which the Americans sought from the start was enshrined in Article Six stating: 'The right of the united Germany to belong to alliances, with all the rights and responsibilities arising therefrom, shall not be affected by the present treaty.' But they had anxieties until the last moment that a change of regime in Moscow before the agreement was ratified could enable

Russian diehards to retain their rights under the Quadripartite Agreement and upset the unification arrangements. These were overcome by
a clever legal ploy devised by the British delegation which won plaudits
from their Western partners – a declaration on signature of the
agreement that all quadripartite rights were suspended pending their
extinction on ratification of the agreement.

However, it was not the completion of the unification negotiations
which ended Thatcher's political isolation from Bush. It was the sheer
coincidence of being with Bush at Aspen, Colorado, at the time of the
biggest international crisis since the Falklands War. Her visit had been
arranged three months earlier so that she could be presented with the
Statesman Award on the 40th anniversary of the founding of the Aspen
Institute. Thatcher had been invited to give an address on the third
day of the celebrations and Bush had agreed to make a speech on the
first day. Nothing could have been better timed for her to make a
return to the sort of close Anglo-American relations which she had not
experienced since her partnership with Reagan. Having been left
stranded for so long, Thatcher was clearly delighted to be there and
catch the bus again.

At seven o'clock in the evening of 1 August Mrs Thatcher was
unpacking her cases at the ranch of America's London Ambassador,
Henry Catto, ten miles outside Aspen, when a flash telegram was
delivered to Charles Powell in his hotel room at Aspen. It was from
London timed 03.00 hours – eight hours ahead of Aspen – stating:
Iraq has invaded Kuwait. He telephoned Thatcher at once and she
began a series of consultations which went on late into the night. By
another strange coincidence Britain's UN Ambassador Sir Crispin
Tickell, at the end of his diplomatic career, was being given a farewell
dinner that evening at the Fairfax Hotel in New York by the American
UN ambassador Thomas Pickering. They had reached the coffee stage
by ten o'clock – three hours ahead of Aspen – when Pickering was
called to the telephone to be told of the Iraqi invasion. In the tradition
of Francis Drake at the time of the Spanish Armada approaching the
English coast in 1588 they treated their coffee in the same way as his
bowls, draining their cups first and then leaving for an emergency
meeting of the Security Council. With the experience of working
together closely over Resolution 598 which brought a ceasefire in the
Iran–Iraq war, the Anglo-American team worked on the 15-member
Council until five o'clock in the morning. Their intense diplomacy
secured by 14 votes to nil with one abstention – Yemen – Resolution

660 condemning Iraq's aggression and demanding the immediate withdrawal of its troops from Kuwait.

When Bush joined Thatcher at the Catto ranch on the following morning her assessment of the crisis was described as 'a bull's-eye shot'. Her immediate verdict that Iraq's invasion was 'absolutely unacceptable' and had to be reversed was enough to ensure that her purdah period of isolation from White House policy on Germany and nuclear weapons was over. General Brent Scowcroft, the National Security Adviser who accompanied Bush, observed a complete meeting of minds: 'They were heading in the same direction and they tended to reinforce each other.' Some British correspondents, carried away by an ebullient briefing by Thatcher's spokesman Bernard Ingham, sent back reports of the Prime Minister stiffening the President's backbone. This was sheer jingoism. In fact on this occasion, Bush was not the wimp he was so frequently portrayed to be. He was resolute from the outset, convinced that this was no minor border incursion but an action which, in his view, 'violated every norm of international law'.

The benefit that both Thatcher and Bush derived from the restoration of the Special Relationship at Aspen was the interaction of their judgements as hardened politicians. They each knew that they had to hype the rhetoric about human rights being brutally crushed and the danger of allowing an aggressor to get away with a land grab. Thatcher spoke for both when she warned: 'If we let it succeed, no small country will feel safe again.' But beyond that was the realistic assessment that the main reason they had to do something drastic was the threat to oil supplies. With Iraq seizing Kuwait and menacing Saudi Arabia with the same fate, President Saddam Hussein could have within his grasp the control of 45 per cent of the world's oil reserves and thereby the power to determine the international price of petrol.

By the second session of talks in the afternoon, after Bush had made his speech at the Aspen Institute, that thought concentrated their attention on the need to defend Saudi Arabia. This was the first time the question of sending troops arose and they both agreed that it was necessary to have Defence Secretary Richard Cheney fly to Riyadh to obtain King Fahd's authorization for troops to go to the aid of Saudi Arabia. They divided the task of enlisting support from friendly states which meant that each had to make long telephone calls to heads of government. While Bush got in touch with Arab leaders, Thatcher worked on her European Community partners – and it was fortunate that her Private Secretary Powell had fluent French and Italian so that her message could be interpreted instantly to François Mitterrand in France and Giulio Andreotti in Italy. When they adjourned their Aspen discussions to continue them in Washington it was significant that Bush put a presidential helicopter at Thatcher's disposal as a mark of the importance he now attached to the British role in the crisis.

That importance was demonstrated at the United Nations where Tickell's experience from the days of tea party diplomacy gave him a key role. He took the lead in making the moves towards sanctions against Iraq since the British had the precedent of drafting UN resolutions for economic sanctions against Rhodesia after Ian Smith's rebellion with UDI in 1965. Because Iraq's economy depended on exporting oil, Tickell worked hard to have all the loopholes sealed under the trade embargoes spelled out in Security Council Resolution 661 passed on 6 August by 13 votes to nil with two abstentions – Cuba and Yemen. In the next seven weeks Anglo-American co-operation – continued by Sir David Hannay on taking over from Sir Crispin Tickell on 7 September – secured the passage of a further nine Security Council Resolutions tightening the screws on Iraq's economy with a series of restrictions including an air blockade and the search of ships.

Despite British expertise at the United Nations, Thatcher was not enthused about allowing the UN the power to decide whether force could be used and the circumstances of its use. She resisted demands in Parliament for assurances that the Government would not commit troops to military action without a specific UN Security Council resolution authorizing it. Thatcher was emphatic that Chapter VII of the United Nations Charter was adequate authorization since it provided for sanctions including the use of force in case of a threat to peace. Not so Bush. While he ultimately insisted on the United States, not the United Nations, running the 29-nation military operations he was a stickler for having specific UN authority on his side. Although there was a protracted debate in Bush's War Cabinet about going to the UN and the risk of not getting authorization, Bush was firm about it and talked Thatcher into going along with him. Scowcroft admitted that she took some considerable time to be convinced in a long telephone call and then she told the President: 'All right, George, all right. But this is no time to go wobbly.' That phrase was to be played back against Bush thereafter in the War Cabinet every time he was hesitant about any course of action. As a result the American draft for authorizing 'all necessary means to uphold and implement Resolution 660' became Security Council Resolution 678 passed on 29 November by 12 votes to two – Cuba and Yemen – with China abstaining.

Thatcher's unwavering support for a firm stand against Iraq's President Saddam Hussein put the British Government in a totally different relationship from that of any other partner of the United States during the Gulf crisis. Throughout the difficult diplomatic evolution from Desert Shield to Desert Storm the main emphasis by the White House team in constant hot-line contact with Downing Street was on 'the two of us'. Thatcher was 100 per cent behind Alan Clark, Defence Minister of State, when he rebuked other Europeans who behaved 'very, very feebly', and 'ran for their cellars'. Although his outspoken remarks angered the Bonn Government, the Americans privately endorsed them. They were thoroughly disillusioned by the behaviour of Bush's 'partners in leadership' from the previous year. The Germans were so engrossed in their national problem of unification that they totally misjudged the importance of the international problem posed by Iraq's aggression.

While they sheltered under the umbrella of a constitution which in theory barred the Government from sending troops outside the NATO area, the Germans were slow in responding to calls for sharing the financial burdens. It was only after criticism that they were sending obsolete East German military equipment that the Bonn Government faced up to their obligations and made a substantial contribution including Patriot missiles worth $826 million for the protection of Israel and a sum of $822 million to defray some of the British costs. The nearest the Germans got to the war was in sending 600 troops to protect Turkey, which had 780,000 men in its armed forces – almost twice the size of Germany's.

Britain's military commitment ensured that the Americans recognized the reality behind the rhetoric of the Special Relationship. In fighting personnel the British force of 40,000 was almost three times larger than any other European ally – the French were the nearest with 14,700. The Belgians, who refused initially to supply artillery shells for the British gunners, eventually had 600 navy personnel on duty in the Gulf. Britain committed 200 main battle tanks compared to 40 from France. Britain had five fighter squadrons available soon after the Iraqi invasion; the French followed with three squadrons. Apart from Canada no other NATO partner of the United States was prepared to place military units under American command and have troops fighting for the liberation of Kuwait.

In political terms Britain's support for the United States was demonstrably more wholehearted than that of any other partner. The Government's predicament was more complicated than others initially by having more Britons in Kuwait as potential hostages – some 4,000 compared to America's 2,500, plus 128 passengers from British Airways flight BA 149 stranded in Kuwait at the invasion and driven to Baghdad as 'restrictees'. It was intensified three weeks after the invasion when 137 Britons were seized in Kuwait for detention as human shields at strategic sites liable to become targets for Western air strikes. In these difficult circumstances Thatcher's commitment to the same tough policy as Bush in refusing to do deals or make concessions strengthened the transatlantic partnership.

Fears that this stand might be undermined by the decision of former Prime Minister Edward Heath to fly to Baghdad on 12 October proved to be unfounded. His mercy mission for talks with Saddam Hussein about releasing seriously ill hostages was dragged out for 11 days and he flew back to London with only 33 British hostages. His mission was seen in Downing Street and the White House more as a minor irritant than an embarrassment in appearing to show that the Baghdad dictator was not diplomatically isolated. Foreign Secretary Douglas Hurd insisted that the Government would not be blackmailed over hostages and delivered an acerbic comment on the outcome of the Heath intervention: 'I find it grisly and repulsive that the Iraqis should set about deciding who is sick and so old that they should be released from a position in which no human being should ever have been placed and in which hundreds still remain.'

Public support was much firmer in Britain than in any other of America's allies. Throughout the six months of the crisis public support for the use of force if necessary never dropped below 50 per cent, which was on average 5 per cent higher than in the United States. In Spain a public opinion poll showed 85 per cent of the people opposed to military action, and when Thatcher rebuked the Madrid Government for its tepid support of the United States Prime Minister Felipe Gonzalez retorted: 'We don't all have the same warmongering ardour she is capable of at times.' In France an opinion poll revealed that 80 per cent did not think it worthwhile fighting over Kuwait. Anti-war demonstrations were largest in Germany with 250,000 marchers on the streets on one occasion. The French were next with 200,000, compared with 50,000 people demonstrating in London.

In spite of a European Community agreement to discourage 'freelance diplomacy', the French and the Germans were active behind the scenes for a compromise solution. Michel Vauzelle, chairman of the Foreign Affairs Committee of the French National Assembly, flew to Baghdad during the countdown to Desert Storm for talks with Saddam Hussein and came back with a message that the Iraqi leader was ready for concessions if there was agreement on a conference on Palestine – a linkage previously rejected in Washington and London when suggested by Foreign Minister Roland Dumas. An earlier intervention by Germany's Foreign Minister Genscher with a proposal for a European Community delegation to work with Algeria, Tunisia and Jordan for a peace formula was also blocked.

There was no questioning Thatcher's solidarity with the United States from the moment they first discussed Iraq's aggression, but she drew the line at one aspect of co-operation and refused to go along with Bush. Originally, he had been as much against it as she was. However, after a great deal of hesitation Bush bowed to pressure from President Hosni Mubarak of Egypt and King Fahd of Saudi Arabia and accepted that Syria's partnership was necessary for Arab unity against Iraq. Although Syria was on America's blacklist as a supporter of international terrorism, Bush swallowed his objections and agreed to meet President Hafez Assad on neutral territory in Geneva. A short communiqué on 23 November said they agreed that the occupation of Kuwait was unacceptable and would co-operate to ensure that the legitimate government should be restored.

In Damascus the Syrians also took it as an agreement on a 'comprehensive and just solution' of the Arab-Israeli dispute. Thatcher, however, was in no mood to bury the hatchet. She had broken relations with Syria on 31 October 1986 following an attempt by Nezar Hindawi, a Palestinian carrying a Syrian passport, to blow up an Israeli airliner leaving Heathrow Airport with 375 people aboard including his pregnant wife in whose luggage an explosive device was placed. British Intelligence claimed Syrian involvement through the London Embassy of Ambassador Loutuf Haydar. Thatcher remained unforgiving until the end of her premiership.

On 28 November, the day after Thatcher's successor, John Major, took over at 10 Downing Street, Foreign Secretary Douglas Hurd restored diplomatic relations with Syria after a successful secret mission to Damascus by his Middle East expert David Gore-Booth, who was subsequently promoted Ambassador to Saudi Arabia. He secured an assurance from the Syrians that they rejected acts of international terrorism and would 'take action against the perpetrators of such action'. On the face of it Major had inherited a clean sheet and was shoulder-to-shoulder with Bush. Thatcher had made a truly remarkable recovery from the isolation into which she had boxed herself by her attempts to put the brakes on the process of German unification. After almost a year of being marginalized by Bush and his White House team, she had re-established Britain as America's main partner with the hot line back in daily use between Charles Powell and Brent Scowcroft co-ordinating policies in the Gulf crisis.

There was even an occasion when the United States appreciated the services of Britain as honest broker in a showdown at the United Nations threatening the unity of the anti-Iraq front over the killing of 21 Arabs at Temple Mount, or as Moslems know it, Haram al Sharif – the Noble Sanctuary – alongside the Dome of the Rock in Jerusalem on 8 October. While Hurd deplored the Israeli violence and 'the misguided policy which believes that the security of Israel must rest on closed universities, illegitimate settlements and even collective punishments', the Americans made anodine comments about the 'saddening' event. Their traditional support for Israel appeared at one stage to be jeopardizing the unity of the alliance with the Arabs required to liberate Kuwait, particularly when Saddam Hussein proclaimed three days of national mourning.

In the course of a four-day deadlock at the UN Security Council, Britain's Ambassador Hannay as current president worked round the clock to prevent the Americans being cornered into using the veto. A compromise text submitted at 3 a.m. modified the American draft and watered down the original Palestine Liberation Organization draft submitted through the non-aligned group. It was tough enough, however, to draw denunciation of Bush from Jerusalem for 'humiliating and endangering Israel' and angry observations that the United States did not insist on the ritual balancing criticism of the PLO. Even though Prime Minister Yitzhak Shamir had no intention of co-operating with the UN Secretary-General's mission of inquiry established in the compromise Resolution 672, he was outraged that the United States accepted the proposition for such a mission. The Americans, however, privately welcomed such criticism since the Hannay resolution kept the Arabs in harness with the rest of the anti-Iraq forces.

For Major such signs of harmony being restored in the transatlantic partnership were a welcome relief from the upheavals of the domestic British political scene after the bitter departure of Thatcher, ousted from Downing Street not by the electorate but by Conservative MPs saying: Enough is enough. Any new Prime Minister would have assumed, as Major did, that taking over the reins of government in the countdown to a war in which Britain was the principal ally of the United States would ensure that the solidarity of the Special Relationship was guaranteed for as far as anyone could see into the future. Certainly, if judgements had to be made on the basis of the warmth of the rhetoric, there was no reason to doubt the strength of the relationship. But the reality was that the end of the Thatcher era coincided with so many other changes in the international political equation that Major was left with an impossible task in trying to keep the Special Relationship alive – a fact of life that he had to face much sooner than he would have liked.

XI

The End of the Affair

*'It was inevitable that questioning voices should be raised in the
United States, for the burdens lie heavy on the American people:
"Why should we be the world's gendarme?"'*

Sir Robert Menzies, *The Measure of the Years*

*'There's almost a psychic wish here to say: "Well, there's another
thing that's gone. Well, we blew that one too. Well, we're no
longer important or relevant."'*

US Ambassador Raymond Seitz: London, March 1993

Twenty-four hours after John Major became Prime Minister the United
Nations gave Saddam Hussein an ultimatum to withdraw Iraqi troops
from Kuwait by 15 January 1991 or else military action would be taken
to oust them. The deadline locked Major into Thatcher's legacy of
close bonds of co-operation with the United States for the next seven
weeks and beyond to the end of the campaign. Not that he was disposed
to waver over Britain's commitment. He had inherited so many difficult
problems from Thatcher on the domestic front – political, economic
and social – that he was relieved to have the experienced hands of
Foreign Secretary Douglas Hurd dealing with international questions.
While the French and the Germans persisted almost to the last minute
with peace bids in an attempt to avert a military showdown, it was
Hurd who stood resolute with Baker in London on 7 January in ruling
out any extension of the deadline for Iraq.

Bush acknowledged the dependability of the British as his leading
ally when Major was invited to Camp David less than a month after
taking office and took the opportunity to extol the partnership with
the ritual rhetoric: 'It is very easy when one comes here to see why
my predecessors have talked of the Special Relationship.' In an effort

to establish his own credentials in the kinship connection, Major recalled that his father had spent ten years in America in the unusual dual capacity of circus performer and minor league baseball player. Although Major did not broach the subject at Camp David, one of his main concerns at this anxious period of the countdown to the UN deadline was the prospect that there might be savage reprisals against Britons in the Middle East and that there could be heavy casualties in the fighting to liberate Kuwait.

Despite threats from Saddam Hussein to attack American and British interests throughout the world, the decision on 6 December to free all the foreigners held hostage in Iraq and Kuwait calmed fears about reprisals. However, the prospect of a large death toll weighed heavily on Major when Desert Storm was launched on 16 January and RAF pilots flying Tornado jets on low-level strikes were among the first to be shot down. These fears were sharpened by a warning in a publication of London University's Centre for Defence Studies entitled 'The Gulf Crisis: Economic Implications'. It came to the startling conclusion: 'Even if Saddam Hussein were defeated relatively quickly, an estimated 60,000 Allied troops might be killed.' Fortunately, such doom-laden forecasts proved to be ludicrously inaccurate. When the Iraqis bowed to a ceasefire on 28 February exactly 100 hours after Desert Sabre, the land war, started and 42 days after Desert Storm began with air attacks the losses on the Allied side were astonishingly light. With over half a million troops fighting in the forces of 29 nations there were only 343 servicemen killed and 133 of them died in accidents. The Americans with 425,000 in uniform lost 266 men while the British casualties totalled 29 dead. After 110,000 air strikes only 36 planes were lost – 27 American, 6 British, 1 Italian, 1 Kuwaiti and 1 Saudi Arabian.

One of the main reasons why the casualties were kept so low was the speed with which the war was ended. Going on to Baghdad and deposing Saddam Hussein was never a serious option regardless of what Thatcher claimed afterwards. The Americans had two good reasons for not continuing to Baghdad: they knew they could not achieve a mandate for it at the UN and, secondly, they were very anxious not to get bogged down in another quagmire like Vietnam. The decision to end the war was not an example of the Special Relationship in action. It was taken in Washington by Bush after discussing the military situation with General Colin Powell, Chairman of the Joint Chiefs of Staff, who took the view that it was immoral to continue with the massive slaughter of Iraqi troops fleeing along the

Jahra–Basra road at Mitla ridge. Hurd, who was in Washington at the time, was told – not consulted – about the decision to end the war. Scowcroft sent the message to Charles Powell who spent most nights during the war sleeping by the hot line at Downing Street – again for information with no consultation – to pass on to Major. There was never any doubt about how far partnership went. It was the Americans in charge; it was their war.

One casualty figure in particular cast a cloud over Anglo-American relations: the deaths of nine British soldiers who were, in the strange euphemism of military jargon, 'killed by friendly fire' when two American pilots of A-10 Tankbuster jets fired missiles at British troop carriers standing stationary, miles from the enemy in the desert. What left a bitter taste was that the Pentagon declined to give an adequate explanation of how the tragedy happened. Their refusal to allow the pilots to testify at the inquest or even give evidence from America by satellite link caused anguish in Britain, especially when the United States persisted with its demand for Libya to extradite two men for trial over the PanAmerican 747 destroyed by a bomb blast over Lockerbie in Scotland. Both Major and Defence Secretary Malcolm Rifkind were criticized for not taking more vigorous action with the US authorities and allowing the relatives' anxiety to be prolonged until an inquest jury at Oxford gave a verdict of unlawful killing 16 months after the event on 19 May 1992. Even though the verdict was tantamount to an accusation against two Americans of manslaughter, it was indicative of the different perspective on the other side of the Atlantic that the report of the inquest, which was front-page news in British newspapers, was given only eight paragraphs on page 10 of the *New York Times*.

All the euphoria over the stunning victory of Desert Storm evaporated soon after the Welcome Home celebrations for the Desert Rats. It was becoming apparent, even if Downing Street declined or failed to recognize it at the time, that the partnership which brought about the victory would not be seen in such action again. While America's vast military machine was going through its final preparations for the liberation of Kuwait, the decision was taken in Washington in January 1991 that the United States' military commitment in Europe would be substantially reduced. Plans were drawn up for 79 of the American bases in Europe – including 13 in England – to be drastically scaled down or closed. The role of the British as a standard-bearer in Europe for the Americans was clearly coming to an end. After four decades in that capacity the British were to discover that one of the main factors in making Anglo-American relations special was no longer relevant when the Cold War was being consigned to the history books.

When the NATO Foreign Ministers' meeting sent out its 'Message from Turnberry' on 8 June 1990 – 'We extend to the Soviet Union and to all other European countries the hand of friendship and co-operation' – no one, least of all Thatcher, who flew to Scotland on her way to Moscow to warn the NATO nations not to drop their guard, expected any dramatic response in the foreseeable future. Yet a year later, on 1 July 1991, the six remaining members of the Warsaw Pact – Bulgaria, Czechoslovakia, Hungary, Poland, Romania and the Soviet Union – met in Prague and disbanded the organization. On the previous day General Eduard Vorobyov left Prague as the last Soviet soldier serving on Czechoslovak soil. The two events symbolized the end of East–West confrontation, and with no enemy to be faced across the plains of Europe it also underlined the fact that Britain was no longer needed by the Americans as the experienced sergeant-major keeping the allied troops in Europe ready for action.

If there had been any doubts about the implications of this development, they were dispelled six months later by a meeting held in Brussels on 20 December 1991. It was the inaugural session of the North Atlantic Co-operation Council at which the foreign ministers of NATO sat down with ministers from the Soviet Union, the Eastern European states and the three Baltic states – Estonia, Latvia and Lithuania – to discuss 'security and related issues'. This called into question the very *raison d'être* of NATO as it had existed since its establishment on 4 April 1949: 'to take such action as it deems necessary, including the use of armed force, to restore and maintain the security of the North Atlantic area.' The essence of the NATO deal with Britain and the other European allies at the outset of the Cold War was that the United States would stand foursquare against any Communist threat to Europe in return for the Europeans acknowledging America's leadership in the international arena. However, once the threat disappeared and those who had been the source of the threat became partners in the North Atlantic Co-operation Council, the case for Europeans automatically accepting American leadership and for Britain, in particular, enjoying a special relationship in the security of Europe became steadily more difficult to sustain. From Washington's perspective there was one significant financial conclusion to be drawn: it was impossible to justify to the American taxpayer why almost 50 per cent of the United States defence budget should be spent on the security of Western Europe at the expense of domestic projects when there was no risk from the Russians.

The point was forcibly made by California's Democratic Congressman Pete Stark of the House Committee on Ways and Means to a Congressional hearing on 31 July 1991: 'For almost half a century the United States has played the world's policeman. We have spent trillions of dollars and lost countless numbers of lives protecting our allies in Europe and the Far East from military threats, real and imagined. With the end of the Cold War we don't need and can't afford to spend $200 billion on more than 300,000 troops overseas. Not when we're experiencing a severe recession, huge federal budget deficits and the prospect of closing military bases here at home. If our allies want us to keep troops overseas, then they should have to pay the cost.' His recommendations were acted upon with an announcement to a North Atlantic Co-operation Council meeting in Brussels that US troop levels were being reduced to 100,000 – but that was almost two years afterwards, on 29 March 1993.

On the same day as Stark talked of force levels Bush was announcing reductions in nuclear arsenals. At the end of his summit in Moscow with Gorbachev there was agreement on a 30 per cent cutback in long-range weapons under the Strategic Arms Reduction Treaty. It was the outcome of a Washington–Moscow deal by which the Americans offered trade concessions with Most-Favoured-Nation status to Russia. However, the Americans kept a tight rein on their allies by rejecting Gorbachev's demand for an easing of the export restrictions on Western high-technology products imposed under the 17-nation COCOM embargoes.

While there were still two superpowers each with 6,000 warheads on strategic nuclear weapons and with 1,600 strategic nuclear delivery vehicles after the cuts agreed under START, it was still possible to argue that crises could yet occur justifying the need for a close Anglo-American partnership. But when the collapse of Communism in Eastern Europe was followed by the first signs of disorder in the Kremlin, the bell began to toll not just for Gorbachev in Moscow but eventually for the Special Relationship in London and Washington. As long as Gorbachev was able to preside over some sort of stability with his heady mix of *glasnost* and *perestroika* there were good reasons for caution about relaxing the watchfulness which Washington and London worked together to maintain. When the fissiparous pressures for the break-up of the Soviet Empire gathered momentum, the changes in the power complex had far-reaching effects not just in the Communist world but also in the West.

The first warning signals for Gorbachev came on 12 June 1991 with the outcome of two polls – one throughout the Russian Federation, the other in the city of Leningrad. A sweeping victory for Boris Yeltsin with 45,552,041 votes against 13,395,335 votes of his nearest rival, former Soviet Prime Minister Nikolai Ryzhkov, made him the first directly elected executive president of the republic. In the other poll the people of Leningrad decided by 55 per cent of the votes to 43 per cent to defy the advice of Gorbachev and change the name of their city to the one chosen for it by Peter the Great in 1703: St Petersburg. That decision plus the Russian Federation's announcement of plans to privatize 70 per cent of government property and assets signalled a radical transformation of the political equation between East and West.

Two months later tanks rumbled through the streets of Moscow on 19 August after an announcement that Vice-President Gennady Yanayev had taken over power 'due to Mikhail Gorbachev's inability to perform his duties for health reasons'. Although the coup – staged 24 hours before the Union Treaty was due to be signed ending central control in the Soviet Union – collapsed in three days and Gorbachev was reinstated, he was a shattered man on his return to the Kremlin and the political barometer was never the same afterwards. Yeltsin's days of defiance in the Russian Federation's White House supported by the elite KGB Alpha anti-terrorist force and the air force commander, Marshal Yevgeny Shaposhnikov, put him in a commanding position as the Soviet Union began its inexorable progress towards total disintegration. Watching it in Washington and London, the two partners, who had assumed for decades that they would be facing a challenge from Moscow that would never be abandoned even if it were scaled down, became aware that they were approaching the end of a chapter.

The formal notification that the world was no longer dominated by two superpowers completely changed East–West and West–West relations and was the death knell of the Special Relationship. It occurred on 8 December 1991 with a 15-word declaration in Minsk by Yeltsin as President of Russia, Leonid Kravchuk as President of Ukraine and Stanislav Shushkevich as Chairman of the Supreme Soviet of Belarus: 'The USSR as a subject of international law and a geopolitical reality ceases to exist.' The last remains of what had been the Evil Empire were quietly interred without ceremony. The Soviet Union was replaced on 21 December by the CIS – Commonwealth of Independent States formed by 11 of the former Soviet republics – and Gorbachev resigned on 25 December. As evidence of the unchallenged position of the United States as the sole remaining superpower, Yeltsin's deputy in charge of economic affairs, Yegor Gaidar, declared that the Vneshekonombank, the Soviet bank for international economic transactions, was bankrupt and that Russia as the largest republic would start its independent existence with 61.34 per cent of the debt.

Confusion over the military arrangements in the wake of the disintegration of the Soviet Union argued for a continuing alertness among Defence Ministers of the West. While Yeltsin announced a 90 per cent pay rise for the armed forces in an attempt to ensure the generals' support for the CIS, there was strong resistance in the other new independent republics to centralized control of the armed forces. Although Gorbachev handed over the codes for pressing the nuclear button to Yeltsin on his resignation, the existence of nuclear weapons in four republics – Russia, Ukraine, Kazakhstan and Belarus – created doubts about where the authority over them really resided. After visits to the four republics for talks with political and military leaders, James Baker assured NATO ministers that arrangements were being made to ensure that the nuclear arsenals were under single control. His assurances did not put all their fears to rest.

Bilateral deals by the Americans with Russia, Ukraine, Kazakhstan and Belarus caused concern in the capitals of Western Europe. There was anxiety that the main emphasis appeared to be on cutting the long-range inter-continental ballistic missile stocks – the principal danger to the United States – while there was little effective control over the dissemination of nuclear expertise and the export of high-tech conventional weapons to Third World countries. Further reductions in nuclear warheads to 3,500 and the total elimination of land-based ICBMs with multiple warheads by the year 2003 were agreed under the START II treaty signed at the Bush–Yeltsin summit in Moscow on 3 January 1993, but other republics prolonged the uncertainty of the East–West security problem by bargaining the implementation of the denuclearization process against external aid programmes. Tensions between Yeltsin and Kravchuk, which were exacerbated by the dispute over the control of the former Soviet Black Sea fleet and the transfer of short-range nuclear weapons, created further complications for the changing East–West political equation.

Other factors producing chaos in many areas of the former Soviet empire encouraged a steady drift away from close transatlantic co-operation, since it was felt that nothing was liable to emerge from any of the new republics which could seriously affect the wellbeing of the Western world. The governments in Washington and London watched with a sense of detachment the protracted constitutional struggle for power between Yeltsin and the Congress of People's Deputies – although they wondered what the repercussions inside and outside Russia might be after Yeltsin crushed opposition inside the Congress by having the army storm Moscow's White House on 4 October 1993. They saw Russia further weakened by fighting in the Abkhazia autonomous region where Georgia's President, Eduard Shevardnadze, retreated accusing the Russians in September 1993 of 'unconcealed interference in the internal affairs of sovereign Georgia'.

Wherever they looked in the new republics they saw problems: ethnic upheavals in the Caucasus and Moldova, the long-standing conflict over Nagorno-Karabakh, and in all of them poverty, unemployment, shortage of goods, rampant inflation and social services badly run-down for lack of equipment and funds. In Russia prices had risen by 2,500 per cent in the course of 1992, and although inflation was curbed to 15 per cent a month by mid-1993 that amounted to 435 per cent a year. While the governments in Washington and London were concerned at the dangers posed to the process of democratization and the transition to a market economy, they were able to take heart from the fact that apart from demands for billions of dollars in aid from the West these problems presented no serious consequences for them.

That assessment led them to the conclusion that they should go their own way and concentrate on other issues until the new republics had reorganized themselves into a position of some economic and political stability from which they could properly utilize an international aid package. It was a recognition that the New World Order proclaimed by Bush amid the triumphalism following Desert Storm had been built on shifting sands. There was no community of interest between East and West when so much tension was erupting all over Eastern Europe and the former Soviet Union. The theory that America and Russia had enough leverage between them to ensure stability was shown to be invalid when one of the partners became hopelessly unstable itself, leaving the United States to contemplate the new world disorder.

In pursuing other questions outside the East–West context, the British began to find themselves either at odds with the Americans or set aside by them as no longer being entitled to partnership status.

One of the most bitterly contested issues between the two governments was the problem of the Vietnamese boat people flooding into Hong Kong which soured relations over a long period. Although only 5,000 of the 64,000 people in the overcrowded camps in the Crown Colony had been accepted as genuine refugees in 1991 and only a trickle were granted immigration permits by other countries, the United States opposed any mandatory repatriation to Vietnam. Despite the routine expulsion of illegal immigrants from Haiti and Mexico by the American authorities, the US Government regarded the involuntary return of boat people to Vietnam as immoral and even refused a British request to make room for 9,000 boat people on the Pacific island of Guam. They stuck to the principle of a right to asylum at the first port of call regardless of the burdens imposed upon the tiny colony.

The British went to great lengths in attempts to get co-operation from the Americans, right up to the President who was a long-standing friend of Ambassador Acland – they had been next-door neighbours when Bush was Vice-President and the two of them would relax over meals together after playing tennis. Despite his persistence with formal representations at the White House and to Scowcroft, Baker and Congressional leaders, Acland found it impossible to change their views. For Americans, in the light of the Vietnam War, to return Vietnamese who had taken great risks to escape was as heartless as sending Cossacks back to Stalin's Russia. So long as public pressures on the Administration remained strong on the missing-in-action issue over American servicemen not being properly accounted for in casualty lists, British appeals on behalf of Hong Kong fell on deaf ears.

After one frustrating meeting in Washington with Baker, when the Americans had blocked an agreement at a Geneva refugee conference, Hurd made no attempt to hide his anger: 'People here draw a distinction between returning people to Vietnam and returning people to dictatorships in any other part of the world. Well, I know what any other government would do in our circumstances because they already do it around the globe.' Even on 29 October 1991 when an accord was reached by the British, the Vietnamese Government and the UN High Commissioner for Refugees that all boat people in Hong Kong who did not qualify as refugees would be compulsorily repatriated, the US Government remained strongly against deportations.

The one area of international affairs where the Americans were most reluctant to co-operate with the British – even at times to the point of cutting them out and relegating them to observer status with no right to partnership – was Middle East peacemaking between Israel and the Arabs. This reached a climax over Baker's peace missions which culminated in conferences in Madrid and Washington, but it could be traced back to the resentment aroused by Carrington over his initiative with the European Community's Venice Declaration proclaiming the right of Palestinians to self-determination. Anglo-American relations on Arab-Israeli issues were always overshadowed by a history of American mistrust of the British as traditionally pro-Arab, matched on the British side by a resentment at the way American Administrations were so heavily influenced by the Jewish lobby in the United States.

British initiatives on the Middle East were difficult to carry forward in the face of American resistance, as Howe found in December 1988 when he was planning to send his Minister of State William Waldegrave, who had made his mark with Arab leaders, on a mission to try to break the current stalemate. Under heavy pressure from the Jewish lobby, Secretary of State George Shultz barred Palestinian leader Yasser Arafat from addressing the United Nations General Assembly in New York by refusing him a visa on the grounds that he 'knows of, condones and lends support to terrorism'. The Americans had not raised the matter in the tea-party diplomacy sessions among the Big Five at the Security Council since they knew they would be outnumbered four to one. But as Ambassador Tickell was the Security Council chairman at the time, he played a leading role in ensuring that Arafat's voice was heard saying what the Palestinians wanted the world to hear when the UN General Assembly session was transferred to Geneva on 13 December 1988.

The fact that Tickell spent hours with the Palestinians working on the draft of the Arafat statement so that it was clear that the PLO leader accepted UN Security Council Resolution 242 – and thereby the existence of Israel – and that he 'condemned terrorism in all its forms' did nothing to ease the Anglo-American rift. But Tickell persisted with his behind-the-scenes diplomacy after the State Department shrugged off the Arafat speech because it 'continued to be ambiguous on the key issues'. Following further British and Swedish interventions, Arafat held a Press Conference in Geneva on 14 December to make it completely unambiguous that he acknowledged 'the right of all parties concerned in the Middle East conflict to exist in peace and security and this included the state of Palestine, Israel and other neighbours according to Resolutions 242 and 338'. Tickell's reward was Shultz's decision to authorize the US Ambassador in

Tunisia, Robert Pelletreau, to open a dialogue with Yasser Abed Rabbo of the Palestine Liberation Organization on 16 December.

However, any British hopes of being able to influence the Americans to be more flexible towards Palestinian proposals for a Middle East settlement were crushed two months before the Iraqi invasion of Kuwait. The Americans broke off the dialogue because of the PLO's failure to take action against extremists who made a seaborne attack on the Israeli coast. The PLO then made it even more difficult by Arafat's extraordinary decision to align himself with Saddam Hussein after the invasion of Kuwait. The only other key player with influence on an Israeli–Palestinian settlement and with whom Britain had traditional links was King Hussein of Jordan, but his ambivalent role towards the Kuwait crisis left him on the sidelines when the peace process resumed. This meant that after the success of Operation Desert Storm, Baker was in a strong position with the principal leaders in the Arab world to conduct the search for an Arab–Israeli settlement without turning to the British for any assistance. With his 'Gang of Four' – Robert Zoellick, Dennis Ross, Margaret Tutweiler and Jack Lorenz – Baker had all the expertise he required and had no need of advice from anyone else.

Baker's Middle East peace shuttle, which began a week after the Gulf War ended and took him seven times to the region in the next six months, focused on selling the framework of a deal to Israel and Syria as the two main protagonists who were required to make concessions. The British were left in the margins so much that at Hurd's instigation the European Community's foreign ministers sent a message from their meeting in Luxembourg on 16 April 1991 to Baker that Europe wanted a place at any Middle East peace conference resulting from his initiative. It did not appear to carry much weight with Baker. In seeking assistance outside the area he turned to the Russians and a week later, after meeting Foreign Minister Aleksandr Bessmertnykh at Kislovodsk, secured Russia's agreement to be a co-sponsor with America of a Middle East peace conference.

When Baker finally manoeuvred the four principal negotiating groups – Israelis, Palestinians in a joint delegation with Jordanians, Lebanese and Syrians – into accepting the agenda for a conference it began with a spectacular opening at the Royal Palace in Madrid on 30 October 1991. There was, however, no place for the British as Spain's Prime Minister Felipe Gonzalez welcomed Bush, Gorbachev, Israel's Prime Minister Yitzhak Shamir and foreign ministers from Jordan,

Syria and the Lebanon. The nearest the British came to the conference table was through observer status accorded to a representative of the European Community, the place being taken by Netherlands Foreign Minister Hans van den Broek as current President of the EC Council. In the months that followed before the talks ran into stalemate the process remained entirely in Baker's hands as his Russian co-sponsor was dumped on the sidelines like the British.

While the end of the Cold War and the disintegration of the Soviet Union would have been sufficient in themselves to highlight the reality behind the rhetoric of the Special Relationship, there was one other factor that had a dramatic impact upon the transatlantic partnership – the emergence of the European Community as a global power bloc. Major's first decision of cardinal importance to his government's domestic and international position was to commit himself to the European Community in a way that Thatcher refused to contemplate. His description of his vision of Britain during a visit to Bonn on 11 March 1991 as being 'at the very heart of Europe' set the country on a course which was eventually to confirm that the old transatlantic partnership was over and that if anything were to take its place it would have to be a United States–European relationship based on the European Community.

The United States had already braced itself for radical changes in its preparations for intensified economic competition as a result of the Community's decision to inaugurate the Single European Market on 1 January 1993. Its fears of a serious protectionist clash with 'Fortress Europe', however, proved to be exaggerated despite many anxious episodes during the bargaining over the Uruguay Round of the General Agreement on Tariffs and Trade. Nonetheless, the economic strength of Europe had by then reached the point where the EC was almost at superpower status with the United States. Its gross domestic product was the same as America's at $6.5 trillion. The Community had become America's biggest trading partner and was taking around 25 per cent of all American exports. Over 40 per cent of America's direct foreign investment was lodged in the Community. Direct investment by European companies in the United States stood at over 55 per cent of all foreign investment. As each provided a huge market for the other, the Americans had good reason to become increasingly concerned about the Community's burgeoning economic power.

However, the most fundamental shift in the transatlantic balance came with the agreement on the Maastricht Treaty on 11 December

1991. In the most significant development since the Treaty of Rome in 1957 it established a coherent identity for the European Community as something much more than a trading bloc. It provided the framework for a new Europe as a power bloc with the evolution of political as well as economic and monetary union. The treaty which Hurd signed on 10 February 1992 committed Britain to a European Union registering its identity 'through the implementation of a common foreign and security policy which shall include the eventual framing of a common defence policy'. Although a common foreign policy was destined to remain more of an aspiration than actuality for a long time beyond ratification of the treaty, the British undertaking to work towards it ruled out any prolongation of the Special Relationship on foreign policy co-ordination. It became increasingly obvious in Washington that the first priority in London was no longer to get an Anglo-American policy harmonized wherever possible. When problems arose, Britain's main aim was to achieve a consensus in the Community and then examine whether the Americans could be encouraged to follow a similar line of action. Naturally, when the British found themselves at odds with their European partners it was sometimes helpful to be able to revive some of the former close links. That occurred over differences within the Community about the way the Western European Union should be reactivated as 'the defence component of the Union'. Britain and the United States were both concerned at the creation of a Franco-German army corps as a separate military wing from NATO. Defence Secretary Rifkind's proposals, worked out in collaboration with the Pentagon, ensured that the WEU would become the main security pillar of the European Union and be linked to NATO. Yet the principal concern was to keep the 12 members of the Community harnessed in the closest co-operation, an aim which Major worked hard to achieve at the Edinburgh summit on 12 December 1992 after the first Danish referendum rejecting ratification of the Maastricht Treaty threatened stalemate.

By the time Major as EC Council President had found a formula for solving the Danish problem over ratification and paved the way for a successful second referendum in Denmark, he was confronted with a change in the transatlantic partnership which put paid to any prospect of reviving the nostalgia of the Special Relationship. In winning the presidential election in November 1992 the Democratic Governor of Arkansas, Bill Clinton, who was born a year after World War II ended, was the first President at the White House without any memories of the wartime Roosevelt–Churchill alliance. He was in a position to wipe the slate clean and determine the new perspectives of the United States for the twenty-first century. However, one part of the slate might have proved awkward to wipe clean. What could easily have resulted in a tetchy start to the new relationship were Clinton's memories of the assistance his Republican opponents received from England in the 'dirty tricks' operations against him during the election campaign.

Clinton might well have stored up resentment at the way officials in Whitehall trawled through Home Office files checking on him while he was a Rhodes scholar at Oxford from 1968 to 1970. Instead, he brushed it off with a joke afterwards: 'I'm just glad that I got through the campaign with most of my life in Britain still classified.' Conservative Party help given to the Republicans was not so lightly dismissed. It led Major to have a denial issued from Downing Street that he had any knowledge of the visit to America by Sir John Lacy, Conservative campaign director, and his deputy, Mark Fulbrook, to help Bush's campaign team. Ambassador Renwick in Washington was much more diplomatic in planning his strategy. He sent one of his bright First Secretaries, Jonathan Powell, brother of Thatcher's former right-hand man, to follow the Democratic campaign round the country and become known to the new leaders. Not surprisingly, when Vice-President Al Gore gave a dinner for the Prince of Wales Clinton broke away from policy meetings to attend – and he took time for a talk with Renwick.

Largely because of Renwick's influence it was arranged that Major should be the first European leader to visit the White House after Clinton's inauguration – a race Major was desperate to win. His 36-hour visit on 24–5 February 1993 was not one which registered as a highly significant event in the minds of many Americans, to judge by the Press coverage. The *Los Angeles Times* referred to Major as 'a flawed partner in an uncertain transatlantic partnership'. The *Washington Post* assessed him as someone who 'seems to have an uncanny instinct for making a beeline to the brink of political disaster'. However, Clinton went out of his way to dispense all the sugary rhetoric of old, which was just what Major wanted to hear. With the practised skill of a politician who knows where votes are gathered and which clichés pay most dividends for a visitor, Clinton came out in front of the television cameras with the assurance: 'The relationship is special to me personally and will be special to the United States as long as I am serving here.' Clinton could justify claims that he arrived at the White House as an

Anglophile. He was one of only two American presidents ever to have lived in England. The impact of being a Rhodes scholar could not be lightly dismissed, since Clinton gave senior appointments to 22 Rhodes scholars when he came to office, but the rhetoric about Anglo-American relations had really passed its 'use by' date. As a new-generation occupant of the White House, Clinton moved in with a totally different set of priorities from his predecessors who were preoccupied with the Cold War. While he was prepared to observe the niceties of protocol to a visitor like Major, he established himself as an 'America First' President who put jobs and prosperity for Americans before the challenges of international diplomacy.

One of the biggest lessons Clinton learned early in the presidential campaign was that Bush's political undoing was his concentration on the problems of the world at the expense of America's economic problems. After winning the nomination at the Democratic Convention, Clinton devoted only 141 words out of 4,250 in his acceptance speech to international affairs. Whenever he was challenged about his global strategy he retorted that his first foreign policy priority was to restore America's economic vitality, and while he stressed the need for a strong America he added the rider: 'We have learned that strength begins at home.' Not having to face any superpower threatening America, Clinton felt no need for an adviser on international strategy. There was no place for a Kissinger or a Brzezinski.

In transatlantic terms, the lack of any serious challenge to America's security meant that Clinton saw little need to turn to the British for the consultations previous presidents considered necessary. While issues involving the balance of power between East and West gave Britain a key role in American policy-making, that influence became marginal when the dominant questions being faced in Washington were concerned with trade, jobs and industrial expansion. This change in priorities resulted in the British, like other Europeans, being regarded in a different light from before: instead of allies standing together against a common threat they were becoming more often trading rivals and economic competitors. For the United States the threat was no longer from the Communists but from the Community.

Only a month after taking office Clinton served notice to Britain and her European partners that the United States would not stand idly by and let America's air industry become the victim of the market penetration of Airbus – the product of the consortium of British, French, German and Spanish planemakers which won 41 per cent of new orders in its market in 1992. His speech to Boeing workers in Seattle, two days before Major arrived in Washington, was about the real world, not about nostalgia. He blamed countries like Britain for causing 28,000 men at Boeing plants to be made redundant by unfair foreign practices such as the subsidies which helped start the Airbus project. If these practices were allowed to continue, Clinton threatened that a 'tough new discipline' would be imposed on Europeans.

While the British were reconciled to the likelihood of sterner transatlantic confrontation on economic issues, they were surprised by the onset of confrontation on political issues so soon after the Clinton Administration was installed in Washington. They assumed there would be no dynamic foreign policy initiatives when Clinton appointed Warren Christopher, a veteran of the Carter Administration, as his Secretary of State. Yet even before Christopher's appointment was confirmed by Congress he served notice that it was time for structural changes at the Security Council – a proposal which caused dismay in London and emphasized the widening gulf between the United States and Britain.

America's proposals for updating the world body from the framework dominated by the victors of World War II were set out in June 1993 by America's UN Ambassador Madeleine Albright without any advance notice, let alone consultation, with Britain. It was all the more galling for the British since the proposals for increasing the Permanent Members of the Security Council from five to seven with the addition of Germany and Japan opened a debate which threatened Britain's own position. Not only did it prompt demands for others such as India, Brazil, Indonesia and Nigeria to be considered for permanent membership, it raised questions about the status of the European Community.

With Britain and France already Permanent Members, the suggestion of adding a third Community member, Germany, was countered by arguments that one seat was enough for the EC and perhaps the 12 could rotate it among themselves. Since Britain through Ambassadors Thomson, Tickell and Hannay had long taken the initiative to make decision-making more effective in the Security Council, it worried Downing Street that the Americans should seek to introduce extra uncertainty with two more veto powers – especially to governments whose willingness to play a full part in United Nations peacekeeping was open to serious doubt. Japan claimed that her constitution inhibited her from sending troops abroad. The German position was uncertain even after their constitutional court accepted on 23 June 1993 that

1,600 troops could be used on humanitarian duties in Somalia. It was not *carte blanche* approval of German troops being sent anywhere to help the United Nations. Foreign Minister Klaus Kinkel insisted: 'German troops will only be active in peaceful areas.' Germany did not volunteer for UN service in Bosnia, where the British and French were under fire.

With 279 vetoes cast by the five Permanent Members of the Security Council during the Cold War, Downing Street shuddered at the prospect of having to face more than 100 extra vetoes in the years ahead with an enlargement to seven Permanent Members. However, the Americans indicated their lack of concern at the widening Anglo-American gulf by arguing that the UN Security Council could not cope with the challenges of the twenty-first century by sticking to the rules under which Trygve Lie operated as Secretary-General in 1946. Hurd was not impressed with these arguments and borrowed Bert Lance's famous dictum for his response to the Americans: 'If it ain't broke, don't fix it.'

This hardening of America's attitude towards transatlantic consultations signalled the diminishing importance given in Washington to Britain's role in the international arena. Differences began erupting over a number of issues which formerly would have been resolved by a telephone call to Hurd or a talk with Hannay at the United Nations. The Foreign Office was angered at remarks by Warren Christopher that American policy towards Iraq was being 'depersonalized' by not focusing on maintaining sanctions so long as Saddam Hussein remained in power since it aroused speculation that Britain was softening towards the Baghdad dictator by endorsing it. The White House had to backtrack after Foreign Office statements insisted that there was no change of policy and drew attention to the long list of Iraq's failures to comply with UN resolutions which Hannay had stressed to justify the Security Council's renewal of sanctions in March 1993.

When Clinton decided to take action against Iraq for the plot to assassinate ex-President Bush during a visit to Kuwait there was no consultation with the British on what form the retaliation should take or when it should be carried out. As America's principal partner during the Gulf War and as an ally with three of its citizens serving long prison sentences for inadvertently entering Iraq illegally, Britain had a case for consultation. The only advance notice given to Major was a message 24 hours before the attack on the Iraqi Intelligence headquarters in Baghdad on 27 June 1993 with 23 Tomahawk missiles fired from two American warships. Although Major expressed his support afterwards, there were strong reservations among Labour and Liberal Democrat leaders about the legality of the American action undertaken without any sanction of the UN Security Council.

The big breakthrough in Middle East peacemaking with the 'Gaza–Jericho First' agreement between Israel and the PLO in September 1993 was achieved without any attempt by the Clinton Administration to avail itself of British expertise in Arab affairs. Clinton gave Christopher a free hand since he had none of Bush's interest in the Middle East, and the Secretary of State, having inherited key members of Baker's peacemaking team, felt no need to seek British assistance. The decision of Yitzhak Rabin's Labour Government to deal directly with Faisal Husseini, the senior Arafat lieutenant in the Occupied Territories, made it unnecessary for any third party such as the British to have a mediating role with the Palestinians which Ambassador Tickell had undertaken in the past. When Christopher made his tour of Syria, Egypt, Lebanon and Israel in July to give the final push towards the agreement he did not stop off in London for any consultations. The eventual agreement – brokered not by the United States but by Norway which brought the two sides together in direct negotiations – was signed at the White House on 13 September with Clinton presiding over the ceremony while the British took a back seat.

A sudden call by Christopher for an oil embargo against Libya without advising the British about the move was another signal of the change from the days of transatlantic co-operation. The United States' move cut across other plans for putting pressure on Colonel Muammar Gaddafi to hand over two men suspected of involvement in the PanAmerican 747 explosion over Lockerbie in 1988. Differences also arose between the Americans and the British over the tactics to be adopted towards North Korea in its dispute with the International Atomic Energy Authority over the inspection of suspected nuclear plants. The fact that these rifts came out into the open so easily was a sign that the existence of transatlantic differences was no longer a matter of great concern in Washington.

By far the most serious consequences of the deterioration in Anglo-American relations occurred during the crises which had to be confronted in the course of the disintegration of Yugoslavia. In every respect – political, diplomatic and military – the handling of the problem on both sides of the Atlantic was a shambles. It demonstrated how far apart the British and the Americans had drifted since the withering of the Special Relationship began. Misjudgements and pro-crastination compounded by indecision and hesitation allowed the situation to develop into a vicious civil war which close co-operation by the transatlantic partners in taking firm action could have prevented. Initially, the fault lay with Britain and her European partners in believing that the situation could be contained by tackling it as a purely European problem. The mistake made on the other side of the Atlantic was the Washington decision to leave the problem to the European Community as a 'regional issue'. A credible show of transatlantic force at the outset could have stopped the bloodshed in Yugoslavia.

When Croatia and Slovenia declared independence on 25 June 1991 and the first serious armed clashes occurred, the Europeans were slow to read the signs that President Slobodan Milosevic was using the crisis to achieve a Greater Serbia. An EC troika of foreign ministers – Jacques Poos of Luxembourg, Gianni de Michelis of Italy and Hans van den Broek of the Netherlands – stepped in with a warning that a £600 million aid programme to Yugoslavia would be suspended unless a ceasefire were accepted. European bravado reached a tragi-comic peak when Poos declared: 'This is the hour of Europe, not of America.' But his ultimatum was quickly shown to be totally ineffec-tive.

As the country slid steadily into civil war, the next idea of the British and their EC partners was to call in the assistance of the CSCE – the Conference on Security and Co-operation in Europe. All it achieved at a meeting in Prague on 4 July was another call for a ceasefire. While the United States stayed on the sidelines, the Europeans were pushed into recognizing Croatia and Slovenia by Chancellor Kohl, who had warned that he would go ahead with recognition unilaterally if fighting continued – which was an added incentive for the Croats and Slovenes to keep fighting. The impulsive action of the Bonn Government was doubly damaging since they left it to others – the British and the French – to provide troops for the dangerous humani-tarian duties in the chaos that followed, the Germans claiming that their constitution forbade such involvement by them.

The first serious attempt at peacemaking was made by the EC at a conference which opened in The Hague on 7 September 1991, but the Europeans did not call in the political clout of the United States. Despite the immense patience and diplomatic skill of Lord Carrington as its chairman there was not enough pressure available to command acceptance of a settlement. At this stage, when outside assistance was clearly needed, the United States kept its distance and it was the French who took the issue to the United Nations Security Council where Resolution 713 imposed an arms embargo on Yugoslavia. It was only after further ceasefires broke down that there was the first move towards transatlantic co-operation: a joint declaration on 10 April 1992 that the United States and the EC would improve their co-ordination in response to the Yugoslav crisis. By then, with only nine months to go before the presidential election, there was no disposition in Washington to commit American troops to what was still considered to be a European responsibility.

Ironically, it was only after Bush lost the election that there was any American troop commitment to a humanitarian operation and then it was in Somalia, which in some European quarters was initially regarded as a soft option compared with service in Bosnia. The landing of 28,000 US troops on Mogadishu beaches in operation 'Restore Hope' on 9 December 1992 to stop rebel gangs blocking food supplies to starving Somalis made people wonder why the US Government did nothing to implement UN Security Council Resolution 770 which it helped to sponsor on Bosnia-Hercegovina. That resolution authorized the use of 'all measures necessary' to ensure that humanitarian food and medical supplies reached starving people. It was taken to mean that UN troops protecting convoys in Bosnia-Hercegovina had the right to open fire. The resolution applied to British and French troops wearing the UN blue berets, but there was no enthusiasm in Washington for having American troops alongside them.

The first direct American involvement in the problem of the disintegrating Yugoslav republics came when Lord Carrington resigned his peacekeeping role on 27 August 1992. It took the form of a distinguished American, former Secretary of State Cyrus Vance, operating as a United Nations mediator, not as an American envoy, alongside former British Foreign Secretary Lord Owen as partners in a new peace mission. Nonetheless, it was assumed that the high reputation Vance had in Washington would encourage greater American interest in the issue. Their persistence in the face of enormous difficulties in searching for a formula to bring peace won respect and admiration in capitals throughout the world. When they produced the Vance–Owen plan for dividing the country into ten semi-autonomous provinces, four of the Big Five at the UN Security Council gave it their backing – Britain, Russia, China and France. The attitude of the United States varied from hostile to ambiguous – a factor that served to emphasize how wide the transatlantic divide had become.

Yet there was still optimism in some quarters when President Clinton took office that the moral dimension of the Yugoslav problem might induce a more positive commitment and revive the prospect of transatlantic co-operation. On 28 July 1992, three months before his election, Clinton took a firm stand: 'If the Serbs persist in violating the terms of the current ceasefire agreements, the United States should take the lead in seeking UN Security Council authorization for air strikes against those who are attacking the relief effort.' That appeared to be renewed in his inaugural address when he said: 'When our vital interests are challenged, or the will of the international community defied, we will act – with peaceful diplomacy when possible, with force when necessary.'

After weeks of indecision, however, all that Clinton was prepared to do about Bosnia was to authorize American air drops of food, some of which fell into the hands of the besieging Serbs instead of the besieged Moslems. It took another month – with gruesome television reports of the slaughter arousing public dismay around the world – before there was any further indication of United States willingness to intervene. When it emerged that Clinton was considering air strikes against the Serbs and lifting the arms embargo against the Bosnians, the already strained transatlantic relations reached a dangerous level of tension which Douglas Hurd signalled publicly by stressing his 'deep reservations' about the American proposals in the House of Commons.

The risk of air strikes causing retaliation by the Serbs against the 2,500 British troops in UN berets on humanitarian relief operations prompted so much anxiety that Hurd distanced himself from the proposition with the pledge: 'We would not agree to action which would put British forces at risk.' Former Prime Minister Sir Edward Heath urged even more emphatic distancing from the United States with a warning against Britain being 'dragged stage by stage into a European war or pushed there by Washington'. His assessment about the state of Anglo-American relations was brusque: 'The new President has no experience of international affairs; he has no military knowledge of any kind.' Clinton's apparent conversion to the belief that the West had a moral duty to intervene with force aroused some bewilderment, since there had been no similar compulsion in America over the civil war in Afghanistan. When Heath recalled Kissinger's comment that it was 'easy to get into Vietnam and damn difficult to get out' there were many in Parliament who agreed.

The strength of feeling in Parliament emphasized how far Anglo-American relations had deteriorated. It also reflected a distrust of American leadership. But since there were still some fragile hopes for a time that the Vance–Owen peace plan, which had been accepted by the Bosnians and the Croats, might eventually be palatable to the Serbs there was no disposition to have a transatlantic row in the open. Once the Bosnian Serbs registered a 96 per cent vote against the Vance–Owen plan it was their leader, Radovan Karadzic, who underlined the lessons that should have been learned on both sides of the Atlantic: 'No people has ever relinquished their State without major force being applied against them.'

This was a signal for further bitter hand-wringing about the gulf between the Americans and the British. Democratic Senator Joseph Biden of Delaware was outraged at the British refusal to go along with US air strikes, condemning it as 'a discouraging mosaic of indifference, timidity, self-delusion and hypocrisy'. Republican Congresswoman Susan Molinari of New York called for the United States to lift the arms embargo regardless of European views: 'Let's get the people out of there who were allegedly trying to keep the peace and allow the people to fight their own wars.' Hurd refused to engage in a slanging match across the Atlantic, although he stuck to his view that the objective was trying to 'stop the war, not equipping the parties to fight it out'. Clinton's real regrets over the Bosnian Serbs' rejection of the Vance–Owen plan came out in an NBC television interview with Tom Brocaw: 'I felt really badly because I don't want to have to spend more time on that than is absolutely necessary because what I got elected to do was to let America look at our own problems.'

Hurd was left with the task of finding a formula to paper over the cracks in transatlantic relations, since all the other Europeans, apart from the French and the Spaniards, were too busy with their own national problems to be concerned about bloodshed in the Balkans. There was stalemate over what Warren Christopher wearily called 'the problem of Hell': America refused to send ground troops until there was a peace agreement to monitor; Britain would not support the American twin-track strategy of lifting the arms embargo to arm the Moslems and using air strikes against the Serbs. Hurd put his weight behind a Russian compromise plan for containment rather than cur-tailment of the conflict – in effect a recognition of the new *status quo* by which the Serbs were allowed to control 70 per cent of Bosnia instead of the 43 per cent allocated to them under the Vance–Owen plan. As agreed in Washington by the foreign ministers of the United States, Britain, France, Russia and Spain on 22 May 1993, it designated six 'safe areas' for 1.2 million refugees in Bosnia and provided air protection for the UN forces on humanitarian operations but not for the people taking refuge in the havens. While there was some relief at the illusion of transatlantic unity, the five-nation plan ran into trouble on the ground. NATO defence ministers raised questions about the feasibility of protecting 'safe areas' for Moslems; the two members with the largest armies, Germany and Turkey, withheld support.

Democratic Congressman Harry Johnston of Florida swept aside the platitudes clouding the situation when he said that President Clinton was 'doing a Pontius Pilate and washing his hands of the Bosnian problem'. The hesitations and U-turns in policy by both the Americans and the British were disconcerting to those who had expected resolute action from politicians who had proclaimed that the world was a global village. At the time of UN Security Council Resolution 770 on 13 August 1992, which authorized the use of force to ensure the distribution of humanitarian aid, the United States and Britain were both against sending ground troops. Five days later the British Government did a U-turn and announced that it was sending 1,800 troops – subsequently increased to 2,500 men. Whereas Bush opposed American troop involvement, Clinton had advocated using force. In office Clinton backtracked and by the time the 'safe areas' compromise was worked out he was admitting that there was no clear-cut moral case for intervention.

Nonetheless, Clinton persisted with the idea of arming the Bosnian Moslems in a series of diplomatic moves which fuelled the bitterness between London and Washington. There was deep resentment in the British delegation at the European Community summit in Copenhagen on 21 June 1993 when Chancellor Kohl disclosed that he had received a letter from Clinton seeking support for an appeal sent to the White House by Turkey's President Suleiman Demirel. As the meeting had Bosnia at the top of its agenda, Prime Minister Major was angered that the Clinton letter was not sent to the Danish Prime Minister, Nyrup Rasmussen, as the summit host presiding at the debate. The dismay was increased by State Department spokesman Michael McCurry stating that the letter went to Kohl because he was the one 'most likely to make the argument on behalf of lifting the arms embargo'.

It was seen as a calculated move since Kohl was anxious to improve relations with Turkey after the anger in Ankara over his absence from a memorial service for Turks killed in racist attacks in Germany. It was also regarded as a crude challenge to test whether Britain would be ready to take its opposition to arming the Bosnians to the point of using the veto to block a Security Council resolution for lifting the UN embargo temporarily. In the end a veto was not necessary. The resolution, which was sponsored by the non-aligned nations and vigorously supported by the United States, failed on 29 June because it secured only six of the 15 votes. Even so, the Anglo-American split was registered by Britain's abstention – a stance taken by the three other Permanent Members.

The disarray worsened at the Group of Seven summit in Tokyo on 8 July when the major industrial powers showed themselves incapable of taking any coherent action over Bosnia as it faced division into ethnic mini-states following the final abandonment of the Vance–Owen plan. With both the United States and Germany still in favour of lifting the arms embargo for the Moslems, the British felt the argument slipping away from them as the Serbs and Croats relentlessly went ahead with a carve-up. Hurd indicated the anguished shift in position to be faced if British forces with the United Nations had to be withdrawn and negotiations were impossible: 'Then it might be a situation in which the friends of each side said: "Here is the kit, fight it out." ' For Hurd this was not an occasion to admit that Clinton's argument was being proved right. Making it a fight to the finish was 'a policy of despair'. After more than 50 years of close co-operation, both the Americans and the British had come to the end of the road in their joint endeavour.

This was not a conclusion that politicians were prepared to admit publicly. The rhetoric about the Special Relationship continuing just as Ol' Man River keeps rollin' along is easier to sustain in politics than the reality that the affair is over. The embarrassment of going public about the situation was highlighted by a flurry of denials from the White House after an 'off-the-record' speech was leaked into an 'on-the-record' account of the *realpolitik* of the Clinton Administration's foreign policy. Since the speech on 25 May 1993 was given by Peter Tarnoff, Under-Secretary at the State Department and regarded as the brains behind Clinton's policy-making, it could not be shrugged off as a few maverick shots from a loose cannon.

When Tarnoff set out his theme, saying 'We're talking about new rules of engagement for the United States and new limits', it was obvious that there had been a serious review of the transatlantic co-operation which had been taken for granted since the days of Franklin Roosevelt. Although the reason why the United States would have a much diminished world leadership role in future was given as 'We don't have the money', it was equally clear that America was turning its back on an interventionist policy as much because of a lack of political will as of a shortage of economic resources. That was explicit in Tarnoff's reference to the Yugoslav crisis: 'We are determined not to go in there and take over Bosnia policy. The approach is difficult for our friends to understand: it's not different by accident; it's different by design.' A loaded question as to whether people might die in Bosnia because the United States could do more if it wanted brought a blunt affirmative answer.

America's allies were warned not to imagine that what happened in a crisis during the Cold War would continue: 'that at the end of the day we will do it, or we are going to have a plan that we want to impose, and that we would provide the resources and the manpower – that's rarely going to be the case now.' Even if there were no reversion to isolationism, Tarnoff indicated that America was backing away from any role as the world's policeman: 'We simply don't have the leverage, we don't have the influence, we don't have the inclination to use military force.' The change of priorities was crystal clear: America's side of the Atlantic took precedence over what happened on the other side. Unless the President was 'secure at home and confident that he has his domestic base covered and has the kind of domestic support for internal programmes that he needs', it would be difficult for him to have 'an active profile' in the world at large.

Immediately after the speech started to be leaked, Warren Christopher made some anxious telephone calls to newspapers in an attempt to assure them that American leadership in the world was considered essential and that the international role of the United States was not being diminished. But it was too late for damage limitation. The damage had been done long before Tarnoff made his analysis of the new political equations. Once the Berlin Wall came down the entire pattern of international relations changed. Nothing survived as it had been before, not even the Special Relationship. The problem that had to be addressed on both sides of the Atlantic was how to live with the reality of the end of the affair while the British public was still being deluded by rhetoric about the Special Relationship which the politicians at Westminster were reluctant to eliminate from their vocabulary.

XII

The Lessons and the Legacy

'*It is not easy for the British people, after their long sense of security and their supremacy in many fields – in trade, in industry, in monetary stability, and in undisputed naval power – the country of the Pax Britannica, with ever growing imperial and colonial responsibilities, to adjust themselves to the new conditions.*'

Harold Macmillan, *At the End of the Day*

'*It is not easy, in the psychological sense, for a people living in the afterglow of a great empire and unquestioned power and authority to exist without these things.*'

Alexander Haig, *Caveat*

'*Only as one of the leaders of Europe could Britain continue to play a major role on the world scene.*'

Henry Kissinger, Lecture

At every turning point it is considered prudent to look backwards as well as forwards before tackling the road ahead. In Britain's case there are good reasons for looking back over the five decades of Anglo-American relations in terms of the Special Relationship before assessing what lies ahead in the new era of international relations. The interim period, which could be a prolonged one as the global jigsaws take time to settle into new shapes after the upheavals of the end of the Cold War, can be used to assess the lessons of the past decades and the legacy from them as Britain and the United States brace themselves for the twenty-first century. In starting afresh there is a chance to jettison all the unnecessary baggage – in this instance the now irrelevant nostalgia and the web of myths woven around the relationship between the United States and Britain.

While sentiment played a part in moulding the relationship nurtured by Churchill and Roosevelt in the wartime days, the sort of sentimentality which has been employed since then in an attempt to sustain it has usually been counter-productive. Norman Mailer's observation that 'Sentimentality is the emotional promiscuity of those who have no sentiment' is an apposite judgement on the attitude of many misguided Atlanticists. It was that attitude which encouraged the belief that the Americans were doing the British a great favour in having bases in the United Kingdom during the Cold War. The reality is that the stationing of troops in Europe and the siting of air bases in Britain was the outcome of a coincidence of self-interest on both sides of the Atlantic.

Britain wanted the Americans in Europe as a deterrent against the Russians moving westwards and a shield against the Communists' vast superiority in conventional forces. The United States wanted their troops on the ground in Europe not just to draw the line against the spread of Communism but as a tripwire in their own first-line defence. It proved an added advantage when the Americans carried out their 1986 bombing raid on Libya to have bases in Britain. But coincidence of self-interest did not mean total trust between the partners. While American U-2 planes were spying over Russia and Cuba, there were other American flights over factories in Britain. Their task was to keep an up-to-date record of possible targets for the contingency, incredible though it may seem now, of the United States being at war with Britain. When the British authorities realized what was happening Sir Ralph Murray, the Deputy Under-Secretary of State at the Foreign Office, called in the American Ambassador, David Bruce, to point out that the low-flying operations were making people on the ground nervous. 'If you want pictures of our factories just let us know what you need and we'll send them to you,' the Ambassador was told.

One of the myths to be discarded was that the state of Anglo-American relations depended solely or even principally on the relationship between Prime Minister and President. This concept was fostered by what the pollsters call the 'feel good factor', particularly during the Kennedy–Macmillan era and the eight years of the Reagan–Thatcher partnership. While it was true that a good relationship at the top did make it easier for the British in their dealings with Americans at all levels, there were many occasions when officials had close working relations even though their political leaders were not on very good terms with each other. Ambassadors often exchanged telegrams at their posts and worked out ways of co-operating with each other regardless of state of the political barometer between the leaders in London and Washington.

The extent of the collaboration depended upon the individual relationships; there was no automatic co-operation from the Americans for any diplomat just because he was British. Jeanne Kirkpatrick was not disposed to be of assistance to the British. During her entire time at the United Nations she never helped the British on any resolution over the Falklands unless it was ordered from Washington. She did not give the British any advance consultation on American draft resolutions; information about any proposal being made by Kirkpatrick was given to the British by other delegations. In Geneva Jock Dean, the American delegate at the negotiations with the Russians on mutual and balanced force reductions, behaved in such a secretive way to his British partner, Sir John Thomson, that the row over it caused ructions at a high level. It transpired that Dean put proposals to the Russian legal adviser, Vladimir Khlestov, which he had not disclosed to Thomson although they were presented as an agreed Western position. In the vast majority of posts, however, Americans went out of their way to be helpful to the British and that assistance was reciprocated.

Sir Michael Palliser, as the first head of the Foreign Office Planning Department in 1964, initiated a consultation process with the Americans which developed into a system of collaboration with the State Department in Washington that operated smoothly irrespective of rough patches between the White House and Downing Street. For three days in Washington Palliser and his successor, Thomson, had ten members of the State Department Planning staff in no-holds-barred discussions over the entire range of policy-making and the interrelation with other government agencies in Washington. Even when NATO brought all planning staffs from member countries together twice a year the discussions were never as frank and open as those between the Americans and the British. They were not merely valuable to the British; the Americans appreciated the depth of research undertaken by the British planning teams and came over to London for joint sessions. Thomson hosted meetings at Admiralty House with Henry Owen and Zbigniew Brzezinski. In Washington, Henry Kissinger and Walt Rostow would make themselves readily available to senior British diplomats. It established a pattern of close co-operation which continued throughout the lean years of the Special Relationship.

Heath's coolness did not inhibit Kissinger from maintaining close relations with senior advisers in the Foreign Office and Cabinet Office whose expertise he valued. At one stage Kissinger claimed that he kept the Foreign Office 'better informed and more closely engaged than the American State Department'. Recalling the co-operation in his memoirs, he described it as 'a pattern of consultation so matter-of-factly intimate that it became psychologically impossible to ignore British views.... They used effectively an abundance of wisdom and trustworthiness of conduct so exceptional that successive American leaders saw it in their self-interest to obtain British advice before taking major decisions.'

Where the British were able to make the most of their influence in the policy-making process was through their expertise in being on the inside track in Washington at what is termed in diplomatic parlance the 'Munchkin level'. The munchkins are the experts working at the grass roots of policy-making, preparing papers assessing the options and setting down recommendations for decisions to be taken at the top. The ponderous inter-agency system in the United States Administration means that teams of munchkins are competing against rivals in the various agencies – State Department, Pentagon, National Security, Arms Control and Disarmament, and Trade. While ambassadors maintain top-level contacts with the Administration, it is the Politico-Military Counsellors at the British Embassy who do the rounds of the munchkins at their desks three times a week which enables the Foreign Office to know the way American policy is shaping and where to direct pressure to influence the outcome.

The importance of dealing with the munchkins can be gauged from the calibre of the people who have been picked as Politico-Military Counsellors at the Washington Embassy, men such as Robin Renwick, John Kerr, John Weston and Michael Pakenham, all of whom went to the top in the Diplomatic Service. If the Foreign Office became concerned at a trend in American policy these experts could pull levers at various levels from munchkin upwards. They were often so respected for their expertise that one American agency would use information from them as leverage in the struggle against another agency for winning approval from the White House. This close co-ordination, with the British gaining insights into the policy process in Washington and feeding ideas from British policy advisers into the American machine, continued across a wide spectrum of issues regardless of the state of relations between the two heads of government.

By far the most important aspect of co-operation was the outcome of a secret treaty in 1947 called UKUSA by which the Central Intelligence Agency, set up in that year under the National Security Act, agreed to work closely with Britain's Secret Intelligence Service. It proved to be the most fruitful joint venture of the Anglo-American partnership, with extraordinary dividends for both sides. Under the agreement a vast network of Sigint – Signals Intelligence – was established without parallel anywhere else in the Western world. The operations enabled an unrestricted stream of intelligence information to flow into and out of two centres: the National Security Agency headquarters at Forte Meade, Maryland, and the Government Communications Headquarters – GCHQ – at Cheltenham in Gloucestershire. With a staff of 7,000, GCHQ has its function officially described as 'the reception and analysis of foreign communications and other electronic transmissions for Intelligence purposes.' Because of the value of GCHQ to the Americans, a substantial share of its budget has been funded from Washington.

As well as having American officers work alongside the British at GCHQ units at Oakley and Benhall, the NSA was secretly authorized to establish its own outstations for additional eavesdropping operations. Two were sited in Scotland – at Edzell, six miles north of Brechin, and at Kirknewton, eight miles south of Coldstream – and two in England, at Menwith Hill outside Harrogate and at Chicksands in Bedfordshire. Britain's global listening posts proved of immense significance for America's information gathering, particularly the Middle East station in the British sovereign base in Cyprus and the China station at Little Sai Wan on Hong Kong. Military Intelligence was also co-ordinated. The Royal Air Force undertook surveillance flights alongside the US Air Force over Soviet activities in Eastern Europe and the eastern Mediterranean. This collaboration on Intelligence matters was sustained with an unusual degree of harmony which not even the bitter political rift over the Suez War in 1956 undermined – for a time, in fact, it was the only surviving element of the partnership with any warmth. Nonetheless, there were limits to this sharing of confidences from which all other American allies were excluded. These parameters were illustrated on one occasion when Major-General Sir Kenneth Strong, head of the Joint Intelligence Bureau at the Ministry of Defence, went to the CIA headquarters for a meeting with its Director, General Walter Bedell Smith, a close friend from their days together on General Eisenhower's staff in North Africa in 1943. In a gesture of cordiality Bedell Smith pushed his in-tray across to Strong and invited him to take a look at the contents, saying: 'Kenneth, there are no secrets between you and me.' Strong took up his offer but found nothing in the documents to make him raise his eyebrows. 'All rather routine,' he observed. Unabashed, Bedell Smith replied: 'Of course. Do you think I would have left anything there that was really secret?' It was all said jokingly but behind the smiles was the basic assertion that while the British were trusted far beyond other partners, the Special Relationship did not mean that they were completely trusted.

There were many testing times for the Americans' trust in the British. The first blow to their confidence came three years after the UKUSA agreement with the arrest of the atomic physicist Klaus Fuchs on 2 February 1950 for passing nuclear secrets to Moscow. After that setback to atomic co-operation there was even more Anglo-American friction over the defection of the two Foreign Office diplomats Guy Burgess and Donald Maclean on 25 May 1951 after years of working for the Russians. The gnawing suspicions about Britain's reliability as a partner kept surfacing through the 1960s when Kim Philby fled to Moscow in January 1963 and again in the 1970s with the unmasking of the former Surveyor of the Queen's Pictures, Sir Anthony Blunt, in 1979.

These ideological betrayals, however, were less serious in their impact upon Anglo-American relations than treachery in the communications field. The worst damage was done by a former RAF corporal from Signals Intelligence at Gatow in Berlin, Geoffrey Prime, who infiltrated himself into GCHQ in 1968 and worked there for the KGB for nine years. Not only did he pass the names of agents to the Russians but he indicated which parts of the KGB Sigint had been penetrated by the British. What angered Washington was the inefficiency of the British vetting process which enabled Prime to give the Russians information about America's most advanced intelligence-gathering satellites year after year without being at any time under suspicion. They were furious that it was only three years after Prime left GCHQ and was arrested for sexual offences that his work for the KGB was exposed.

The effect upon the Special Relationship in the Intelligence field would have been considerably more severe had it not been for the fact that the Americans could not take a holier-than-thou attitude because of KGB penetration of the US Intelligence system on a much larger scale. Within a few days of Prime offering his services to the Russians in January 1968 a US Navy Chief Warrant Officer, John Walker, began a long espionage career for the KGB. As a communications officer with the Commander of Submarine Forces in the Atlantic – COM-SUBLANT – at Norfolk, Virginia, he had access to cipher machines and provided the Russians with a cornucopia of material. His operations, which lasted for 17 years until his wife alerted the FBI, covered a wide area because he was able to hand over cipher keys which enabled Russian cryptanalysts to decode messages involving the State Department and the CIA.

Since there were far fewer penetrations of the British Intelligence network than of the American system there was no disposition in Washington to have a protracted post-mortem on security breaches. Once tighter screening was established in Britain following the upheavals caused by the so-called Magnificent Five, the reputation of the British on security was greatly enhanced. If corroboration were needed it was supplied by Russia. When the KGB archives became available after the disintegration of the Communist system it was shown that there had been only one major case of penetration into the British Intelligence system. America's problems in having a more open society with a greater tendency towards leaking in the various govern-ment agencies have made the US Intelligence establishment more appreciative of Britain in recent years as a secure ally who can be trusted.

One Intelligence coup put the British in a class of their own: the acquisition of Oleg Gordievsky, the senior KGB officer at the heart of espionage operations in the West. His 11 years as a double agent for the SIS, from his recruitment in Copenhagen in 1974 until he came in from the cold after three years as the KGB's London Resident, made him the most valuable source on Intelligence available to the West and elevated Anglo-American relations to a unique level of confidence. Even so, there was a limit to the trust which the British had in the ability of the Americans to keep a secret. Only four people in Downing Street knew that Gordievsky had been 'turned' and was supplying such a wealth of material from the Kremlin: Prime Minister Margaret Thatcher, Foreign Secretary Sir Geoffrey Howe, Head of the Foreign Office Sir Antony Acland, and the Intelligence Co-ordinator Sir Antony Duff. Nothing was put in writing, so no one else in the Cabinet knew about the Intelligence coup. Richard Stolz, the London chief of the CIA at the time, knew that Gordievsky was his KGB opposite number, but he did not know that the Intelligence material he received about the Russians was being supplied by Gordievsky. Not even CIA Director William Casey was told about Gordievsky until after he made his daring escape from Moscow.

In two matters of vital importance Gordievsky made significant contributions to the Special Relationship which boosted beyond measure Britain's status in Washington. It was Gordievsky's inside knowledge of the apprehensions in Moscow which halted a dangerously escalating nuclear crisis over a NATO exercise called Able Archer 83 planned for 2–11 November 1983 to rehearse the procedures for a nuclear alert. Half-way through the NATO manoeuvres Gordievsky, who was London Resident at the Soviet Embassy in Kensington Palace Gardens, became aware of anxieties bordering on panic at the KGB headquarters in Moscow's Dzerzhinsky Square. Although the NATO operations were a tactical exercise without troops, signals were transmitted at one stage as if units were being moved to a state of alert preparatory to a nuclear strike. When Russian espionage agents picked up signs of heightened activity at US bases in the NATO area, the KGB became alarmed that they were about to face a pre-emptive nuclear strike by the Americans.

It was a time of mounting East–West tension. American Secretary of State George Shultz had recently clashed bitterly with Russia's Foreign Minister Andrei Gromyko in Madrid and asked him to leave the US Embassy after accusing him of blatant lies over the shooting down of a South Korean airliner with the loss of 209 lives. The manoeuvres also coincided with Russian anxiety over the imminent deployment of Cruise and Pershing missiles in Europe as a deterrent against the Soviet SS-20 missiles targeted on the West. The tension reached such a peak that the KGB sent urgent messages to its stations in the 16 NATO countries calling for instant reports on the changes in the pattern of behaviour around bases or emergency meetings of ministers at Cabinet offices. When Gordievsky received his instructions from Moscow he immediately contacted the SIS to warn them of the dangerous consequences of the KGB's mistaken fears that the Soviet Union was about to face an American surprise attack. Downing Street's Intelligence chief, Sir Antony Duff, got in touch at once with Prime Minister Margaret Thatcher who was about to leave for Bonn for an Anglo-German summit.

The assessment in Downing Street was that if nothing were done quickly to dissolve the paranoia at Dzerzhinsky Square then drastic counter-measures might be ordered by the Kremlin. Washington was urged to take immediate steps to reassure the Russians that their fears of a pre-emptive nuclear strike were completely groundless. Gordievsky, who knew precisely what the KGB surveillance agents were instructed to monitor, advised on the best way to leak indications that the manoeuvres and the training on the nuclear alert system were genuinely routine. The American Service chiefs tailored the exercises in the final stages of Able Archer 83 so that there was no question of it being misunderstood as the countdown to a nuclear strike. When the amended signals were studied by the Russians the tensions eased.

Gordievsky's second intervention of crucial importance to the Special Relationship was in the political sphere – the briefings he provided for Thatcher's first meeting with Gorbachev at Chequers in December 1984 and for Reagan's first meeting with the Soviet leader a year later in Geneva. The Chequers session was an extraordinary double-sided operation. Gordievsky supplied the KGB with political guidance notes for Gorbachev to study before his discussions with Thatcher – subtly angled by Downing Street's Soviet experts. At the same time he contributed large sections to the briefing papers for Thatcher so that she would be aware of the parameters within which Gorbachev had to work because of the hardliners in the Kremlin.

Even more vital was Gordievsky's contribution to the success of the first Reagan–Gorbachev summit four months after he ended his double role and escaped to England. When Reagan sat down in his armchair at the Waterflower Villa in Geneva on 19 December 1985 alongside Gorbachev with only interpreters present, he had memorized a short list of do's and don'ts plus an assessment of how best to handle the Soviet leader. They were drawn up by his advisers on the basis of discussions at an American debriefing of Gordievsky in England. Reagan became so fascinated with the insights into the mind of the Russian leader that for the first time he read through the entire White House briefing notes to the last sentence without a pause.

Gordievsky's guidance was extremely valuable to the Americans on two basic points. First, he warned that there would be strong Russian distrust of any American offer presented on the basis of idealism and good faith. This ruled out any heavy-handed attempt to sell Russia partnership in Reagan's Strategic Defence initiative. Reagan was advised to avoid fuelling the Russian fears of Star Wars and stress the idea of a defensive shield to eliminate the risk of a surprise attack. Secondly, Gordievsky enabled Reagan to feel relaxed at having the superior negotiating position since he exposed the weak hand which Gorbachev had to play because the Russians realized that they could not keep up with the Americans in the arms race. Although Reagan was not encouraged to make a major issue of the fact that the arms race was bankrupting Russia, he was not discouraged from letting the Russians know that the United States was aware of the dreadful financial burden it was imposing upon them.

That the British had enabled the American President to be in such a dominant position at Geneva through their Intelligence coup was a dividend of the Special Relationship which was used as an argument for some form of scaled-down partnership afterwards. But it was not the only example of the co-operation which the American Intelligence establishment believed should be continued in the new era. Under the reorganization begun in Downing Street by Sir Antony Duff, and continued by his successors Sir Percy Cradock and Sir Rodric Braithwaite as chairmen of the Joint Intelligence Committee, the British Intelligence assessment system became a highly esteemed addition to the material collated from the various agencies in Washington. It was given a further boost by the incisive mind of Pauline Neville-Jones, the first woman to achieve the rank of Deputy Under-Secretary of State in the Diplomatic Service, when she took over as Britain's Intelligence chief at the Joint Intelligence Committee in the Cabinet Office in January 1994.

The advantage of the British system is that, while the collection of Intelligence is on a smaller scale than that of the Americans, the end product is co-ordinated into one coherent, unified assessment. In the United States the assessment system is much more politicized and is duplicated among rival agencies – Central Intelligence Agency, National Security Council, Defence Department and State Department. There is so much rivalry to be first with daily assessments that the CIA arranged for one of their officers to deliver their global review by hand to Secretary of State Alexander Haig at 7.30 a.m. so that he could absorb the CIA view while he was driven to his office before picking up the State Department assessment from his desk. Because of the competition, the longer weekly assessments vie for the seal of approval from the President and therefore are often modified to meet what are thought to be his political preferences.

British assessments, which are produced by a staff of 20 at the rate of six a week, were significantly sharpened under the eagle eye of Gerald Warner, a former SIS officer who was appointed Intelligence Co-ordinator in the Cabinet Office in 1991. They distil the various strands of Intelligence material from all sources – the SIS, Foreign

Office, Ministry of Defence and other Whitehall departments. Although they are highly classified and intended only for senior Cabinet members, if these carefully weighed analyses of current problems are not of purely national interest they are made available to the Americans. The CIA London Station chief attends the weekly review of the JIC on Thursday mornings for the international items on the agenda and has easy access to the assessment staff in the Cabinet Office in the course of processing raw Intelligence material. These facilities are not available to the French or Germans and it is rare for them to be offered a copy of British Intelligence assessments. The tradition of regular visits by the American Intelligence chiefs to London and the British to Washington, which is a legacy from the Cold War period, was continued by Clinton's CIA director James Woolsey.

One serious problem which threatened to cast a cloud over Anglo-American relations in the Intelligence sphere was a political issue – not on the international front, but in Britain's domestic political arena. It arose from an announcement by Sir Geoffrey Howe on 25 January 1984 that the Government intended to ban the 7,000 employees at GCHQ from trade union membership because the prospect of industrial action was perceived as potentially damaging to security. The CIA was extremely worried that Howe might back down in face of furious opposition in Parliament and the trade union movement. Howe had been Chancellor of the Exchequer during the civil service strike two years previously and was determined to eliminate the risk of such disruption at GCHQ. However, the Americans were far from convinced that he could hold the line and might seek some modification to the plan.

They stepped up their behind-the-scenes pressure when it seemed that a compromise might be devised to head off angry attacks coming not just from Labour MPs but from Conservatives, including Cheltenham's MP Charles Irving who condemned the proposition as a denial of democratic rights. The Americans were just as opposed to the option of allowing GCHQ staff to retain union rights as individuals as they were to allowing collective trade union activity. They were strongly against any formula which depended on a no-strike assurance from trade unions. Feelings in Parliament against the Americans ran high when it became known that the CIA was pressing Downing Street to introduce lie detectors as a condition of service at GCHQ. At one stage the Government accepted the arguments for the lie detector being introduced but then dropped the idea because of opposition from MPs and the general public. However, the Americans were relieved when the Government persisted in proscribing trade union organization completely at GCHQ.

The usefulness of GCHQ to the Americans did not cease with the end of the Cold War. Its value was demonstrated day after day in the Gulf crisis from the invasion of Kuwait until its liberation. Traffic trebled at the height of the crisis as the material from all the Middle East centres flowed into the Cheltenham headquarters. Even so, GCHQ's usefulness was vastly diminished in the same way as Britain's general Intelligence collection and assessment skills were as a result of the removal of the threat to Western security with the end of the Cold War. Just as the armed forces of the United States and Britain were scaled down with the collapse of the Communist challenge, so the Intelligence resources which were required for surveillance and infor- mation-gathering in the Communist world were reduced.

Despite the budgetary pressures for sweeping cuts, however, the Intelligence establishments in both countries have managed to delay drastic reductions until the fluidity of the immediate aftermath of the Communist empire's disintegration is replaced by a more stable pattern of relationships. Although operations have been wound down in Eastern Europe, Intelligence chiefs are cautious about making substantial reductions in activity in the former Soviet republics because of the need to monitor the problem of arms proliferation not only in nuclear, biological and chemical weapons but also in sophisticated conventional weapons. Regardless of Russian protestations that they are not selling their arms stocks for much-needed hard currency, both American and British Intelligence have maintained a large operation monitoring the threatened proliferation from the former Soviet military-industrial complex. This vigilance was justified when a consignment of ammonium perchlorate, which is used to produce solid fuel rockets, was discovered on its way from a Moscow factory to Libya in June 1993.

Where the British have been traditionally better placed than the Americans they have been encouraged to maintain their operations, especially in areas of particular value to the Americans. With only three Intelligence services operating with global interests – CIA, KGB and SIS – the Americans were concerned that Britain's operations should remain as widespread as possible since there was no comparable capacity sustained by the French, Germans or Italians despite their expertise in certain areas. Britain's presence in Hanoi has been of special value to the Americans as have her activities in the Gulf states, particularly those based in Oman. The Americans have always had a high regard for the strength of British resources in places of international significance such as Geneva and Vienna. Even so, circumstances diminish the range of British eavesdropping facilities and, therefore, their usefulness to the Americans, such as the closure of the Little Sai Wan base at the hand over of Hong Kong to China in 1997.

Even though the American Administration became less enthusiastic for global involvement than when President Clinton appointed Warren Christopher to lead 'a foreign policy of engagement', the Americans retain a keen interest in the Intelligence assessments which the British continue to make available to them after the glow of the Special Relationship has gone. While a much smaller percentage of the material than before has a direct relevance to Western security, the Americans rate what remains important as an interesting cross-check on their own perceptions. Although they have great respect for German Intelligence operations, the Americans continue the tradition dating back to the beginning of the Cold War of turning to the British for a second opinion when they want to check out an assessment. For the British it is extremely valuable to continue having access to the panoply of American Intelligence material which has always been at least ten times the volume accruing from Britain's own resources.

How far this legacy of co-operation in Intelligence and other spheres of mutual interest from the days of the Special Relationship will be enhanced or allowed to wither depends upon the nature of a new transatlantic partnership. This relationship is still in the course of evolving from the complex new developments and policy appraisals of them on both sides of the Atlantic. Inevitably, politicians persist in referring to the Special Relationship whenever it so happens that there is a coincidence of interest in London and Washington. It is an example of the type of nostalgia which is useful for politicians to invoke when they are uncertain about the pattern of new partnerships. As long ago as 1966 Lord Beloff, in his monograph 'The Special Relationship: An Anglo-American Myth', suggested that it would be interesting to enquire 'why it has been found psychologically so necessary to dress up in this way a perfectly honourable relationship as though national self-interest were something which should play no part in this branch of international politics'.

Cynics, who were overeager to bury the Special Relationship long before its ultimate demise, argued that the basis of the partnership was Britain's awareness of her steadily increasing economic weakness and consequent loss of status as an influential world power. It was presented as a way to stave off further decline by clinging to America's coat-tails and being the dependable junior partner of the United States. That argument glossed over the fact that the benefits of the arrangement went in both directions, a factor that will determine the extent to which a new transatlantic partnership plays a role in the international arena in the twenty-first century. How any partnership is perceived to serve the interests of both sides will decide the power and responsibility vested in it.

In developing any new relationship both sides will first of all examine how much the partnership is needed and how important it will be in helping to maintain their position in the world. The absence of any direct external threat has had a tendency to make each side of the Atlantic more self-centred. In Washington there has been a significant shift of emphasis since the end of the Cold War with the political focus being concentrated much more on domestic needs. One month after the Berlin Wall came down James Baker assured the people of Berlin: 'The United States is, and will remain, a European Power.' That concept was dropped when President Clinton was installed at the White House. What is termed the 'Come home' factor became a powerful public influence on Capitol Hill. Although there is no serious drift towards isolationism, American policymakers have increasingly seen security issues as regional questions which pose no real challenge to American interests. At the same time neither Britain nor her European partners see themselves as facing any potential adversary with the capacity to threaten their security. In these circumstances, while they would not wish to be suddenly deprived of America's nuclear umbrella, the eventual scaling down of US troops in Europe to zero is not a prospect liable to bring vast crowds onto the streets with placards saying 'Yanks Don't Go Home'.

Changes in attitudes, ethnic patterns and the centre of gravity in the United States influence the calculations of the importance to be attached to a new transatlantic partnership. Japan's increasing economic and financial strength has compelled a reassessment of American priorities towards Europe. Its advances in new technology tend to upgrade Japan's status in American eyes and make Europeans less relevant in the high-tech age. Even more influential is the advance of the Hispanic culture as a result of the rapid growth of the Hispanic segment of the American population – three times faster than the total growth. At present the United States has the fourth largest Spanish-speaking population in the world; early in the twenty-first century, it is estimated, one in four Americans will be of Hispanic origin. Such statistics foreshadow increasing concern for closer links with South America and indicate that whatever survives of the Anglo-Saxon sense of kinship will be increasingly marginalized.

The shift westwards of the centre of gravity – in political and economic terms – in the United States is not a recent phenomenon. There has been a steady drift ever since the beginning of the twentieth century. But the cumulative effect of more people looking westward has eroded the old establishment authority of New England and has given much more influence to the west coast. Trade has expanded dramatically across the Pacific in the past decade and with commercial interest spreading in the north-west Pacific there has been an upsurge of political interest in the Pacific Rim. The new importance of Japan as a pivotal partner of the United States was highlighted by President Clinton at Waseda University during his visit to Tokyo for the G-7 summit on 7 July 1993. 'Our first international economic priority is to create a new and stronger partnership between the United States and Japan. The time has come for America to join with Japan and others in the region to create a new Pacific community,' he stressed. Warren Christopher told the *Washington Post* on 17 October 1993: 'Western Europe is no longer the dominant area of the world', adding the barbed observation that it was time for Washington to abandon its 'Eurocentric attitude'.

The future of the transatlantic partnership depends upon a number of factors, such as whether a new European Union evolves as a loosely or a tightly knit Community with a powerful political influence to match its economic power and whether the Community is prepared to share the burdens of international responsibilities. The enlargement of the European Community from 12 to 16 in 1995 with the addition of Austria, Finland, Norway and Sweden could eventually strengthen the bonds rather than weaken them. However, a large question mark hangs over the effects of any further widening of the Community's embrace to take in six former Communist states in Eastern Europe – Bulgaria, the Czech Republic, Hungary, Poland, Romania and Slovakia. Doubts about European preparedness to share the burdens of out-of-area obligations have frequently been a niggling issue on Capitol Hill, but the record of Europe's responses in a crisis do not support Congressional complaints. Although some European countries were somewhat murine in their attitude to supplying troops for the Gulf War, they were proportionately as generous as Japan and the wealthy Arab states in their financial contributions. By paying their share towards the total of $48.4 billion contributed by America's allies to the costs of Desert Shield and Desert Storm, the Europeans ensured that US taxpayers did not have any extra burdens for the defence funding requirements of the fiscal year 1991–92.

The reverse side of burden-sharing has not demonstrated a strong sense of obligation in the United States to help deal with the new problems in Europe. While the Americans adopted a generous open-door policy to refugees after the Hungarian uprising in October 1956, they have taken the view that the massive migration of populations from Eastern and South-Eastern Europe in the 1990s is a problem for the governments of Western Europe, not the United States. Although over 300,000 people have fled into Germany from the former Yugo-slavia, the Americans, who uphold the principle of freedom of move-ment, have not felt obliged to take any exceptional measures to accommodate refugees from Bosnia and Croatia. American economic assistance to Russia has been very modest compared with the funding supplied by Western Europe.

Over 56 per cent of all aid to Russia in the three years since the Berlin Wall came down was provided by Germany. The United States gave $9 billion and Japan $3 billion but Germany supplied $50 billion. When the G-7 summit in Tokyo announced a further $3 billion in aid for Russia on 8 July 1993, America's contribution was 13 per cent while 50 per cent came in loans from the European Bank for Recon-struction and Development, the World Bank and the International Finance Corporation. The Americans were vigorous advocates of Western expertise being made available to Hungary, Poland and the Czech Republic, but it has largely been provided by Britain and other Community countries with their Know-How funds to stimulate economic revival.

This complementary aspect of sharing obligations will weigh heavily with European governments when they consider the value of any new transatlantic partnership. If major crises in Europe – economic as well as political – are to be met by Washington describing them as regional problems of no direct concern to the United States, there will be strong reluctance to accept the terms of a partnership which is activated only when America decides that issues are global, not regional. Most of the 14 European members of NATO are prepared to see it continue as the framework of Western security since its experience, organization and training are not easily replaceable in an emergency. There would be a sense of unease in many quarters about any moves to consign NATO to a military museum so long as the main provisions of the arms-reduction agreement with the former Soviet Union and its successors are not fully implemented. At the same time there is a large element of caution in many NATO capitals about making its expertise available to the Americans on a world-wide basis.

While European countries may increasingly question the commitment of the United States to co-operate in the areas important to them in future, the Americans may well hesitate to take on a partnership in depth with the Community if its dependability is in doubt. Senior figures on Capitol Hill do not forget the rebuffs which the United States suffered in Europe when seeking support for its retaliatory air strikes against Libya in April 1986. With the admission of three traditional neutrals – Austria, Finland and Sweden – into the Community, many Americans fear that there may be even more difficulty in securing politico-military co-operation from the EC in any future crisis. The United States would be loath to accept a new transatlantic partnership that was hedged around with conditions. It would not wish to be forced into a prolonged search for consensus at a time of crisis and risk taking collaborative action on the basis of the lowest common denominator.

Britain, however, ranks high in the reliability tables in Washington. Even those with short memories remember how quickly Britain committed troops and planes for the liberation of Kuwait while the Germans looked the other way and how Margaret Thatcher was the only Western leader to offer the Americans support and logistical facilities for US air strikes against Libya. But memories, like nostalgia for the hands-across-the-sea days in World War II, are not enough to justify Britain having a priority place in a new transatlantic partnership. That place depends largely, but by no means solely, on the economic and political status which Britain is able to carve out for herself in the new Europe.

In both spheres the British had to start with serious handicaps. By being late in making a decision about being 'at the heart of Europe', Britain was at a disadvantage in many respects compared with the other members of the Community. Having missed the bus in staying aloof from the Treaty of Rome in 1957, Britain had a lot of ground to make up after finally signing the treaty in 1972. By delaying her entry into the Exchange Rate Mechanism until 1989, Britain gave an impression of half-heartedness, which was underlined by her leaving the ERM in 1992. The onset of the deepest economic recession for decades and the exceedingly slow recovery from it encouraged the belief in some circles that Britain was in a state of irreversible decline and for a considerable period was not thought strong enough to play a leading role in a new transatlantic partnership. Political uncertainty over Britain's role in Europe further diminished any optimism in Washington that the British could quickly establish themselves in a prominent position of influence in the European Community. The protracted parliamentary manoeuvres at Westminster by the Major Government to outwit the Euro-sceptics in the Conservative Party over the ratification of the Maastricht Treaty left many Americans bewildered and uncertain about the prospects of Britain being able to stake any claims to leadership in Europe. While the skilful projection of foreign policy by British foreign secretaries and their high-powered diplomats aroused admiration for the way the British 'punch above their weight', many of these admirers in Washington believed that the punch would be far more effective if it were seen to come from Britain weighing in as a full-blooded European.

Those arguments during the agonizing 19-month debate over the Maastricht Treaty were buttressed by recalling the shrewd analysis made by Harold Macmillan in 1962:

> If we remain outside the European Community, it seems to me inevitable that the realities of power would compel our American friends to attach increasing weight to the views and interests of the Community and pay less attention to our own. We would find the United States and the Community concerting policy together on major issues with much less incentive than now to secure our agreement or even consult our opinion. To lose influence both in Europe and in Washington, as that must mean, would seriously undermine our international position.

Since the end of the Special Relationship, one of the main guarantees of continuing close – though not always cordial – Anglo-American relations is for Britain to have political clout as a leading power in Europe. The Americans attach great importance to the European Community developing a thoroughly outward-looking economic and political policy – and this is where they see a key role for Britain. As a traditional free-trade nation Britain is regarded in the United States as either a stalking horse or a Trojan Horse – depending on how right-wing the user of equine analogies is – for the Americans inside a community which they fear could easily become very protectionist in a transatlantic confrontation over the terms of trade.

For the British to be in a position of strength – politically and economically – inside the European Union is considered in the United States the soundest insurance that American interests will not be brushed aside whenever Community regulations and tariffs are discussed. Because the British are reckoned to know America well and understand how its financial and commercial system operates, the United States puts considerable value upon having Britain as an advocate of open market policies who would resist discrimination against American products. However, the assumption that Britain will usually be found on America's side can be a dangerous illusion, as has been shown not just in the transatlantic dispute over the former Yugoslavia but also in agricultural issues and steel policy. As one ambassador assessing the impact of transatlantic trading controversies put it: 'We are in the trenches with the Community when the shooting starts but that is something the Americans don't always hoist in.' Although they usually accept that communication with the Community should be done through its current President, the Americans still like to be able to turn to the British to discuss problems arising between them and the EC

This ability to provide an understanding ear is sustained far beyond Community matters and is a key factor in making continued close consultation with the British highly valued in Washington. The Americans recognize that no other European partner has the range of global interests – besides the Intelligence network – which Britain maintains. They value the extra depth of judgement which the British can bring to international discussions as a result of their Commonwealth connections. The reason why Britain has frequently played a more significant role than the Germans at meetings of the International Monetary Fund, despite the power of the Bundesbank, is that the Chancellor of the Exchequer arrives straight from half a week with some 45 Finance Ministers of the Commonwealth. With the knowledge of what the attitudes of India, Malaysia, Australia and other Commonwealth partners are, a British minister can provide a more profound global perspective to the Americans than they get from any other European.

The Commonwealth connection enables Britain to have a much more detailed knowledge of certain international issues of importance to the United States than America's other allies. Tensions which arise from time to time between India and Pakistan are usually more accurately assessed by Britain through the Commonwealth network than can be achieved through other sources. America's interest in moves to restore democracy to Cambodia was shared with the British who kept a close watch on the situation in reviews of the issue with the Australians. The problem of securing a settlement in Cyprus after the Turkish invasion in July 1974 became a matter of regular consultation between the Americans and the British since Britain was a Guarantor Power of the independence agreement, and there was a former Commonwealth Prime Minister, Joe Clark of Canada, put in charge as UN Special Representative. The Americans have turned to Britain when analysing situations of concern in Commonwealth countries such as Nigeria and Kenya. In many instances Washington experts have been heard to repeat an old diplomatic maxim: 'If in doubt, go to the Brits for a second opinion.'

The skills in giving second opinions and making well-informed political assessments are essential elements of the legacy to be carried forward into the new era of transatlantic relations. The preservation of Britain's military capacity for effective independent action outside the European continent – as was demonstrated in the Falklands War – is important to the United States. As America's London Ambassador Raymond Seitz shrewdly observed: 'People have a predisposition to listen more carefully to your point of view if there are a couple of armoured divisions parked around the corner. Our shared interests will seem less like interests if we aren't willing or able to do anything about them.' Collaborative arrangements which Britain has as a nuclear power with the United States were diminished to some extent by President Clinton's announcement on 3 July 1993 of a 15-month moratorium on nuclear testing, thus denying British scientists American facilities for tests to develop a new warhead for Britain's Trident submarines based on the RAF's WE-177 free-fall bomb. Even so, a substantial amount of nuclear co-operation secured under previous American Administrations continues.

After five decades of partnership in the Special Relationship neither side expected or wanted the slate to be wiped clean for a totally fresh start. That Britain is no longer a factor of prime importance in the formation of American policy is an inevitable consequence of all the changes in the international power ratios since the end of the Cold War and the collapse of Communism. Anglo-American relations will ebb and flow like America's relations with other countries such as Israel or Germany, sometimes convivial, sometimes just correct. Britain, however, is assured of a place in a new transatlantic partnership between the United States and Europe; how significant it turns out to be depends upon what the British Government makes of its place in Europe.

It is inevitable that many people, inside and outside of politics, regret that Britain is 'Special' no more. The generation which grew up in World War II with the sense of kinship which Churchill nourished in his partnership with Roosevelt can be forgiven if at times they feel that history has been harsh in ending a relationship once thought to be enduring for all time. There will be occasions when they feel shocked at the way the interests and the feelings of the British are ignored in the new era of international relations. But of one thing they can be sure: however much the memories fade, Britain will never be *just another foreign country* to the Americans.

Appendix I

US Presidents and British Prime Ministers

US Presidents
4 March 1933
Franklin D. Roosevelt

12 April 1945
Harry S. Truman

20 January 1953
Dwight D. Eisenhower

20 January 1961
John F. Kennedy

22 November 1963
Lyndon B. Johnson

20 January 1969
Richard M. Nixon

9 August 1974
Gerald R. Ford

20 January 1977
Jimmy Carter

British Prime Ministers
28 May 1937
Neville Chamberlain
26 October 1939
Sir Winston Churchill

26 July 1945
Clement Attlee
26 October 1951
Sir Winston Churchill

6 April 1955
Sir Anthony Eden
13 January 1957
Harold Macmillan

19 October 1963
Sir Alec Douglas-Home

16 October 1964
Harold Wilson

19 June 1970
Edward Heath
4 March 1974
Harold Wilson

5 April 1976
James Callaghan

4 May 1979
Margaret Thatcher

20 January 1981
Ronald Reagan

28 November 1990
John Major

20 January 1989
George Bush

20 January 1993
William Clinton

Appendix II

US Secretaries of State and British Foreign Secretaries

US Secretaries of State
4 March 1933
Cordell Hull

30 November 1944
Edward R. Settinius
2 July 1945
James F. Byrnes

8 January 1947
George C. Marshall
19 January 1949
Dean Acheson

21 January 1953
John Foster Dulles

21 April 1959
Christian Herter

21 January 1961
Dean Rusk

British Foreign Secretaries
1 March 1938
Lord Halifax
23 December 1940
Anthony Eden

28 July 1945
Ernest Bevin

12 March 1951
Herbert Morrison
27 October 1951
Anthony Eden

7 April 1955
Harold Macmillan
22 December 1955
Selwyn Lloyd

28 July 1960
Lord Home

21 October 1963
R. A. Butler
16 October 1964
Patrick Gordon Walker
24 January 1965
Michael Stewart

12 August 1966
George Brown
15 March 1968
Michael Stewart

21 January 1969
William Rogers

21 September 1973
Henry Kissinger

20 June 1970
Sir Alec Douglas-Home

5 March 1974
James Callaghan

21 January 1977
Cyrus Vance

22 February 1977
David Owen
5 May 1979
Lord Carrington

8 May 1980
Edmund Muskie
22 January 1981
Alexander Haig

5 April 1982
Francis Pym

16 July 1982
George Shultz

11 June 1983
Sir Geoffrey Howe

20 January 1989
James Baker

25 July 1989
John Major
26 October 1989
Douglas Hurd

8 December 1992
Lawrence Eagleburger
20 January 1993
Warren Christopher

Appendix III

US Ambassadors in London and British Ambassadors in Washington

US Ambassadors in London
17 January 1938
Joseph Kennedy

11 February 1941
John Winant
2 April 1946
Averell Harriman

6 March 1947
Lewis Douglas

12 December 1950
Walter Gifford

2 February 1953
Winthrop Aldrich

11 February 1957
John Hay Whitney
22 February 1961
David Bruce

14 March 1969
Walter Annenberg

British Ambassadors in Washington
29 August 1939
Lord Lothian
24 January 1941
Lord Halifax

23 May 1946
Lord Inverchapel

22 May 1948
Sir Oliver Franks

31 December 1952
Sir Roger Makins

2 November 1956
Sir Harold Caccia

18 October 1961
Sir David Ormsby-Gore
6 April 1965
Sir Patrick Dean
4 March 1969
John Freeman

4 January 1971
Lord Cromer

3 March 1974
Sir Peter Ramsbotham

20 February 1975
Elliot Richardson
29 January 1976
Anne Armstrong
29 April 1977
Kingman Brewster

21 July 1977
Peter Jay
12 July 1979
Sir Nicholas Henderson

7 May 1981
John Louis
11 November 1983
Charles Price

2 September 1982
Sir Oliver Wright

28 August 1986
Sir Antony Acland

3 May 1991
Raymond Seitz

20 August 1991
Sir Robin Renwick

Bibliography

A comprehensive list of the volumes covering the five decades of the Special Relationship would require almost as many pages as the 12 chapters of this book. The volumes which are particularly relevant are listed below.

Acheson, Dean: *Present at the Creation* (London: Hamish Hamilton, 1969)

Ambrose, Stephen E.: *Eisenhower, the President* (London: Allen & Unwin, 1984)

Andrew, Christopher & Gordievsky, Oleg: *KGB: The Inside Story* (London: Hodder & Stoughton, 1990)

Attlee, Clement: *As It Happened* (London: Heinemann, 1954)

Ball, George: *The Discipline of Power* (London: Bodley Head, 1968)

Bayliss, John: *Anglo-American Defence Relations 1939–84* (London: Macmillan, 1984)

Beloff, Max: 'The Special Relationship: An Anglo-American Myth', in *A Century of Conflict*, edited by Martin Gilbert (London: Hamish Hamilton, 1966)

Boyle, Andrew: *The Climate of Treason* (London: Hutchinson, 1979)

Boyle, Peter G. (ed.): *The Churchill–Eisenhower Correspondence* (Raleigh: University of North Carolina Press, 1990)

Brandon, Henry (ed.): *In Search of a New World Order* (Washington: Brookings Institution, 1992)

Bulloch, John & Morris, Harvey: *The Gulf War* (London: Methuen, 1989)

Bullock, Alan: *Ernest Bevin Foreign Secretary 1945–51* (London: Heinemann, 1983)

Bundy, McGeorge: *Danger and Survival* (New York: Random House, 1988)

Callaghan, James: *Time and Chance* (London: Collins, 1981)

Campbell, John: *Edward Heath* (London: Cape, 1993)

Carrington, Lord: *Reflect on Things Past* (London: Collins, 1988)

Churchill, Winston S.: *The Second World War*, vols 1–6 (London: Cassell, 1948–54)

Clifford, Clark: *Counsel to the President* (New York: Random House, 1991)

Cline, Ray: *The CIA under Reagan, Bush & Casey* (Washington: Acropolis Books, 1981)

Cook, Don: *Ten Men and History* (New York: Doubleday, 1981)

Cottam, Richard W.: *Iran and the United States* (Pittsburgh: University of Pittsburg Press, 1988)

Coughlin, Con: *Hostages: The Complete Story of the Lebanese Captives* (London: Little, Brown, 1992)

Dickie, John: *The Uncommon Commoner: A Study of Sir Alec Douglas-Home* (London: Pall Mall Press, 1964)
Inside the Foreign Office (London: Chapmans, 1992)

Dimbleby, David & Reynolds, David: *An Ocean Apart* (London: Hodder & Stoughton, 1988)

Eden, Sir Anthony: *Full Circle* (London: Cassell, 1960)

Edmonds, Robin: *Setting the Mould* (Oxford: Oxford University Press, 1986)

Eisenhower, Dwight D.: *The White House Years* (New York: Doubleday, 1963)

Finer, Herman: *Dulles Over Suez* (London: Heinemann, 1964)

Fleming, D. F.: *The Cold War and Its Origins*, 2 vols (London: Allen & Unwin, 1961)

Freedman, Lawrence & Gamba-Stonehouse, Virginia: *Signals of War: The Falklands Conflict of 1982* (London: Faber & Faber, 1990)

Gantz, Nanette & Roper, John: *Towards a New Partnership* (Paris: Institute for Security Studies WEU, 1993)

George-Brown, Lord: *In My Way* (London: Gollancz, 1971)

Gladwyn, Lord: *Memoirs* (London: Weidenfeld & Nicolson, 1972)

Gore-Booth, Lord: *With Truth and Great Respect* (London: Constable, 1974)

Gowing, Margaret: *Britain and Atomic Energy 1939–45* (London: Macmillan, 1964)
Independence and Deterrence: Britain and Atomic Energy 1945–52 (London: Macmillan, 1974)

Grayling, Christopher & Langdon, Christopher: *Just Another Star?* (London: Harrap, 1988)

Haig, Alexander M.: *Caveat: Realism, Reagan and Foreign Policy* (London: Weidenfeld & Nicolson, 1984)

Harris, Kenneth: *Attlee* (London: Weidenfeld & Nicolson, 1982)

Harris, Kenneth: *David Owen: Personally Speaking* (London: Weidenfeld & Nicolson, 1987)

Hastings, Max & Jenkins, Simon: *The Battle for the Falklands* (London: Michael Joseph, 1983)

Healey, Denis: *The Time of My Life* (London: Michael Joseph, 1989)

Henderson, Sir Nicholas: *The Birth of NATO* (London: Weidenfeld & Nicolson, 1982)
The Private Office (London: Weidenfeld & Nicolson, 1984)

Hiro, Dilip: *Desert Shield to Desert Storm* (London: HarperCollins, 1992)

Hitchens, Christopher: *Blood, Class and Nostalgia* (London: Chatto & Windus, 1990)

Home, Lord: *The Way the Wind Blows* (London: Collins, 1976)

Horne, Alistair: *Macmillan*, vol 2 1957–80 (London: Macmillan, 1989)

Isaacson, Walter: *Kissinger* (New York: Simon & Schuster, 1992)

Johnson, Lyndon Baines: *The Vantage Point: Perspectives of the Presidency 1963–69* (London: Weidenfeld & Nicolson, 1972)

Kimball, Warren F. (ed.): *Churchill and Roosevelt: The Complete Correspondence* (Princeton: Princeton University Press, 1984)

Kissinger, Henry: *The White House Years* (London: Weidenfeld & Nicolson, 1979)
The Years of Upheaval (London: Weidenfeld & Nicolson, 1982)

Kyle, Keith: *Suez* (Weidenfeld & Nicolson, 1991)

Lewin, Ronald: *Ultra Goes to War* (London: Hutchinson, 1978)

Louis, W. Roger & Bull, Hedley: *The Special Relationship: Anglo-American Relations Since 1945* (Oxford: Clarendon Press, 1986)

McCullough, David: *Truman* (New York: Simon & Schuster, 1992)

Macmillan, Harold: *Memoirs: Winds of Change; Tides of Fortune; Riding the Storm; Pointing the Way; At the End of the Day* (London: Macmillan, 1964–73)

Monroe, Elizabeth: *Britain's Moment in the Middle East* (London: Chatto & Windus, 1981)

Moran, Lord: *Churchill: Taken from the Diaries of Lord Moran* (London: Constable, 1966)

Nicholas, H. G.: *The United States and Britain* (Chicago: University of Chicago Press, 1975)

Nixon, Richard: *The Memoirs* (London: Sidgwick & Jackson, 1978)

Ovendale, Ritchie: *The English-Speaking Alliance: 1945–51* (London: Allen & Unwin, 1985)

Owen, David: *Time to Declare* (London: Michael Joseph, 1991)

Pahlavi, Mohammed Reza Shah: *Mission for My Country* (London: Hutchinson, 1961)

Parsons, Sir Anthony: *The Pride and the Fall: Iran 1974–79* (London: Cape, 1984)

Pimlott, Ben: *Harold Wilson* (London: HarperCollins, 1992)

Pogue, Forrest C.: *George C. Marshall: Statesman 1945–59* (London: Penguin, 1989)

Ranalegh, John: *The Agency: The Rise and Decline of the CIA* (New York: Simon & Schuster, 1986)

Reagan, Ronald: *An American Life* (New York: Simon & Schuster, 1990)

Reeves, Richard: *President Kennedy* (New York: Simon & Schuster, 1993)

Regan, Donald T.: *For the Record* (London: Hutchinson, 1988)

Roosevelt, Kermit: *Countercoup: The Struggle for the Control of Iran* (London: McGraw Hill, 1979)

Rusk, Dean: *As I Saw It* (London: Tauris, 1991)

Schmidt, Helmut: *Men and Powers* (London: Cape, 1990)

Sherwood, R. E.: *The White House Papers of Harry L. Hopkins* (London: Eyre & Spottiswoode, 1948)

Shuckburgh, Sir Evelyn: *Descent to Suez* (London: Weidenfeld & Nicolson, 1986)

Smith, Geoffrey: *Reagan and Thatcher* (London: Bodley Head, 1990)

Smith, Michael & Woolcock, Stephen: *The United States and the European Community in a Transformed World* (London: RIIA/Pinter, 1993)

Sorensen, Theodore C.: *Kennedy* (London: Hodder & Stoughton, 1965)

Thatcher, Margaret: *The Downing Street Years* (London: HarperCollins, 1993)

Thompson, Robert Smith: *The Missiles of October* (New York: Simon & Schuster, 1992)

Truman, Harry S.: *Years of Trial and Hope* (New York: Doubleday, 1956)

Watt, D. Cameron: *Succeeding John Bull* (Cambridge: Cambridge University Press, 1984)

Weinberger, Caspar: *Fighting for Peace* (London: Michael Joseph, 1990)

Wilson, Harold: *The Labour Government: 1964–70* (London: Weidenfeld & Nicolson, 1971)

Woodhouse, C. Montague: *Something Ventured* (London: Granada, 1982)

Woodward, Admiral Sandy: *100 Days: Memoirs of the Falklands Battle Group Commander* (London: HarperCollins, 1992)

Young, Hugo: *One of Us* (London: Macmillan 1989)

Index